CHRONICLES OF OLD LOS ANGELES

EXPLORING THE DEVILISH HISTORY OF THE CITY OF THE ANGELS

JAMES ROMAN

Published in the United States by:
Museyon Inc.
1177 Avenue of the Americas, 5th Floor
New York, NY 10036

Museyon is a registered trademark.
Visit us online at www.museyon.com

ISBN 978-1-940842-00-4

1451117

Printed in China

*L*A's vibrant culture comes from the diversity of its people, and the challenge of merging their diverse ideas.

From the hard lives of the early settlers, a new thinking emerged, where creativity and spontaneity prevailed, where individuals joined forces to overcome risk. That sensibility continues to define the City of the Angels today. As the epicenter of the entertainment industry, but also in its architecture and industry, its foods, fashions, and even its surfboards, Los Angeles is notoriously unique.

These Chronicles bring those previous generations and the uniqueness of their bright ideas to vivid life, explaining to a new generation how Los Angeles became the world capital we know today.

Hon. John J. Duran
Mayor, City of West Hollywood

CHRONICLES OF OLD LOS ANGELES

CHAPTER 1. **BAY OF SMOKES**
The Birth of Los Angeles
1781 10

CHAPTER 2. **FANDANGOS IN THE PUEBLO**
Wealthy Mexicans and the Siege of Los Angeles
1786–1848 18

CHAPTER 3. **CULTURE CLASH**
The Racial Tensions of Statehood
1850s–1860s 26

CHAPTER 4. **THE MASSACRE**
Chinese Tong War Ends as a Historic Tragedy
1871 34

CHAPTER 5. **HUNTINGTON'S BOOM**
The Iron Horse Pokes Its Head through San Fernando Tunnel
1876 42

CHAPTER 6. **OIL!**
Doheny, Canfield, and the Oil Queen of California
1890s 50

CHAPTER 7. **TAKE A RIDE ON THE RED CARS**
LA Sprawls with an Electric Railway
1901–1961 56

CHAPTER 8. **TROUBLED WATERS**
Mulholland Builds an Aqueduct
1905–1941 68

CHAPTER 9. **HOLLYWOOD PIONEERS**
Movie Makers Remake Los Angeles
1914–1928 76

CHAPTER 10. **HOLLYWOODLAND**
The Neighborhood Beneath the Iconic Sign
1923 100

CHAPTER 11. **SISTER AIMEE**
Los Angeles Gets Religion
1922–1944 106

CHAPTER 12. **GREYSTONE MANSION**
Doheny and the Teapot Dome Scandal
1921–1929 112

CHAPTER 13. **SUNSET STRIP UNINCORPORATED**
Mickey Cohen's Territory, a.k.a. West Hollywood
1925–Present.. 122

CHAPTER 14. **PENTIMENTO**
The Controversial Art of David Siqueiros
1932 130

CHAPTER 15. **THE LEFT COAST**
Reinventing the Democratic Party
1934 138

CHAPTER 16. **THE PARTY IN LITTLE TOKYO**
Dancing in the Face of Hardship
1934–Present 146

CHAPTER 17. **ON THE AVENUE**
Jazz Nights at the Dunbar
1928–1948 154

CHAPTER 18. **LOVE ON THE LOT**
Romances at the Studios during Hollywood's Golden Age
1930s–1950s 162

CHAPTER 19. **SWITCH HITTERS**
The Dodgers' Home Run at Chavez Ravine
1957–1962 170

CHAPTER 20. **SURF CITY**
Freeth, Kahanamoku, Blake, Gidget, Dora and The Beach Boys
1907–1964 178

CHAPTER 21. **BOBBY KENNEDY AT THE AMBASSADOR**
A National Tragedy
1968 186

CHAPTER 22. **NEW VIEW**
LA's Architectural Innovations
1921–2003 194

CHAPTER 23. **THE VILLA AND THE ACROPOLIS**
J. Paul Getty Changes the Art World Forever
1954–Present 204

CHAPTER 24. **LAST STOP HOLLYWOOD**
Where Fame Rests in Peace
1946–2012 212

WALKING TOURS 220

TOUR ONE   EL PUEBLO AND CHINATOWN 222

TOUR TWO   BUNKER HILL 230

TOUR THREE HOLLYWOOD 242

TOUR FOUR   HOLLYWOOD HEIGHTS 254

TOUR FIVE   SUNSET STRIP AND BEVERLY HILLS 270

TOUR SIX   SANTA MONICA AND VENICE BEACH 284

INDEX 292

For the Arlens,

who gave my Los Angeles chronicle its start

James Roman

CHRONICLES OF OLD LOS ANGELES

Sites that appear in the chapters

CHAPTER 1.　❶ San Gabriel Mission

CHAPTER 2.　❷ The Pueblo

CHAPTER 3.　❸ Fort Hill

CHAPTER 4.　❹ Chinatown

CHAPTER 5.　❺ Wharf at Wilmington (San Pedro)

CHAPTER 6.　❻ Colton Street and Glendale Boulevard (Doheny well)

CHAPTER 7.　❼ The Huntington

CHAPTER 8.　❽ San Fernando Valley

CHAPTER 9.　❾ Lasky-DeMille Barn

CHAPTER 10.　❿ Hollywoodland

CHAPTER 11.　⓫ Angelus Temple

CHAPTER 12.　⓬ Greystone Mansion

CHAPTER 13.　⓭ Sunset Strip in West Hollywood

CHAPTER 14.　⓮ Watts Towers

CHAPTER 15.　⓯ The *Los Angeles Herald Examiner* Building

CHAPTER 16.　⓰ Little Tokyo

CHAPTER 17.　⓱ The Dunbar

CHAPTER 18.　⓲ Hollywood Studios

CHAPTER 19.　⓳ Dodger Stadium

CHAPTER 20.　⓴ Malibu Beach

CHAPTER 21.　㉑ Ambassador Hotel (RFK Community Schools)

CHAPTER 22.　㉒ Hollyhock House

CHAPTER 23.　㉓ The Getty Center

CHAPTER 24.　㉔ Lake Shrine

Los Angeles

CHAPTER 1.

BAY OF SMOKES
THE BIRTH OF LOS ANGELES
1781

For 227 years, nobody told the Native Americans they were living in the Viceroyalty of New Spain.

First, the Spanish won *Alta California* when they conquered the Aztecs in Mexico. Then, their explorer Juan Rodriguez Cabrillo headed north, the first European to set eyes on the land that is today's Los Angeles. He staked a claim for the Viceroyalty of New Spain in 1542. What did Cabrillo see? Smoke. A fragrant cloud, stoked by two-dozen Native American campfires, permeated the area. Cabrillo named this indentation in the coastline *Bahia de los Fumos,* "Bay of Smokes." (Yes, LA's "discovery" was also its first smog joke.)

The natives called their home Yang-na, but their story is no joke. When the Spanish first arrived, the Yang-na people were scattered in little clusters between the ocean and the Los Angeles River; their center stood where City Hall stands today. They spoke a language similar to the Shoshones (on the other side of the Sierra Nevada); they lived on fish, small game and the flour they milled from acorns; they wore almost no clothing. The Yang-na believed in an afterlife, they practiced cremation and they savored hallucinogens

The first recorded baptisms in Alta California were performed in The Canyon of the Little Christians.

during coming-of-age rituals. *Temescals*, ceremonial sweat lodges, were used for cleansing and for communion with their god Chinigchinich, but most rituals revolved around cycles of life. They had no demons.

Compared to their colorful relatives the Aztecs and the Great Plains Indians, the Yang-na were lackluster natives. They didn't farm the land, didn't make war, didn't build, didn't weave blankets or make terra cotta pottery. Yet, unlike the Aztecs and Mayans, these simple natives held onto their land and their lifestyle for hundreds of years beyond those sophisticated civilizations. California was one of the last habitable places on earth that wasn't being planned for the white man's empires. However, in 1781, more than two centuries after Cabrillo first smelled smoke, the Viceroy needed a plan.

Russian fur trappers were venturing too far south from their northwest trading posts; this concerned the King of Spain and his Viceroy in the New World. To protect Spanish holdings in California, the Viceroy appointed a governor. That governor, Gaspar de Portolá, was a romantic. Instead of lining *Alta California* with soldiers awaiting confrontation, Portolá installed an army of a different sort: the Franciscan Friars. They planned for the construction of 21 missions along an Indian path that was soon called *El Camino Real*, the Royal Road, from San Diego to San Francisco 500 miles away. Of course, every mission still had a military *Presidio* attached to it to keep the peace, but the king got his wish. The missions took 42 years to build; no nation challenged the Franciscan Friars or their Spanish sponsors, not even the local Yang-na. Roman Catholics would build California, mission by mission.

Situated just six miles from the San Gabriel mission, Los Angeles was not a mission. It was to be a *pueblo*, a community. On an expedition in 1769, Governor Portolá named the local river *El Rio de Nuestra Señora la Reina de Los Angeles de Porciúnculá,* "the river of Our Lady, Queen of the Angels of Porciúnculá." The expedition's journalist wrote that on August 2 they encountered "eight heathen," the local Yang-na, who gave the strangers gifts of baskets "and strings of beads made from shells." This friendly exchange marked the end of an era for the native people. In 1779, Portolá's replacement, Governor Felipe de Neve, would populate *El Pueblo de Nuestra Señora la Reina de Los Angeles de Porciúnculá.* It would no longer be the Bay of Smokes.

When word went out across Mexico that *pobladores,* settlers, were invited to this new land, the response was limp. Eventually, 11 impoverished farmers were recruited with promises of seven-acre farms, along with seed, tools, horses, 10 pesos a month and a plot of land 20 *varas* (55 feet) by 40 *varas* (110 feet) facing the plaza they planned to build. With their wives and children, they formed a community of 44 *pobladores,* the first settlers in Los Angeles. Two were full-blooded Spaniards, plus four Indians, one Mestizo, two Negroes and two Mulattos. Twenty-two were children. Governor Neve designed a traditional pueblo where each residence faced a common plaza with a church in its center. September 4, 1781, the day that Governor Neve completed his plan, is recognized as the birthday of Los Angeles. (The LA County Fair coincides each year to celebrate this date.)

As the *pobladores* went to work on the community, the friars at the San Gabriel Mission went to work on the Indians. While learning to communicate with the Yang-na, they produced foods from seeds never seen before by the natives; they provided shelter to the native people in exchange for their labor. Then the friars introduced stories about evil, about Satan, and why the red man was destined to a place called Hell unless he was baptized immediately. An entire culture was lured into submission.

San Gabriel Mission

The friars were organized; they planned industries

The Founding of Los Angeles (mural at LA Public Library), Dean Cornwell, 1932

at the mission. They taught the native hunter-gatherers about farming, and the appeal of harvesting crops instead of scavenging for them. They soon had the Indians building a dam that diverted fresh water to irrigate the fields for the mission. They introduced citrus trees; they made olive oil. They built a granary and kept it stocked. Chickens and roosters held in captivity provided a steady supply of meat and eggs — captivity being a foreign concept to the natives. Eventually, the mission even expanded to include cattle for the manufacture of cowhides and tallow. Friars gave the orders, but natives did the work. Free Indian labor was the basis for nearly all the mission's achievements. With the friars and the *pobladores* controlling all the suitable farmland, Native Americans were forced to work the lands they once occupied with abandon.

Journalists who visited during those early decades decried what they witnessed. The Native Americans were slaves on their own land. In 1786, just five years after the founding of Los Angeles, visiting French sea captain Galaup de la Pérouse wrote: "The moment an Indian allowed himself to be baptized he relinquished every particle of liberty and subjected himself body and soul to tyranny from which there was no escape. The church then claimed him as its own . . . and enforced its claims with the strong hand of power."

If a baptized Indian ran away in an attempt to return to native independence, he was hunted down by soldiers from the *Presidio*, brought back and lashed into submission. There were stocks and a whipping post in the mission courtyard for discipline. Despite the broken spirits of the Yang-na, the success of the pueblo actually attracted *more* Native Americans into the mission. Indians from the outlying islands and from San Diego found their way to Los Angeles, where they too learned about eternal damnation, then offered themselves up for baptism. The captain continues: "In a short while after the establishment of the mission, resistance was almost unknown. Three or four hundred [Native Americans] were driven to their labors by three or four soldiers like so many cattle."

The following year, in an effort to break the friars' monopoly on free labor, the new governor delivered his "Instructions for the Corporal Guard of the Pueblo of Los Angeles." It set some rules for engaging the Native Americans, who now had the freedom to choose between employment at the missions or the sprawling pueblo-associated ranchos.

What the natives didn't get was land or wages. They also didn't get their god *Chinigchinich*, for the friars destroyed every trace of pagan idolatry they encountered. In 1830, the U.S. Congress passed the Indian Removal Act, when Native Americans were shoved and slaughtered across the states, but there was no Trail of Tears in Los Angeles. With barely a skirmish, the land had been out of Yang-na control for decades. Its people were raped, beaten and exploited, completely dependent upon the missionaries and the rancheros for their survival. Even children worked. In 1836, the last of the independent Yang-na abandoned the ancestral land, and the native

Native women watch men play a game at a mission.

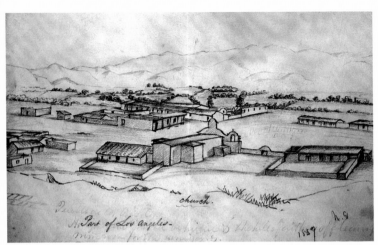

Drawing by William Rich Hutton depicting a section of Los Angeles, c. 1847

culture ceased to exist in Los Angeles.

Torrential rains flooded Governor Neve's original pueblo. The natives moved the *pobladores* to higher ground in 1818, where they built a new plaza and a new church that still stand today at historic Olvera Street. It was added to the National Register of Historic Places in 1972. For generations, the plaza was the cultural gathering place for Los Angeles.

A tragic surprise lurked when the natives mixed with the Catholics: syphilis, smallpox, measles and every other European disease to which the natives lacked immunity. Living in crowded, unsanitary conditions, they died in droves. More than 6,000 indigenous people are buried at the San Gabriel Mission, ravaged by diseases. By the time the missions were secularized and the last Franciscan departed in 1852, the Yang-na were decimated. Though the Franciscan Friars came to *Alta California* with high ideals, their efforts resulted in genocide.

From this sad start, one of the world's most vibrant cities was born. Native American muscle built the first structures, providing the grist for subsequent generations. At the same time, *pobladores* invested their souls to make Los Angeles work, and happily for us, they succeeded. Many generations later, this indentation off the coastline is still renowned as a Bay of Smokes!

IN THE MOVIES:

Much of Charlie Chaplin's film *The Kid* (1921) is filmed in the rundown pueblo. Also, *Double Indemnity* (1944), *Lethal Weapon 3* (1992) and, on television, *The Roy Rogers and Dale Evans Show* (1962).

CHAPTER 2.

FANDANGOS IN THE PUEBLO
WEALTHY MEXICANS AND THE SIEGE OF LOS ANGELES
1786–1848

Joy was in the air on September 4, 1786. The founding fathers were honored by the governor on this fifth anniversary of *El Pueblo de Nuestra Señora la Reina de Los Angeles de Porciúnculá*.

After five years of grueling labor, building the pueblo from the ground up, it was time to get paid. Each man had earned the title to a generous parcel of land, plus his small plot facing the plaza. One by one, the *pobladores* were called forward, then ceremoniously presented with a deed and a branding iron. Each neighbor signed for his property with an X because none of them knew how to read or write. Then, each one learned the unique insignia he would burnish into his livestock, enabling cattle to mingle across property lines in communal pastures (since barbed wire wouldn't be invented for another 100 years). From this day forward, the Spanish-speaking residents of the pueblo would be known as *Californios*.

Prior to this day, the governor dismissed three of the original 11 heads of families for being "useless." Only eight of the original settlers witnessed this memorable day, though property was awarded to two sons of a dismissed

Old Spanish and Mexican ranchos of Los Angeles County, 1830

black man, Luis Quintero. One of those parcels eventually expanded to become the 4,500-acre *Rodeo de las Aguas*, known today as Beverly Hills.

It was also the day that the stipends from Spain officially ended. Now each family was expected to harvest wheat and grain for profit, and to pay taxes to the king. But after years of living in huts they made from willow branches, the prospect of a solid one-room, windowless adobe on the plaza was reason to celebrate. The *pobladores* gave thanks.

As the pueblo's good news attracted more residents, even bigger celebrations would follow. Twenty more families soon joined the pueblo, bestowed with spectacular land grants by the governor, thanks to their political connections. Chief among them:

Juan José Dominguez, one of Governor Portolá's original foot soldiers back in 1769, was granted 75,000 acres of land; he is acknowledged as the first *ranchero* in Los Angeles. He drove his herd of horses and 200 heads of cattle from San Diego to the site he named Rancho San Pedro, overlooking today's port at San Pedro Bay, a distance of more than 100 miles. Dominguez was an instant celebrity, as every enterprising *ranchero* in the pueblo had to haul their goods through his vast territory to reach the port. (Today, it's home to Boeing; Honda; California State University, Dominguez Hills; and the busiest seaport in America.)

Corporal José María Verdugo and his brother Mariano were granted 36,000 acres that make up today's Burbank and Glendale neighborhoods. (Today, The Walt Disney Company stands on Buena Vista Drive, part of the original Verdugo territory.) Their Rancho San Rafael became even more famous for its rodeos and fiestas than for the voluminous cowhides they delivered to the port at San Pedro for shipment to Boston and New York. They set the pace for a generation of revelers.

By 1790, the pueblo's official population was up to 139 residents. The pueblo had a chapel, a town hall, a guardhouse, granaries, irrigation canals, a protective wall that surrounded the central pueblo and even an *alcalde*: a mayor to oversee justice and morality, who was constantly busy.

Since the *Californios* regularly produced more grain, cattle, horses and sheep than any other community in California, suddenly there was . . . wealth. Los Angeles gained a reputation as one big party town. There was revelry in the Plaza, and celebrations on the sprawling acres recently awarded to *rancheros*.

Like a lord overseeing a European manor, a ranchero owned a self-contained community that employed craftsmen, herdsmen, leatherworkers, harness-makers, sheepshearers, cooks, seamstresses, housekeepers, a few freeloading relatives and a small army of Indians who cared for the crops and everything else. A large spread required the efforts of hundreds, all living outside the confines of the central pueblo.

With so much free labor, the wealthy rancheros did little work. They dressed in fancy silks and velvet suits embroidered with gold threads. They lived for their *fandangos*: each month brought fiestas, birthdays and holiday celebrations. On Sundays, they fenced in the Plaza for bullfights, eventually constructing a bullring on *Calle del Toro*, near today's Chinatown. (The

'Californios' during the Mexican Rancho period

bull was rarely killed; sacrificing a bull was too costly.) At the annual rodeo, cattle were divided by their rancho brands. Horses bore ornate saddles bedecked with silver mountings and rawhide reins. As the *aguardiente* brandy flowed, wagers were placed and emotions ran high when competitions in bronco riding and horsemanship measured the skills and daring of each rancho community.

Celebrations got even louder when Mexico declared its independence from Spain in 1821. No more scrutiny from the judgmental friars at the San Gabriel Mission. All Spanish-born priests were ordered out of California. Across the state, the government took control of an estimated $78 million worth of land and chattel (that's more than $1.5 billion today) developed by European ingenuity and the lives of overworked Indians. At the time of the transfer in 1834, Mission San Gabriel had 3,000 Indians, 20,000 horses, more than 100,000 cattle and eight million acres of land. Half the land was supposed to go to the Indians, but that didn't happen. Political connections with Mexico prevailed. The governor awarded land grants to only 800 families who assumed control of eight million acres. Spacious ranchos soon followed.

In 1835, the pueblo was declared a *ciudad* (city), and designated as the state capital. The transfer of power took years, however, because a succession of Mexican governors were reluctant to exchange the comforts of Monterey in the north for an unruly town in the south.

There were no public buildings to run the government in LA, yet it had saloons, bordellos and gambling dens as new and permanent fixtures. Until government buildings were constructed, the home of Judge Olvera, who occupied the largest house on the north side of the Plaza, served as the local courtroom. (Today's Olvera Street is named for the respected Mexican judge.) Across the street, Gibson's Gambling House's green table was frequently piled high with $50-gold ingots, while wealthy *rancheros* risked their increasing fortunes.

The first Yankee to see LA was also the first one to stay. Joseph John Chapman was arrested as a pirate, but he proved to be a skilled Jack-of-all-trades, with talents as a carpenter, blacksmith and amateur surgeon. He converted to Catholicism, married into a prominent Mexican family and was welcomed among the *gente de razon*, society's upper crust.

Other Anglos followed. John Temple and George Rice opened the town's first general store in 1828 (at the corner of today's Temple and Main streets). According to the census, there were more than 2,000 residents, but only 250 women. Temple labeled 15 of those working girls as "M.V." (*Mala Vida*—Bad Life.)

Another Anglo who could write was Richard Henry Dana, Jr., a sailor in the 1830s. He penned the classic *Two Years Before the Mast*, recounting his two-year journey from Boston to *Alta California*, around the tip of South America. Highly critical of the relaxed *Californio* culture, he found *rancheros* to be "thriftless, proud and extravagant, and very much given to gaming." Dana anticipated the culture clash that was to come: "Yankees can't afford the time to be Catholics . . . . In the hands of an enterprising people, what a country this might be!"

From left: Joseph John Chapman and Gaudalupe Ortega y Sánchez c. 1847; Pio Pico family: Marianita Alvarado (niece), Señora Pico, Pio Pico, Trinidad Ortega (niece), c. 1850

Battle of Rio San Gabriel, Mexican-American War, 1847

His words proved to be prophetic. Governor Pio Pico saw the firestorm approaching, too. He urged secession from "the mock republic of Mexico," advocating alignment with England or France, "the two great powers in Europe," but he failed to rally support. On May 13, 1846, America declared war with Mexico. Ninety days later, American troops led by Captain John C. Frémont and Commodore Robert F. Stockton took control of Los Angeles, the state capital, without firing a single shot. With 50 men left in charge, Commodore Stockton chuckled over the bloodless "Siege of Los Angeles" as the American flag with 28 stars (not yet including a star for California) was raised over the Plaza.

To make friends, Stockton's military band provided the first full concert in California during the next sunset on the Plaza. As wide-eyed children and stunned adults peered from their darkened homes, the delight was apparent. The following sunset, they performed again, and this time a large circle of *Californios* surrounded the musicians, offering more heartfelt *¡Vivas!* at each song's conclusion. An elderly priest sat by the church door, near tears. He disclosed that he hadn't heard a real band since he left Spain 50 years earlier. "Ah," he admitted, "that music will do more service to the conquest of California than a thousand bayonets."

He was right. As the crowd was enraptured by the one-hour concert, Stockton's men assessed the adobe on the Plaza that was left unoccupied by the widow Ávila, who fled to safety away from the Plaza. They promptly commandeered the place for Stockton's new home and central headquarters for the remainder of the war.

Abruptly, there was a new kind of party in town, and it was no longer a *fandango*. Governor Pio Pico is remembered as the last Mexican governor of California. Today, a major thoroughfare bears his name. (An entire town is

Los Angeles (looking northeast), 1850

named for Captain Frémont.) The Mexican-American War raged for nearly two years, with just one skirmish in Los Angeles that was suppressed when Captain Frémont returned with reinforcements. There were no additional conflicts in the conquest for Los Angeles.

When the war ended in 1848, Stockton's music stopped. For *Californios* in Los Angeles, the party was over.

Today, Olvera Street and the Plaza are national landmarks open to the public daily. For free guided tours of LA's historic pueblo, visit elpueblo.lacity.org to make reservations.

IN THE MOVIES:
Restored Olvera Street is seen in *Runaway Jury* (2003), *Death Wish II* (1982), and on the hit TV series *Beverly Hills 90210* (1993).

CHAPTER 3.

CULTURE CLASH
THE RACIAL TENSIONS OF STATEHOOD
1850s—1860s

"Eureka!" was the cry in 1848: Gold in California! It was the beginning of a new era, drastically reinventing the state.

Dreamers from around the world plotted their routes to reach remote California. Miners from New Mexico, from Ireland, from China; they came on boats or on the backs of mules. On their way to fortune, thousands of prospectors passed through Los Angeles, a Spanish-speaking town similar to Tucson or Santa Fe, with about 1,600 residents and a reputation as the toughest town in the nation. Blood flowed when four diverse cultures converged, violently, on the Wild West Coast.

Latinos
First, the American Army captured Mexico City in the Mexican-American War; now the Mexicans had surrendered. They set the date to sign the treaty that would cede all territory north of the Rio Grande, the new national border. The U.S. was about to annex all or part of 10 states in this massive Mexican Cession, but nine days before the signing, gold was discovered at Sutter's Mill on the American River, not far from Sacramento.

Westward the Course of Empire Takes Its Way (detail) by Emanuel Gottlieb Leutze, 1861. The title is from a 1726 poem by George Berkeley about Manifest Destiny

Anglos, Native Americans, Latinos and Chinese engaged in gold prospecting, c. 1850

Suddenly, all eyes turned to Northern California, where dreams of personal fortune overtook national allegiance. It was every man for himself.

In 1850, California became America's 31st state. More than 100,000 English-speaking Americans arrived, vastly outnumbering the 13,000 Spanish-speaking residents. Banks, gambling dens, gun shops and prostitutes all set up business. The *Californios* were treated as a conquered people. They chafed at the injustices, but also joined the fray, dropping their genteel lifestyle for even greater wealth. Somebody had to feed those 100,000 Anglos, and the *Californios* controlled all the property and the food supply now that the missionaries were gone. The price of beef skyrocketed; cattle went from $2 a head in 1848 to $70 a head in 1849.

Racial hostility escalated at the gold mines. Hateful mobs harassed Mexican miners and burned their living quarters. Passing the Foreign Miners Tax Law of 1850, the new state government legally extorted $16 from every Spanish-speaking miner (that's more than $400 today), even if they were born in California. Legalized racial profiling drove the Latinos from the northern California mines. Where did they land? Many chose Los Angeles, which soon became home to both extremes, the wealthiest and the most desperate Mexican expatriates in the U.S.

Anglos

"Manifest Destiny" was the lofty term used by journalists, intellectuals and politicians: the belief that America was on a divine mission to build a free nation "from sea to shining sea." The acquisition of California served as proof; the nation now spanned the entire continent. Anglos were in charge, as destined by God. The *alcalde* was out, and the Mayor was in.

In the first years of statehood, industrious new overlords were determined to suffocate *Californio* culture. Bullfights were out; baseball was in. The first building erected with public funds was a jail. Next, the Anglos built the first public school, the first post office, the first Protestant church and the first synagogue; they established the first newspapers and opened the first stagecoach company.

Not everyone was so civic minded, however. Anglos also introduced extraordinary violence. The New York Volunteers who kept the peace at the end of the Mexican-American War were inner-city thugs from the Bowery and the Five Points in Manhattan. When their battalion disbanded at the war's end, many chose to stay in Los Angeles. Some found responsible positions in society; the rest were sharpshooting thugs. They mixed with another brawling crowd of Anglos—the con men and swindlers driven out of the gold mines in northern California. All of them populated a place that the *Los Angeles Times* called "the wickedest street on earth."

A short distance from the Plaza was the *Calle de los Negros*, Street of the Blacks, allegedly named for the dark-skinned *pobladores* who first settled there. With statehood, many street names were Anglicized. The place was renamed Nigger Alley, a moniker that stuck for more than 40 years. The street was lined with saloons, gambling halls, dance houses and brothels. America's rowdiest slum averaged one homicide a day, not including Indians. Stabbings and gunfights were so common that even the local law officials didn't attempt to make an arrest there.

When Samuel Colt invented his new six-shot revolver "for civilian use," the violence spread. Lawyers and judges proved to be reckless with firearms, too. California's first attorney general, Edward J. C. Kewen, tried to shoot the opposing lawyer during a criminal trial. Instead, he wounded a spectator, which sent

The Colt Caliber .45, Model 1873, was used by lawmen and outlaws alike in the Wild West. It garnered the nickname 'Peacemaker.'

the jury fleeing to the streets. In another incident in 1855, the mayor quit his job so he could take part in a lynching, after which he was immediately re-elected.

By 1860, Los Angeles was squalid. A force of only six officers could not keep the peace. Stray dogs roamed the streets. The open ditches that irrigated the town now served as laundry stations, hog wallows, even latrines. The unpaved roads were dusty in summer, then turned to mud troughs when the rains came. And, everyone avoided the plaza at night for fear of being robbed or assaulted. *Californios* had to ask: Was this part of America's Manifest Destiny, too?

Chinese

No one of African descent lived on Nigger Alley. (African Americans migrated to Los Angeles in the decades after the Civil War.) Instead, the Chinese population dwelt among the rackety saloons because they were permitted no place else. America may have been founded on principles of religious liberty, but worshipping a different deity was never an option. California's rejection was swift. The *Los Angeles News* editorialized that the Chinese, with their hair braided in long, odd *queues* were "an alien, an inferior, idolatrous race."

The Chinese weren't here to seek religious liberty. California was *Gum Shan*, 金山, Gold Mountain. They were dreamers like everyone else from around the world who came to seek their fortunes. When that fortune failed to materialize and hostilities increased, Chinese immigrants sought better conditions elsewhere. Many found their way to Los Angeles. They were joined along the way by Chinese laborers who were set adrift as the Transcontinental Railroad neared completion.

Chinese laundry, c. 1878

Most Chinese men envisioned years of modest living while

working and saving in Los Angeles, then retiring on that savings back in China, surrounded by old friends and family. First, they had to find a way to get ahead in LA's booming economy.

Some Chinese opened shops in their rowdy neighborhood, selling tea, preserves and Chinese goods, mostly to the other Chinese. They made overtures to the local press to broaden their businesses, but faced a harsh reality: Readers only seemed interested in the peculiarities of Chinese culture that could give them a few laughs.

That's when the Chinese laundry was born. In the mining camps, Chinese were amazed that other miners shipped their clothes all the way to Hawaii for washing and pressing, then waited months for the parcel of clothing to return. With no experience, Chinese men set up hand-laundry shops, providing a faster service at a lower cost. They had no particular affinity for the laundry; it was a business that required a minimal investment. They liked the math: they could earn $4 a month toiling in Chinese rice fields back home, or make $15 to $20 a month working in a Los Angeles laundry. That equation motivated more Chinese laundries to open across America.

Tensions increased within the Chinese community. They adopted the local method for settling disputes: six-shooters. The steady violence even prompted one Chinese man to apply for the first life insurance policy in 1871. Since most Angelenos weren't in the crosshairs, they dismissed these violent outbursts as entertainment.

Indians

When Mexico signed the Cession treaty, it required the U.S. to grant citizenship to the California Indians, a detail that the U.S. government managed to overlook for 80 years. Instead, the California Constitution considered the Indians to be non-persons, with no protection under the law. It was impossible to bring an Anglo to trial for killing an Indian or for forcing Indians off the land.

With the secularization of the San Gabriel Mission, 3,500 Native Americans in Los Angeles were now crowded into a *pueblito* between Aliso and First Streets, a block away from Nigger Alley. Thousands of Native American children were kidnapped and put to work as child laborers.

Drunken Indians were sold in a slave mart each week. When Indian laborers in the vineyards were paid with *aguardiente* brandy, those laborers with little tolerance for alcohol wound up inebriated. On Saturday night, the town marshal would round up the drunks, then corral them overnight, awaiting someone to pay their fines. In the morning, they were offered for sale, as slaves for the next week. According to Horace Bell in his *Reminiscences of a Ranger,* " . . . the slave at Los Angeles was sold 52 times a year. Thousands of honest, useful people were absolutely destroyed in this way."

For Native Americans in Los Angeles, this was the last gasp. With no property, no money, and the laws stacked against them, they relied on others for survival. But their choices were limited to the Spanish-speaking people who treated them like slaves, or the English-speaking people who wanted them to disappear.

The Clash
Before the outbreak of the Civil War, Los Angeles was locked in a race war. Rampant crime led the Anglos to assert themselves with vigilante committees. If law enforcement couldn't keep the peace, then it was time for civilians to take control. Organizations like the Los Angeles Rangers, 23 men on horseback, including some former Texas Rangers, exerted their form of justice. With Anglos in control of the laws, the courts and the prisons, the only criminals they brought to justice (or lynched, shot or imprisoned) were Latinos and Indians. Public hangings were well attended.

From left: Joaquin Murrieta Carrillo was considered either an infamous bandit or a Mexican patriot in the 1850s; robbing a stage wagon, *Hands Up,* 1897

Los Angeles Plaza, 1869

Latinos had an angry response to the Anglo ideas of justice. Teams of *bandidos* soon terrorized the countryside. They robbed the Wells Fargo wagon nearly 300 times in a decade. Fifty *bandidos* killed an Anglo rancher in 1857. That started a rumor that 500 Mexicans were about to invade. The LA sheriff took six deputies to investigate, only to be ambushed and slaughtered. Los Angeles Rangers leapt to the rescue. With a posse of 119 bloodthirsty rangers and Indians, they overtook the *bandidos*, lynching nine of them before handing over the rest to the courts. From the brand-new gallows at Fort Hill (near today's Cathedral of Our Lady of the Angels), the *bandido* leader was hanged before a crowd of 3,000 spectators. Hispanophobia continued unabated, with Anglos fearing that a revolt might reunite California with Mexico.

There was one topic on which Anglos, Indians and Latinos agreed: Everyone hated the Chinese. Newspapers incited that hatred through libelous editorials, falsely claiming that the "heathen Chinee" were usurping work from local residents. The Chinese were taunted on the streets, pelted with stones; their windows were smashed, their houses were torched. An Anglo hit a Chinaman on the head "because I wanted to." The *Los Angeles News* celebrated the opening of the first Anglo laundry, inviting customers who were "not partial to Chinese labor." Vigilante culture reigned.

The Chinese responded by preparing for battle. Instead of uniting, however, they split into *tongs*, factions competing for dominance within their community. The internal conflict between these gangs took an epic twist in 1871: It instigated a massacre of the Chinese people.

CHAPTER 4.

THE MASSACRE
CHINESE TONG WAR ENDS AS A HISTORIC TRAGEDY
1871

There were not enough women. In 1870, there were a reported 172 Chinese people living in Los Angeles, and 90 percent of them were males. Most of the Chinese women were brought from Asia to work in the sex trade. In Los Angeles, Chinese men in love with their American spouses were a rarified few.

Instead, Chinese men married young women to set them up as prostitutes; their nuptials put the illicit business beyond the reach of law enforcement. It was no surprise, then, when beautiful Yut Ho married a wealthy man who was greatly her senior. But in March 1871, her dashing young lover arrived by carriage bearing a legal wedding certificate; with help from three friends, he successfully abducted her.

The newspapers had a ball with the romantic caper, but it was no laughing matter. A decade earlier, all Chinese people were united in one *huiguan* society. Now, their unity was split along clan lines into three separate *tongs*, all competing for income from prostitution. That dashing young lover was employed by a competing gang, a detail the newspapers glorified. The *Los*

The Chinese Question, Thomas Nast, *Harper's Weekly*, 1871. Columbia tells an angry mob, "Hands Off, Gentlemen! American means fair play for all men."

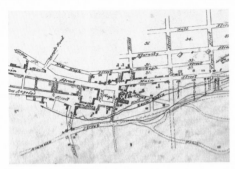

Los Angeles, 1868

Angeles News called the *tongs* "rival companies, which hated each other like Christians."

The enraged old husband went to court, but that backfired when the judge acknowledged the young lover's wedding certificate and ordered Yut Ho to remain with her abductor. So the old man called for reinforcements from San Francisco. *Tong* warfare would soon escalate.

When the steamship *California* docked in San Pedro in September 1871, tong fighters from San Francisco disembarked; professional hitmen with a job to do. The Chinese community knew this showdown was coming. Nearly 50 handguns were sold to Chinese men in the four days prior to the steamship's arrival.

On Tuesday October 24, with Yut Ho apparently hidden out of town, the bullets started flying. No longer a grudge match between two competing grooms, this was a battle for dominance between the Hong Chow (to which Yut Ho's new groom belonged) and Nin Yung *tongs*. A local tong fighter drew first blood when he overtook a San Francisco hitman, shot him in the neck, then fled as the dead body dropped to the dust on Nigger Alley.

Officer Jesús Bilderrain, one of LA's seven policemen, heard the gunshots. He and Police Officer Esteban Sanchez raced to Nigger Alley on horseback. As the gangs faced off with pistols in the street, Bilderrain charged through them to break up the fight. When the horse reared, he pursued the hitmen on foot, heading into the dilapidated Coronel Building at the end of Nigger Alley. Bilderrain blew his whistle with all his might to summon support, then faced a barrage of bullets. He staggered out into the street, clutching his bloody shoulder. The hitmen continued to shoot indiscriminately, still locked in tong warfare, but the rest of Los Angeles saw something very different: For the first time ever, a Chinaman shot a police officer.

When Robert Thompson, a beloved former saloonkeeper, joined Officer Sanchez in coming to Bilderrain's aid, he was shot and killed next. At that instant, race relations in Los Angeles took a furious twist. As Robert Thompson's body was carried into Wollweber's Drug Store on Main Street, every white man within view put his hand on his gun. It was time to eradicate the Chinamen.

Saloons emptied immediately. Shops closed their iron shutters. When one Chinese attempted to escape from the Coronel Building, his body was riddled with bullets. Mexicans and Anglos surrounded the building, taunting the Chinese who had barricaded themselves inside. Both City Marshal Frank Baker and County Sheriff James Burns begged for calm, but the frenzied crowd was determined to avenge Thompson's death. No one knew that almost all the professional *tong* fighters from San Francisco, who smelled trouble and knew when to leave, had already escaped from the neighborhood.

Before sundown, the mob had grown to nearly 500 people. They shot at the

Lafayette Hotel stagecoach near the adobes in Calle de los Negros (now it's Alameda Street near Union Station and Terminal Annex Building). Old Coronel Building in the background, c. 1871

An anti-Chinese riot, 1880

adobe walls of the Coronel Building; they climbed onto the roof and fired down inside. Eventually, they broke in by battering down the doors to adjoining buildings. Innocent Chinese people anywhere in the vicinity were wounded and killed by the wild mob in a bloody rampage that raged for more than four hours. Chinatown's highly respected physician, Chee Long Tong, begged for his life in fluent English and in Spanish. He volunteered his gold ring to buy his life, but he and five other victims were dragged to Temple Street, where they were hanged from the gates of a corral.

Nooses were placed around the necks of four Chinese men as they escaped from the Coronel Building. Others were dragged by their *queues*, poked, jeered and stabbed on their way to Commercial Street, where they were shot and hanged from the bows of freight wagons. Six more were hanged from the awning of a wagon shop and a saloon. Chinese-owned shops were looted and ransacked. Approximately $30,000 in cash, jewelry and merchandise was stolen within hours (that's more than half a million dollars today).

When the mob finally wore itself out, countless people were wounded; 19 bodies, more than 10 percent of the Chinese population, lay dead. By 11 p.m. that night, the streets were empty and the saloons were filled. Blood-spattered men celebrated their massacre. Some held up the queues they sliced from Chinese napes for souvenirs. It's the moment when LA's vigilante culture reached its climax.

Pride turned to revulsion the next morning when Angelenos got a good look at the devastation in Chinatown, with rope fragments and bloodstains still fresh on the streets. It was the biggest lynching in American history; the first time that a story from Los Angeles made international news, knocking the Chicago Fire off the front page of the *New York Times*. The reputation for all of California suffered as a result. The *San Francisco Examiner* chided that the "ruthless slaughter" was a "disgrace to the State." Publications across the country condemned lawless Los Angeles; one East Coast editorial recommended that "certain portions of California" should be "placed under martial law."

The bodies were laid out in double rows on the northern side of the jail (near today's City Hall), some with the ropes still taut around their necks. Dr. Tong's finger was severed to steal his gold ring; his pockets were torn to steal his money. In the intimate Chinese community, everyone had a direct connection to at least one of the dead. The eyewitnesses who placed the bodies into coffins told the newspaper reporter that just one of the dead men was a *tong* warrior. Everyone else was innocent. The Chinese men were buried in the non-denominational City Cemetery, with Dr. Tong's coffin leading the procession.

Newspapers eulogized Robert Thompson as "a generous hearted, liberal man" with a wife and young daughter. He was "killed while aiding an officer in the discharge of his duties." Three weeks later, Mrs. Thompson gave birth to twins, and went on to raise three fatherless children.

Forty-nine rioters were indicted, but just seven were found guilty. Judge Robert M. Widney, the founder of the University of Southern California, had been hastily appointed to fill a vacancy on the bench, but he was ill prepared. On appeal, his indictment failed on a legal technicality: From the language of his indictment, the appellate court could not reach the conclusion that anyone

Chinese corpses at the LA jail, awaiting coffins and burial, 1871

The Dragon Parade and the Chinese New Year's Day celebration in old Chinatown, c. 1900

was actually murdered. The seven defendants served less than one year in jail before their convictions were overturned and all men were set free. No one was held accountable for the massacre in Chinatown.

A steady stream of immigrants continued to arrive from China, unperturbed by this violent incident. Chinese men married Chinese brides and started families. Buildings were rebuilt and Chinatown expanded for a decade. Then a harsh new federal law intervened: The Chinese Exclusion Act prohibited Chinese immigration for decades (until the U.S. needed soldiers for World War II). Nigger Alley and Old Chinatown were demolished to make way for Union Station in the 1930s. A new Chinatown was erected to the west of the historic Plaza where it continues to flourish today.

Beautiful Yut Ho was never heard from again. Los Angeles reporters apparently lost interest in her story, and the city fathers were happy to keep it that way. Los Angeles was about to get connected to the Transcontinental Railroad, a chance to inject new blood into the hotheaded community. From this tragic ebb, Los Angeles would reinvent itself again in a new chapter of prosperity and growth, though race relations continued to simmer.

IN THE MOVIES:

The sites in this chronicle were used (many years later) in the following films; *Gangster Squad* (2013), *The Green Hornet* (2011), *Fast and Furious 4* (2009), *Made of Honor* (2008), *Rush Hour* (1998), *Lethal Weapon 4* (1998), *Chinatown* (1974), *The Dragon Seed* (1944) and many more.

The Anti-Chinese Wall; the American wall goes up as the Chinese original goes down, F. Grätz, 1882

CHAPTER 5.

HUNTINGTON'S BOOM
THE IRON HORSE POKES ITS HEAD THROUGH SAN FERNANDO TUNNEL
1876

When a golden spike was driven into a railroad track in Promontory Summit, Utah Territory in 1869, the Transcontinental Railroad united America from New York to San Francisco. By then, the whole nation had gone a little train-crazy. Boosters even hailed railroads as the "triumph of civilization." Speculators constructed railroads seemingly everywhere ... except Los Angeles.

Collis P. Huntington is credited with the first transcontinental link. The intense New York City businessman was one of the Big Four moguls who controlled the "octopus," the Union Pacific and the Southern Pacific Railroads. It was their Union Pacific that provided the final tracks on the Transcontinental Railroad, terminating at San Francisco. Now, a federal charter empowered Huntington to link it with the Southern Pacific, too. A railroad tentacle finally reached Los Angeles, reversing the city's fortune and reputation with a most welcome boom. Huntington brought civilization to the Wild West Coast, not to seek heroics, but to seize extraordinary wealth.

Southern Pacific train to San Francisco entering San Fernando Tunnel, c. 1898

Across the Continent: Westward the Course of Empire Takes Its Way, 1868

In the 1870s, the railroad industry was big business, the era's major economic force. Then a bank that backed the railroads went broke. The Panic of 1873 was a financial catastrophe that drove railroad speculators and just about everybody else to ruin. Prices fell so fast on the New York Stock Exchange that it closed early and didn't reopen for 10 days! Credit dried up. Huntington's brokers went bankrupt.

Not Huntington. The world's loss was his gain. The Big Four were robber barons, owners of a massive asset financed largely by other people's money, a railroad that could now acquire others at bargain rates to link them or cut them off altogether. The Big Four monopolized rail construction and travel for a huge section of the continent, then lined their pockets. The cash outlay to build a railroad was so astounding that it even broke a bank, but the payoff to former California Governor Leland Stanford, hot-tempered railroader Charles Crocker, numbers cruncher Mark Hopkins and hard bargainer Huntington was even more astounding because it grew exponentially. Still, when pondering potential routes for expansion, the Big Four were ruthless. They approached city officials to enquire how much their communities were willing to pay for a railroad, and then, if a town failed to meet the Big Four's suggestion, the tracks were laid many miles away. Some Western towns turned to dust while others sprang up practically overnight near railway stations.

Collis P. Huntington

Los Angeles—a violent pueblo of just 6,000 people that were policed by vigilantes—was no contender for a railroad terminal. The city fathers approached Huntington twice, and failed twice to agree. Besides, the Big Four observed, the Cajon Pass was a natural route through the rugged terrain. A route to Los Angeles would require a tunnel. They planned to make San Bernardino into a western metropolis on the Southern Pacific line and end the route at San Diego with its large, natural seaport.

The U.S. Congress disagreed. An 1871 bill stipulated Southern Pacific must build its track from San Francisco "by way of Los Angeles" without the Cajon Pass. When Huntington met with LA's former governor John G. Downey on the third approach in San Francisco in April 1872, Huntington agreed to take the money: a subsidy of more than $600,000 from Los Angeles (that's almost $13 million today), plus 60 acres for a depot, and something dirtier. An upstart was already running a new railroad from LA's Bay of Smokes itself, the port at San Pedro; it linked the city to its port. Huntington demanded that, too. In exchange, the Southern Pacific would build a minimum of 50 miles of track through Los Angeles County in 15 months, including a spur to the groves in Anaheim—but they would only collect the subsidy if the railroad was delivered on time.

The race was on! A task force of 350 Chinese tunnel diggers went to work on a staggering piece of construction. The tunnel through the San Fernando Mountain, at more than 7,000 feet, would be the fourth longest in the world. Predictably, it was dangerous work; before electricity, equipment was powered by steam stoked from flaming coal. It necessitated the use of high-pressure drainage pumps and artificial ventilation 400 feet below the earth's surface. Cave-ins were frequent, and the air was so humid that the

torchlights could barely stay lit. The project's pace ratcheted up. Another 1,500 workers, mostly Chinese, were added to the project. Even veteran workers found the project frightening, yet the tunneling progressed about 24 feet per day. Final cost: two million dollars; far more than the amount they were racing for.

Finally, on July 14, 1876, barely 90 days before deadline, the headings met under San Fernando Mountain. When a telegraph operator wired, "The Iron Horse poked his head through the San Fernando tunnel at six o'clock this evening and neighed a long, loud and hearty greeting," the people of LA fired the cannon in front of the opera house repeatedly. A spontaneous, torchlit parade rejoiced through the pueblo streets. The Transcontinental Railroad would link Los Angeles, land of bountiful orange groves and eternal sunshine, with the rest of America.

Another golden spike, driven by Huntington's partner Charles Crocker on September 5, 1876, marked the ceremonial delivery of one new railroad: the day that LA was reborn.

The city's boosters wasted no time. Tons of publicity flooded the East and Midwest. Settlement agents, land bureaus, lectures, exhibits and news stories all touted the City of the Angels, part of a grand plan to get paying customers onto trains bound for California. It worked. Some came for "the Cure" in LA's glorious climate; others came to raise families and grow oranges. All of them relied on Huntington's trains.

Southern Pacific map (detail), 1876

He attempted to monopolize the freight routes in and out of the port on the little San Pedro & Los Angeles Railroad, but the courts put an end to that. Years later, the Supreme Court forced the divestiture of the Union Pacific and Southern Pacific Railroads to break up its monopoly.

Meanwhile, the economy of the dusty little *pueblo* went boom! With the railroad's arrival, Los Angeles County planned 100 new townships, including Hollywood, Burbank, Santa Monica and Glendale. (An even bigger boom would come when the movie camera was invented.)

The Los Angeles and San Pedro Station, the first railroad into Los Angeles, c. 1880

Epilogue:

The golden spike was replaced with a plaque, and the site at Promontory Summit was designated as a Registered National Landmark in 1957. Today, the spike is kept in a vault at the California Historical Society in San Francisco (though a commemorative reproduction is on display at Stanford University). It is engraved: Last Spike Connecting Los Angeles And San Francisco By Rail. The date is engraved on its head, Sept. 5, 1876.

The little railroad from San Pedro to Los Angeles expanded to Las Vegas in 1904, becoming the San Pedro-Los Angeles and Salt Lake Railroad.

The city of San Bernardino was eventually connected by rail to the Atchison, Topeka & Santa Fe Railroad.

Leland Stanford, the first Republican Governor of California, became U.S. Senator Leland Stanford in 1885. He donated more than $40 million (that's more than $1 billion today) to establish the vibrant university that bears his name.

At the end of his life, the severe, implacable Collis P. Huntington reminisced, "I have never failed to do anything I set out to do." Buried in a grand mausoleum in New York's Woodlawn Cemetery, he is also remembered as a fierce Abolitionist and a generous philanthropist who served on the Board of New York's Metropolitan Museum of Art for much of his life. He encouraged his nephew Henry Huntington in the ways of philanthropy, too.

CHAPTER 6.

OIL!

DOHENY, CANFIELD, AND THE OIL QUEEN OF CALIFORNIA

1890s

The City of Los Angeles had a problem. As downtown real estate was parceled into lots, what should be done with the putrid puddles of tar that bubbled up throughout the region? Sure, the climate was ideal for the burgeoning citrus industry throughout LA County, but these gooey black pools near downtown LA hindered growth. That land was useless.

In 1892, Edward L. Doheny solved LA's problem with a lucky hunch. It also made him the wealthiest oilman on earth.

At age 18, dreaming of prosperity from stories he heard around a campfire, Doheny set out from Fond du Lac, Wisconsin, to prospect for silver in the New Mexico Territory. Working with a pick and a shovel for over a decade, he lived a rough-and-tumble existence during the 1880s. At the poker tables in Kingston, New Mexico, he met two lasting, life-altering friends: Albert B. Fall, the future Secretary of the Interior (in President Harding's cabinet; more about him later), and Charles Canfield, who would soon become Doheny's business partner.

Two men standing amidst oil derricks in an LA oil field at Court Street and Toluca Street, 1904, not far from today's Walt Disney Concert Hall.

Albert B. Fall and Edward L. Doheny, 1926

It was Canfield who had the smarts to give up prospecting so that he could speculate on Los Angeles real estate instead. Doheny sold his mining claim too, then followed Canfield to Los Angeles in 1891, where, assuredly, their fortunes beckoned.

Instead, life at the Bellevue Terrace Hotel on Sixth and Figueroa Streets in downtown Los Angeles was dire. Canfield promptly lost all his money when LA's real estate boom went bust. A penniless 36-year-old Doheny wandered the streets looking for work, or at least an inspiration.

That inspiration arrived on a spring morning in 1892. Doheny watched from the hotel steps as a wagon passed, transporting a pungent black cargo. When he called out, "What are you hauling?" the Mexican driver replied, "*brea*," the Spanish word for "pitch," the problematic tar that blemished the land around them. At the *brea* source, Doheny soon learned that the slimy stuff could replace coal as a more efficient fuel. As Doheny would later recall, "I had found gold and I had found silver, but this ugly looking substance was the key to something more valuable." It was the lucky break he'd sought for nearly two decades.

With Canfield as his partner, they borrowed $400, then leased three undeveloped lots on Patton Street (not far from today's Dodger Stadium) that were swampy with *brea*. As experienced miners, they hitched a horse to a pulley that raised and lowered their buckets into the slime, then they went to work with picks and shovels once more.

The noxious fumes could have killed them. Ignorant of the dangers they faced, toiling manually for months, gasping for air in the reeky tar, they burrowed to an incredible 155 feet beneath the earth's surface. When their shovels finally hit hard shale, another loan secured them a drill. Suspended from what would soon be known as the first oil derrick in Los Angeles, the drill bored for seven days, to a level of 200 feet. That's when the hunch paid off: The partners struck oil. On April 20, 1893, the hole on Patton Street became the first free-flowing oil well in Los Angeles. Canfield and Doheny would prosper for the rest of their lives.

They followed the *brea*, eventually establishing 81 wells in Los Angeles. Over the next decade, however, Canfield and Doheny disappeared for months at a time while their business flourished. They made their greatest fortune in Mexican jungles, creating the Mexican Petroleum Company with the blessings of Mexico's long-term president, Porfirio Diaz. Their big win came on Easter Sunday, April 3, 1904, as oil gushed sky high when their drill bored 1,450 feet below the Mexican surface. The drill tapped into an oil deposit of unfathomable magnitude. "Mexican Pete" became the most prolific oil-export on earth, generating more than 100,000 barrels *per day*. In a land of unpaved roads, the formerly destitute partners soon found themselves masterminding an international oil enterprise: They built a network of pipes to transport the crude oil to their refineries, then into their tankers for overseas shipments. The global demand for oil during World War I increased production and profits exponentially, attracting ambassadors, entrepreneurs and influential politicians as investors. For a time, it was estimated that Los Angeles resident Edward L. Doheny was wealthier than John D. Rockefeller himself, the owner of Standard Oil and Doheny's primary competitor.

Signal Hill in Los Angeles County, c. 1923

Emma Summers

Meanwhile, central Los Angeles was now a boomtown for oil. Miners and speculators descended; motivated homeowners tore down their houses to make way for oilrigs. In the 160 acres surrounding Doheny's first field on Patton Street, dozens of start-up companies drilled more than 300 wells. Teams of mules, sometimes four abreast, rutted the roads and destroyed the lawns as they dragged oil tanks and equipment to yet another site. Neighbor was pitted against neighbor as the "Law of Capture" permitted individuals to draw oil from under an adjoining property if the underground deposit flowed across the property line. The neighborhood became an incongruous collection of residences shoehorned between oil derricks. The stench was everywhere and the noise was nonstop. Every amateur dreamed of becoming the next Doheny, winning an accidental fortune by drilling into a lucky puddle of *brea*.

Even the local piano teacher joined in the speculation. Mrs. Emma Summers, a graduate of Boston's New England Conservatory of Music, invested $700 for half-interest in a well near her house at 517 California Street. (Today it's the 101 Freeway, not far from the Music Center.) By day, she learned how oil equipment worked and did the bookkeeping; in the evenings, she continued to teach piano. But Emma Summers soon became a cunning and wealthy entrepreneur, buying stakes in more wells, putting competitors out of business and consolidating her industry through economies of scale.

Although Doheny and Canfield initially convinced executives at the Atchison, Topeka and Santa Fe Railroad to convert their locomotives from coal to oil, it was Emma Summers who provided the steady oil supply to California's railroads. Her enterprise soon expanded to include trolley companies too, then downtown hotels, laundries, machine shops and even the Pacific Light and Power Company (the forerunner of today's Southern California Edison). By 1900, her oil wells were producing 50,000 barrels per month. Summers expanded her enterprise to include new oil strikes in nearby Long Beach, Torrance, and Inglewood. She diversified her investments, creating the Summers Paint Company that was run by her brother; she opened a blacksmith shop, bought theaters, ranches and apartment buildings, all financed by her oil exploits. Satisfied customers proclaimed Mrs. Summers "the Oil Queen of California." She exploited that title, too, erecting a hotel at 529 California Street, aptly named Queen, then made it her residence.

The oil boom was impossible to maintain. There were simply too many companies with too many wells operating within a concentrated location. In 1895, oil from Los Angeles accounted for half the production in the entire state of California, but that output crested in 1901. With 1,150 wells pumping oil for more than 200 separate companies, they drained the oil reservoir and diminished its pressure, making extraction more difficult. The price of oil fluctuated wildly, from a high of $1.80 per barrel in 1901, plummeting to 15¢ per barrel in 1903 due to the overabundance of oil on the market.

With no regulatory agencies and practically no record keeping, lawlessness prevailed. Desperate thieves drained tanks, stole equipment and sabotaged the wells of competitors. As wells went dry, they were simply abandoned. In 1961, the Los Angeles Urban Renewal Association restored most of the oil producing acreage to residential use. However, the supply is not depleted completely. A few remaining oilrigs scattered throughout Los Angeles continue to extract the remaining fossil fuel today.

Epilogue:

When the Queen Hotel was demolished to build the 101 Freeway, Emma Summers moved her residence to the Biltmore Hotel on Pershing Square. She died in 1941 at age 83. But Edward Doheny? His next chapter crackles with bribery and repentance, a messy Senate investigation, an Act of Congress and some lurid deaths. Read on!

The Queen Hotel, c. 1940

CHAPTER 7.

TAKE A RIDE ON THE RED CARS

LA SPRAWLS WITH AN ELECTRIC RAILWAY

1901—1961

Gertrude Stein's famous line, "There's no *there* there," turns up (too often) when comedians mock LA's sprawl. That's when Angelenos recite this mantra: "LA was once united by a magnificent network of streetcars, but the routes were bought by General Motors, Standard Oil and Firestone Tires, then dismantled to be replaced by cars and buses." That mantra reached such a crescendo by 1988 that Hollywood screenwriters actually turned it into the plot for the classic animated film *Who Framed Roger Rabbit*? The truth is darker than that mantra; the streetcars were doomed long before General Motors enters this chronicle.

The story starts and ends with Henry E. Huntington, a multi-millionaire who was groomed to run a railroad by his uncle Collis Huntington, a founder of that famous "octopus," the Southern Pacific Railroad. Young Huntington worked for more than a decade on the Southern Pacific, and thought he'd inherit the railroad when the old man died. Instead, its Board of Directors voted him out.

Unfazed, Huntington envisioned an enterprise of his own. Huntington Sr.

Henry (1907) and Arabella Huntington (1905)

bequeathed $15 million to 50-year-old Henry Huntington, and the rest to his second wife, Arabella. Fifteen million dollars in 1900 equals about $400 million today, enough to build . . . a railroad!

Huntington knew from experience that real estate prices soar when the railroad comes to town. Now that the Southern Pacific had turned Los Angeles into a major railroad hub on his watch, it was the time to buy property, thousands of acres of property. Then, he'd sell it in small parcels and watch his real estate profits soar by bringing the railroad to one community after another.

Unlike large-scale railroads with steam-powered locomotives, fueled by coal or oil, streetcars are powered by electric traction. Every destination for Huntington's streetcars needed a steady supply of electricity first. To guarantee that steady supply, he formed the Pacific Power and Light Company to generate energy for his railroad and the communities it served. At the same time, he pieced together a streetcar network by purchasing five fledgling electric railways, then merged their routes to create the Pacific Electric Railway.

It was genius. He inverted the business model for railroads. Instead of connecting existing communities, he installed the railroad and electricity *first* in undeveloped territories where the property was dirt cheap, then marked up the price, and the community followed. Since he owned the railroad, the real estate and the electricity, another Huntington stuffed his pockets in LA.

It was also a disaster. Most cities develop from one central core, then logically build in rings emanating from its center. Not in LA, where city planners were myopic, where Huntington was welcomed as a philanthropic hero with the freedom to put his trolleys just about anywhere. For a few thousand dollars (that Los Angeles desperately needed in the era before income tax) he would propose a route, face little opposition, then acquire the right-of-way to another far-flung real estate tract. City planning in early twentieth-century Los Angeles meant opening a new streetcar route wherever Huntington planned. He ran the streetcars on Broadway and Main Street, but Huntington had no particular loyalty to a central core. He installed trolley tracks to the places where he landed the best deals, eventually rambling across four counties. New communities sprang up anywhere.

The Pacific Electric never made a profit, though it was hailed for decades as a success. Its network was efficient, affordable and fast; a pleasant ride past fragrant orange groves on the way to the ocean, mountains or city. There were discounted routes like the pre-dawn Fisherman's Special, and on Sundays: A Day for a Dollar. The Big Red Cars, as they were known, delivered the mail and the morning newspapers. They were even decorated as floats in the annual Festival of Flowers Parade.

Never satisfied, Huntington purchased the West Coast Land and Water Company; he merged several small gas companies to form the Southern California Gas Company, and his Pacific Power and Light Company financed the largest hydroelectric-generating facility in the country. Huntington's enterprises would now deliver the gas, electricity, transportation and even the water to new communities he was buying up like penny candy. From 1904 to 1913, Huntington opened more than 500 new subdivisions each year. He bought a town called Pacific City, renamed it Huntington Beach, and built a wharf into the Pacific enabling his streetcars to transport freight and produce by rail to the sea, competing directly with the Southern Pacific.

The first Red Car that went to North Hollywood, 1911

To keep up the building boom, Huntington and his friend Harry

Huntington Beach Municipal Pier, c. 1914; Pacific Electric Railway Car (upper left), concession stands (lower left), bandshell (right), and pier in background

Chandler, publisher of the *Los Angeles Times*, went on a media blitz with other "boosters" to attract more settlers to Los Angeles. They blanketed the Midwest with advertisements that promoted Los Angeles as a paradise: no smelly factories, just orange groves in a climate that allegedly cures almost any affliction. The pitch ended with a specially priced streetcar vacation package, luring many future residents to LA.

The population in turn-of-twentieth-century Los Angeles exploded thanks to Huntington and his remarkable rapid transit system. The boosters were so successful that, for a while, Long Beach was known as Iowa By The Sea because so many people from America's heartland settled there. LA's population doubled between 1910 and 1920 to almost a million-and-a-quarter residents, overtaking San Francisco as the largest city in the West. To keep pace, the Pacific Electric grew from 600 Red Cars carrying nearly a quarter-of-a-million passengers in 1910 to a network of more than 900 Red Cars on more than 1,100 miles of track in 1920 (that's about 25 percent more track than New York City subways today).

It was too good to last. In hindsight, Pacific Electric's business model had one fatal flaw. Huntington was willing to take losses to run an efficient railway as long as profits from land sales offset it, setting up a sort of Ponzi scheme from which he couldn't escape. The railroad only worked if real estate sales supported it. When there was no more real estate to sell, the railroad would crumble.

And so it did. As Huntington's massive acquisitions drove up real estate prices, the number of transactions diminished, apparently not a major concern. Although the Pacific Electric ran at a loss every year, Huntington's company still managed to pocket a million-dollar profit. Eyeing that bottom line, the Southern Pacific applied pressure to buy the Pacific Electric; they claimed the electric railroad encroached on Southern's already established businesses. In September 1911, Huntington's Board of Directors agreed to The Great Merger. Huntington received millions in cash and bonds from the giant Southern Pacific Railroad plus a seat on its Board, while the railroad got stuck with the Ponzi scheme: electric trains that would never profit.

There was a bigger problem. LA was now so spread out that the Red Cars were incapable of providing service to all the undeveloped pockets between Huntington communities. If new trolleys could not service these areas without losing more money, then burgeoning communities would have to be reached by—cars!

Pacific Electric Railway map 1920

Red Cars stacked at Terminal Island, waiting to become scrap metal, c. 1956

A political spin was inevitable. New York and Los Angeles had the two most sophisticated trolley lines in America. The liberals that ran New York saw such grave importance in public transportation that the City acquired the private trolley lines, then ripped up the streets and installed them as the City-run subways that are still in use today. In contrast, the conservatives that ran Los Angeles took the small-government approach: In a capitalist system, let market forces determine the railroad's future. In 1926, the Southern Pacific, as owner of the Pacific Electric streetcars, offered to build a network like New York's, moving the trolley tracks underground in downtown LA and elevated trains that would not interfere with automotive traffic in outlying areas. The catch: The public, not the railroad, would finance it. The plan was put to a referendum and, in the end, Los Angeles voters rejected the plan. They saw no reason to pay to replace what they already took for granted. They would rather spend their money on cars.

To reduce its losses, the Southern Pacific began to convert its electric lines into bus routes, following the original right-of-way to Huntington's disparate communities. But now, new surface streets for cars were inserted along the way to accommodate the growing population. Enter General Motors, Standard Oil and Firestone Tires, investors that had no choice but to maintain Huntington's routes to transport large numbers of people to the Main streets he'd already built. That's why today's major thoroughfares still resemble the Pacific Electric routes.

In his zeal to reap more profits, Huntington destroyed any hope for a central downtown Los Angeles. Since he didn't own it, the historic *pueblo* was just another stop on the streetcar. Instead, Huntington created his own series of downtowns all along the trolley routes to compete with the *pueblo*. That's one way to remember Henry Huntington, providing the punchline one century later to jokers who taunt there's no *there* there.

Of course, that's not the way Huntington would choose to be remembered. In 1913, he had an enormous change-of-heart. The U.S. government passed the Sixteenth Amendment; wealthy people like Henry Huntington and his Aunt Arabella were now required to pay income tax. So, recently divorced Huntington married Collis Huntington's trophy wife, Aunt Arabella, to consolidate the family fortune and dodge some taxes. Both Henry and Arabella Huntington were in their sixties. The bride spent most of her time in the Manhattan mansion she inherited; the groom lived in his California estate. Together, they discovered the perfect antidote to paying taxes: They became inspired philanthropists operating from both Coasts. They collected rare books and European art for display in the West Coast estate.

Before their deaths, the Huntingtons transferred their California estate and priceless collections to a nonprofit educational trust, creating The Huntington Library, Art Collections and Botanical Gardens. Displayed in Henry Huntington's sumptuous estate, the collection and the gardens are open to the public today.

Henry Huntington's date with death was a metaphorical irony. He died on May 23, 1927, just as word reached the U.S. that Charles Lindberg had successfully completed his famous flight across the Atlantic Ocean. The railroad man passed away as the aviation era literally soared.

IN THE MOVIES:
See the Red Cars simulated in *Who Framed Roger Rabbit?* (1988), *L.A. Confidential* (1997), *Hollywoodland* (2006), *Gangster Squad* (2013).

THE HUNTINGTON

Henry and Arabella Huntington deeded their residence and private collection (more than seven million items) to the public trust in 1919. The Huntington estate, situated about 12 miles northeast of downtown Los Angeles, is a place of jaw-dropping splendor that is open to the public.

The Huntingtons' priceless art collection is displayed in five buildings spread across 120 landscaped acres. Among the treasures: Thomas Gainsborough's famous *Blue Boy* painting (in the European Art building). There are tapestries and decorative arts, as well as new American art (including a Warhol soup can).

The Library building contains many treasures: rare publications from William Shakespeare, Geoffrey Chaucer, Benjamin Franklin, Thomas Jefferson and Abraham Lincoln; there's even a Gutenberg Bible.

Visitors are invited to spend the afternoon and dine in the café or tea room. Reservations are recommended.

You'll need a car or a bus, though. The Red Car doesn't stop there anymore.

For visiting hours and tour information, visit: huntington.org

ABBOT KINNEY AND VENICE BEACH

Abbot Kinney was an heir to a fortune. The family firm manufactured cigarettes in New York City for the American Tobacco Company. Sent on a search to locate exotic tobaccos, young Abbot Kinney traveled the world.

He also suffered from asthma. When his travels finally brought 30-year-old Kinney to Los Angeles, he awoke the next morning completely free from asthmatic symptoms. Kinney knew he had found his new home.

The following years were a boom time for real estate speculation in Los Angeles, now that trains and streetcars increased everyone's mobility. Investing a share of his tobacco inheritance, Kinney bought a one-and-a-half-mile stretch of soggy marshland along the Pacific Coast in 1891 that most speculators dismissed as worthless. To provide stable ground for construction, engineers told Kinney that canals must be dredged to reclaim the land. Kinney's imagination was swept away with a grand vision of the canals he'd seen in Venice, Italy. He'd build a residential theme park, a real community networked by canals and linked to the ocean nearby, revitalized with each high tide. Gondoliers could transport residents through his unique, seaside resort. Kinney's workmen spent three years digging trenches 40-feet wide to create the grid of canals that would define the new community of Venice, California.

Kinney also saw this as an opportunity to infuse Los Angeles with culture. Recreating Italian artistry, he had colonnades constructed along the commercial streets, complete with a hotel modeled after the Doge's Palace. Kinney was proudest of his 3,500-seat theater, where the most sophisticated entertainers performed, from actress Sarah Bernhardt to the entire Chicago Symphony.

From left: Abbot Kinney, c. 1900; crowds stroll from the streetcar to the ocean on Windward Avenue, c. 1905

Fashionably dressed men and women on a gondola on a Venice canal, 1908

On opening day, July 4, 1905, 40,000 people reportedly attended the festivities (that's almost half the population of Los Angeles at the time). Visitors were predictably dazzled by the sparkling canals that were traversed by actual gondolas from Italy. They were especially drawn to the enormous amusement pier that featured rides, games and side-show attractions. Prior to the opening, Pacific Electric laid new streetcar tracks to provide direct service from downtown to Venice in 40 minutes for just 25 cents. The route to Venice Beach became *the* most popular destination on the entire streetcar network, frequently surpassing its own records on the balmiest beach days. No other LA beach could rival Venice as a popular attraction.

It didn't last long. Kinney's high-brow aspirations failed fast. Angelenos wanted a day at the beach, not a night at the opera. Though Kinney presented some of the world's finest entertainers, the first summer lost $16,000 dollars (that's nearly half-a-million dollars today). To make Venice solvent, Kinney gave up his lofty ambitions; he spent even more of his rapidly depleting fortune to construct more rides and freak show exhibits. Privately, Kinney was appalled, but the public loved the tawdry new attractions; Venice became known as the "Coney Island of the Pacific."

Meanwhile, ocean silt clogged the water's circulation; the stagnant canals began to stink. In 1912, the State Board of Health declared the canals to be a health menace, putting Kinney on the defensive for the rest of his life. In 1917, the first polluted canals were filled in and paved. Streetcar rails were replaced by a bus route. Kinney died in 1920, saddened that his cultural ambitions failed. Four weeks later, a fire destroyed the amusement pier. Though it was rebuilt, Venice was never the same. It sparkled for a few years on Kinney's dime, but ultimately, it was destined to thrive as a beach town, not a temple of culture.

Today, the remaining canals near the ocean compose an expensive and precious community with large, modern houses on tiny lots. Abbot Kinney Boulevard, the neighborhood's main shopping street, commemorates its founder, and a gigantic mural of Kinney celebrates his memory on North Venice Boulevard. The Venice Canal Historic District was added to the National Register of Historic Places in 1982.

Mack Sennett's bathing beauties promote Venice Beach, including film stars Carole Lombard and Gloria Swanson, 1920s. Beginning in 1915, Sennett invited women who came to be known as the "Sennett Bathing Beauties" to appear in bathing costumes, provocative for the times, in comedy shorts, in promotional photos, and to appear at events like beauty contests on Venice Beach.

A Pacific Electric car rolls along the shore line of the blue Pacific

CHAPTER 8.

TROUBLED WATERS
MULHOLLAND BUILDS AN AQUEDUCT

1905—1941

Thanks to the climate, the railroad and all those orange groves, suddenly LA was a boomtown! Its population doubled between 1890 and 1900 as boosters crisscrossed America, successfully luring new residents. Did anyone think about the increasing demands on the local reservoirs?

Luckily, Water Superintendent William Mulholland was a man of vision. He and former mayor Fred Eaton had a solution to LA's rapidly depleting water supply. Former friends for 25 years, they would become bitter rivals while collaborating on a project that brought much-needed water to Los Angeles in the early twentieth century.

Los Angeles was built near a troublesome river named for the Queen of the Angels. The product of melted snow from the Sierra Nevada, it dried to a trickle in summer months, and overflowed with such rage at other times that the first settlers were forced to relocate the *pueblo* to higher ground in 1818.

By 1905, LA was one of America's fastest-growing cities, but its water supply was hopelessly unreliable. With Henry Huntington building new

The three fathers of the LA Aqueduct: Joseph B. Lippincott, Fred Eaton and William Mulholland, 1906

communities in any direction, and farmlands converting to commercial or residential use, Mulholland realized that LA's water supply must increase exponentially. At the suggestion of former Mayor Fred Eaton, (borrowing a famous idea from New York of 50 years earlier), he proposed to the city fathers: Build a giant aqueduct. Divert water from another river with greater abundance.

That greater abundance was found in the Owens Valley, 250 miles away. What Mulholland didn't know (and Eaton didn't tell him) was that the federal government had notified all Owens Valley residents that their land was being reclaimed, and the river diverted. They would soon be paid for their riparian rights, which made the ranchers eager to cooperate. Now here came Eaton, creating a conflict by delivering Water Superintendent Mulholland to the same spot, presenting it as the solution to LA's water shortage, secretly setting up Mulholland as a pawn among LA's robber barons. For ten days, Mulholland charted the river and the terrain for a massive aqueduct.

He did the math. The Owens River flowed at a rate of at least 400-cubic-feet of water per second—enough water to support a city of two million. LA was not yet a city of 200,000. The best surprise was the physics: LA sits at sea level; Owens Valley is in the Sierra Nevada foothills, more than 4,000 feet above. Despite the rugged terrain between the two points, the water would run downhill. Diverting water from the Owens River wouldn't even require a pump.

Idealistic Mulholland envisioned a dam that would collect a bountiful, citizen-owned water supply, generating energy from its power plant to support commercial and residential growth. Not motivated by profit, Mulholland's everlasting reward would be the construction of the waterway that saved his city from drought. For Eaton, this was just a ruthless opportunity to exploit the Owens Valley for financial gain. When Mulholland assured Eaton that his Board of Water Commissioners would work with the City Council to finance a great aqueduct, Eaton raced back to Owens Valley on his own. He hoodwinked the ranchers into selling their riparian rights to him, which they believed they were selling to the federal government.

Behind closed doors, Eaton announced to Mulholland and the Water Board that he planned to control all hydroelectric power generated by LA's new aqueduct. The use of his property would be leased to the city. Mulholland was stunned by the betrayal and abandonment of the public trust. Eaton's scheme to hold the city's water supply hostage jeopardized their project's construction. They wrangled for two furious days over Eaton's exorbitant demand of $1 million. Eventually, the City of Los Angeles accepted most of Eaton's demands for a sale, not a lease. He got $450,000 (that's more than $11 million dollars today); he also got to keep 12,000 acres, and he was rewarded with a $100,000 commission for assembling all these properties on behalf of the city.

Eaton's land grab thwarted Mulholland's plans for the massive dam LA needed at that site. He could have provided a water supply that withstood LA's lengthiest droughts while still providing Owens Valley with enough water to cultivate thousands of acres of farmland. Now, a smaller dam would be built elsewhere, guaranteeing insufficient water for both LA and the Owens Valley. Though prickly in private, Mulholland and Eaton were forced to unite publicly if they were to sell the project to the voters and the press. They were forcibly cordial.

Mulholland had another reason to be furious. In this early stage, the aqueduct hadn't been disclosed to the public yet. Eaton's sparring with the Water Board breached the secrecy surrounding the aqueduct plan. Now, land speculators could drive up the project's cost.

Too late. Moses H. Sherman from the Water Board whispered the inside story to some of LA's wealthiest boosters, including *Los Angeles Times* publishers Harry Chandler and Harrison Gray Otis; E. T. Earl; publisher of the *Herald*; Henry Huntington of the Pacific Electric Railway; and E. H.

From left: mule teams of up to 52 animals pulled the pipes over the mountains and through the desert, 1912; workmen posing in front of a new section of the aqueduct pipeline, 1912

Harriman of the Southern Pacific Railroad, among others. They formed a syndicate that bought up vast acres of parched, almost-worthless land in the San Fernando Valley for as little as $5 an acre in some places. The newspapermen intentionally suppressed the news that they were buying the land where the aqueduct would terminate. It wasn't until the City scheduled a bond election to raise the $25 million dollars needed to build the aqueduct that voters finally learned of the project. With barely 60 days to scrutinize the plan, they voted overwhelmingly in its favor, believing what they read in the newspapers: that they could not survive without the aqueduct bringing water in abundance to Los Angeles.

Meanwhile, Mulholland performed something of an engineering miracle, guiding 5,000 laborers through five years of desert heat to accomplish one of the most difficult civic projects undertaken by an American city. Fifty-seven camps housed men and supplies along the route. They built a railroad 120-miles long to carry tons of machinery. More than 500 miles of roads and trails were opened to reach the line of the aqueduct. Teams of 52 mules hauled steel pipes to the construction site. When completed, the aqueduct included 142 separate tunnels through the mountains. It was the fourth-largest engineering project in U.S. history (to that date) and the longest aqueduct in the western hemisphere.

The aqueduct was dedicated in a ceremony on November 15, 1913 at its open-ended terminus in the San Fernando Valley. At the climax of the flowery orations, it was Mulholland's turn to speak. Apparently disgusted by the robber barons who populated his audience, he delivered one of the shortest speeches in U.S. history: "There it is. Take it!"

Mulholland speaks to the crowd at the opening ceremonies, 1913

And did they ever! The San Fernando Valley syndicate saw their irrigated property values soar. It is estimated that the syndicate made a profit of more than $100 million dollars. (That's well over $2 *billion* dollars today.) As Mulholland predicted, the population exploded. Huntington added more streetcar routes.

There was one major flaw that the city fathers overlooked while their friends bought up the San Fernando Valley. The voters passed a bond issue to bring water to Los Angeles, not that uninhabited, unincorporated acreage 20 miles away. In stepped President Theodore Roosevelt, who attempted to block the profits of the syndicate by prohibiting the sale of Owens Valley water outside the Los Angeles city limits. To solve the oversight, the City of Los Angeles sidestepped the U.S. president. It annexed more than 100,000 acres of the San Fernando Valley. The newly incorporated territory nearly doubled the city's size to be in compliance, bringing Los Angeles to the aqueduct.

Back in Owens Valley, the raw deal would not go away. Mulholland was right. Los Angeles needed the land controlled by Fred Eaton in order to build a suitably sized storage dam. By the 1920s, LA's population was approaching one million residents; the city was desperate again for more water. On behalf of Los Angeles, Mulholland returned to Owens Valley, seeking to purchase additional water rights. Instead, the local bankers met him with opposition, sparking a bitter feud that lasted for years. In May 1924, 30 boxes of dynamite were set off, destroying one of the ditches that supplied water to LA's aqueduct. Mulholland was warned that if he returned, he'd be lynched.

Map of the Los Angeles Aqueduct, its route and facilities, report
from the City of Los Angeles, 1971

Next, the bankers and 70 armed supporters took control of the aqueduct.
They staged a sit-in occupation for four days during which Los Angeles
received no water, as they challenged LA to buy the entire irrigation district
or get out of the valley. When Los Angeles agreed that it was time to buy
up the remaining properties, a war ensued with the last holdouts. The city
sent a trainload of World War I veterans to protect the aqueduct, but that
wasn't enough; it was still blown up 14 times. Mulholland's inferior storage
dam, built on weak bedrock formations, collapsed in 1928, a disaster that
killed nearly 500 people when a 75-foot wave crashed its way to the sea,

miles away. Unsuspecting residents were buried alive in mud. Mulholland was forced to resign in disgrace.

The bankers who led the opposition were indicted for embezzlement when their bank failed; they were convicted and sent to San Quentin. The Great Depression took care of

Two men find dynamite and wire during sabotage incidents of Owens Valley Aqueduct, CA, c. 1924

the rest. Eaton's finances collapsed. Along with the Owens Valley farmers and ranchers, he faced the inevitable: Los Angeles must assume full control of their properties and the Owens River. They taunted with words, buying full-page ads in the LA newspapers stating, "We, the farming community of Owens Valley, being about to die, salute you." With that final volley, the Los Angeles electorate voted $12 million in bonds in 1930 to buy up what was left of the Owens Valley properties at pre-Depression prices, and the war was over. Towns were demolished to create the Owens River Gorge Dam that opened in 1941, still in service today. Eaton didn't live to see it. LA's 24th mayor died, a broken man, in 1934. Mulholland died one year later.

Today, William Mulholland's name is commemorated by the beautiful winding drive that spans the crest of the mountains. Some of LA's priciest real estate, it separates the San Fernando Valley from the west side of Los Angeles, home to movie stars, industry titans and many swimming pools. Eaton Street is a dead end in Eagle Rock, on LA's east side.

The City of Los Angeles built a second aqueduct from the Owens River in the 1940s. Together, these aqueducts deliver almost 40 percent of today's water supply in Los Angeles. Nobody even thinks about drinking the water from the river that was named for the Queen of the Angels.

IN THE MOVIES:
Chinatown (1974), *Waterworld* (1995)

CHAPTER 9.

HOLLYWOOD PIONEERS

MOVIE MAKERS REMAKE LOS ANGELES

1914—1928

In 1895, arts and sciences merged. The movie camera was invented by the Lumiére brothers. A French physicist gave birth to an art form.

Soon, inventors on both sides of the Atlantic were experimenting with the new medium—and on both sides of the camera. Scientists improved the technology while artists explored new forms of expression. Horizons were broad for a lucky generation of artists and scientists early in the twentieth century. Their imaginations gave birth to an industry that completely redefined the meaning of entertainment.

At the same time, Los Angeles had boosters traveling America to attract new settlers and new businesses. When filmmakers discovered the ease of filming in LA's 300 days of sunshine, a match was made. LA's wide, open spaces were ideal for an industry that needed to sprawl. The film industry remains one of America's largest and most lucrative exports.

Here's the chronicle of how the movie business got its start, told through the start-up tales of some film industry pioneers.

THE FIRST COMEDIES: SENNETT AND CHAPLIN

In Hollywood's earliest days, filmmakers wore many hats. That suited Mack Sennett.

Sennett was the most productive filmmaker in a fledgling industry. At his Keystone Studios, he served as an actor, director, screenwriter, cinematographer and producer. His rise to fame also launched the careers of silent film stars and filmmakers for decades.

On a visit to New York in 1913, Sennett saw a British touring company on Broadway. He howled at the physical comedy of a 24-year-old actor named Charles Chaplin, and offered the young actor triple his salary to make movies in Hollywood. Untested and unknown, Charlie Chaplin signed a one-year contract at $125 a week (that's about $3,000 today), and then boarded the Transcontinental Railroad bound for California. Chaplin was one of Hollywood's highest-paid actors from the day he arrived.

The problem: In front of his first movie camera, Chaplin wasn't funny. In a long coat and droopy mustache, he looked downright villainous in his first comedy, *Making A Living*. Sennett, a master of slapstick, explored movie comedy with the young stage actor, as they both learned to tell their tales without sound.

Movie making was anything but silent. Most filming at Keystone took place outdoors on two-and-a-half acres of today's Glendale Boulevard, or in its barnlike structure. Directors talked to their actors as they filmed; everyone worked without a script because the plot was always the same. As

Charlie Chaplin in 1916 at the age of 27

From left: Keystone Studios, c. 1917; Charlie Chaplin with the founders of the Triangle Film Corporation, Thomas H. Ince, Mack Sennett and D. W. Griffith, c. 1915

Sennett plainly put it, "Comedy is an excuse for a chase." Action had to be fast, like his Keystone Kops, climbing on streetcars and falling off piers, or like Fatty Arbuckle, the studio's biggest star, being frequently slammed in the face with a pie.

Chaplin played a reporter in his next film, *Mabel's Strange Predicament*, but he wasn't thrilled with the costume. At rehearsal, he tried on the trousers of the rotund Fatty Arbuckle, who laughed at the site of Chaplin in baggy pants. He put on Charlie Avery's jacket, which was far too small, some giant shoes and a derby hat. To add some age to his character, Chaplin applied a tiny mustache. Then grabbing a bamboo cane, he stepped into the light and tried some tricks with the cane, hooking it on things, tipping his hat with it.

Sennett laughed out loud. He announced, "There are kid's auto races down in Venice. Keep that outfit on and go with the guys."

When Chaplin asked for a hint about the plot of this movie, "Just make something up," was Sennett's reply, defining the entire spontaneous, unregulated movie business of 1914.

The Little Tramp made his first appearance in *Kid Auto Races At Venice*, a short, improvised film in which Chaplin's character wrangles with a cameraman while go-carts whiz past in an actual race. With the cane as his prop, the Little Tramp shuffled out of the crowd of real spectators and into the hearts of millions.

From left: *Making A Living*, 1914; *Kid Auto Races at Venice*, 1914

Recognizing the potential for the Little Tramp to become a recurring character at Keystone, Chaplin begged Sennett for the chance to write and direct for himself. As he reports in his autobiography, when Sennett asked, "Who's gonna pay for the film if we can't release it?" Chaplin posted a bond of $1,500 for Sennett to keep if the film was not releasable.

Of course, the film was released, and many more followed. Demand was so great that Chaplin's films set records for the number of prints in circulation. He set the standard for improvisation on screen, devising physical gags on the fly while cameras rolled. Unlike Sennett's frantically edited chase movies, Chaplin devoted hundreds of feet of film to a single sequence, imbuing his character with depth that all other comedies lacked.

And he kept those one-reel movies coming, practically one every week. Scenery changed but the character didn't. In 1914, Chaplin made 35 movies at Keystone. He later reminisced, "I had confidence in my ideas, and I can thank Sennett for that."

Though Chaplin was a contract player earning a handsome weekly salary (and fame), it was Sennett who reaped unfathomable rewards. Chaplin's film *Mabel at the Wheel*, for example, cost $1,800 to make; it earned $130,000 in its first year. As their contract's one-year expiration approached, Chaplin told Sennett that he wanted $1000 a week in the next contract. Sennett balked, unconvinced that the 25-year-old could milk many more years from the Little Tramp. He wouldn't pay. Another upstart called Essanay (for Spoor and Anderson) offered 10 times his salary: $1,250 a week (about $30,000 today) to make longer movies of the Little Tramp at their studio instead. It was the end of a chapter. Sennett and Chaplin had set the precedents for comedy on film, the iconic Little Tramp was born, and a friendship ended. The Little Tramp appeared in 41 more films.

In 1938, Mack Sennett was presented with a special Academy Award "for his lasting contribution to the comedy technique," and in 1972, Chaplin accepted one "for the incalculable effect he has had in making motion pictures the art form of this century."

The Keystone Studio building still stands, now a storage facility, at 1712 Glendale Boulevard, near Effie Street.

ON THE WALK OF FAME:

Charles Chaplin: 6751 Hollywood Boulevard
Mack Sennett: 6710 Hollywood Boulevard

Douglas Fairbanks Sr., Charlie Chaplin, Thomas Edison and Mary Pickford on the set of *The Gold Rush*, directed by Charlie Chaplin, 1925

THE FIRST FEATURE: INTRODUCING CECIL B. DEMILLE

Samuel Goldfish was driven. As Shmuel Gelbfisz, he walked across Poland at age 16 to get to England, and eventually made his way to America. By 1910, he'd anglicized his name, landed a job as a salesman in the glove business, learned to think in English and married Blanche Lasky.

In his travels, he'd seen some of the earliest films ever made. Now, completely bedazzled, he was convinced that it was a business opportunity like no other. Blanche's brother was Jesse L. Lasky, Mae West's producer on Broadway. He listened to the persistent Goldfish and eventually agreed to take a risk: They'd pool their money to gamble on this popular new attraction called Movies.

But they needed another opinion. They turned to a young actor on Broadway named Cecil B. DeMille, who now worked for Lasky. DeMille confessed that he, too, knew nothing about making movies, but it sounded like a great idea. With that, the three novices went into business as the Jesse L. Lasky Feature Play Company. For Goldfish, the gamble was literal; he wagered his life savings. Combined with Lasky, they had $15,000 to invest in making a movie and promoting it.

They were determined to stand out from the pack; there'd be none of those 10-minute lowbrow comedies from *their* company. They wanted to compete

From left: Cecil B DeMille (far left) and *The Squaw Man* cast. Dustin Farnum in white shirt; Cecil B. DeMille shooting *The Squaw Man* in 1913 at Lasky-DeMille Barn

with Broadway, exploiting the theatrical potential of the new medium. DeMille suggested that they acquire the rights to a popular play called *The Squaw Man*. It had been revived on Broadway recently with handsome Dustin Farnum as the lead. DeMille knew that this tragic love story

The Squaw Man, 1914

between an Indian girl and an Englishman in the American West would be popular with both men and women. And, since most of its action takes place outdoors, they could keep costs low. They simply had to go film it out West somewhere.

For $4,000, they acquired the rights from the playwright, and convinced Dustin Farnum to reprise his stage role in their movie. Thirty-three-year-old DeMille would direct. But where? Lasky had been all the way to Flagstaff, Arizona, once. He instructed DeMille to transport the New York actors by train to Flagstaff to shoot their movie. Goldfish stayed in New York, selling gloves to remain solvent, while Lasky stayed in the East to hustle up his next theatrical venture, in case movies were a passing fad like everybody said.

Flagstaff wasn't what DeMille envisioned. He couldn't film there. He telegraphed Lasky and Goldfish: He wanted to relocate the production all the way west to Los Angeles, where he could "rent barn in place called Hollywood for $75 a month."

The first feature film was already a runaway production. Goldfish agonized, for he realized that the cost was now beyond their company's assets. When Lasky gave DeMille the green light to proceed, Goldfish launched a scheme to keep the business afloat. He bought newspaper ads that touted their company's long roster of upcoming feature-length films, pledging that their first film, *The Squaw Man*, was such a breakthrough that theater owners could charge a full 25 cents a ticket instead of the mere nickels and dimes collected at other movies.

An advertisement for *The Squaw Man* in a trade magazine, selling distribution rights

Goldfish had another brilliant idea. As the promotions caught on, he sold "state's rights" in advance, letting distributors buy up territories where they could play the film exclusively. What the distributors didn't know was that the money they were anteing up was desperately needed to finish the film!

February 17, 1914 was the film's opening night at the Longacre Theater in New York (on West 48th Street, now a Broadway landmark). The film broke six times, but it didn't matter. The invited audience knew they were the first to witness a new form of artistry: This 74-minute movie proved the viability of a feature length narrative.

Sight unseen, Louis B. Mayer offered $4,000 to distribute the movie in his chain of theaters. Prospective distributors surrounded Sam Goldfish, all seeking to show *The Squaw Man* in their movie chains, too. In the spring, Lasky, Goldfish and DeMille caught their breath. Their little movie company had grossed almost a quarter of a million dollars!

The company eventually became Paramount Pictures. Goldfish changed his name to Goldwyn and teamed with Louis B. Mayer to form Metro-Goldwyn-Mayer, today's MGM (Goldwyn had no role in management or production there). Goldwyn produced eight films that were nominated for Best Picture Academy Awards, none of them released by MGM.

Members of the Famous Players-Lasky Corporation. From left, Jesse L. Lasky, Adolph Zukor, Samuel Goldwyn, Cecil B. DeMille, and Al Kaufman, 1916

The Squaw Man put Hollywood, California, into the imaginations of filmmakers everywhere. Today, Jesse L. Lasky's barn is a National Landmark and a delightful museum. It was moved and restored on North Highland Avenue, across from the Hollywood Bowl, and is open daily.

ON THE WALK OF FAME:

Jesse L. Lasky	6433 Hollywood Boulevard
Samuel Goldwyn	1631 Vine Street
Cecil B. DeMille	1725 Vine Street (for film)
	6240 Hollywood Boulevard (for radio)

THE FIRST COSMETICIAN: MAX FACTOR

Rags-to-riches tales have been a Hollywood staple for generations, but few fictional screenplays can top the real life adventures of make-up man Max Factor.

As one of 10 children born to peasants in Eastern Europe, there was no money for education. Max was put to work at age eight at the local apothecary. At age 14, he was hired by the Russian Grand Opera to make wigs and apply make-up on opera divas. They were like wicked stepsisters who frequently vented their rage on Max, their convenient whipping boy. However, his artistry so beguiled the Czar and his family that young Factor was commanded to work for the royal family instead. At age 22, the peasant boy found himself living in storybook castles, kowtowing to Russian nobility.

"I was like a slave," he recalled later. "I had no life. A dozen people were always watching me." Every seventh day he was permitted to leave the palace, but always escorted by guards. With his make-up kit in hand, he'd visit a house in Moscow, supposedly on business, while guards waited in the carriage. In actuality, these visits were romantic trysts with Esther Rosa, whom he soon married with a rabbi's blessing, but without a marriage license that might attract suspicion. The one-day-a-week arrangement continued for nearly nine years. Mrs. Factor gave birth to three children while her husband toiled in the palace.

He had to escape. Russia was a land of famine, pogroms and social unrest. He didn't want his children to grow up

Max Factor applying makeup to Jean Harlow, 1930

without a father, so Factor devised an elaborate scheme. By applying make-up that gave him a sickly pallor, he gained two weeks of ordered rest in Carlsbad. He never got there. Instead, Max, his wife, two daughters and a son trekked by foot through woods and hills to a seaport, where they boarded an ocean liner bound for America. No passports were required. In all his years of labor, with no chance to step out and spend his wages, young Factor had amassed a savings of $40,000.

Max Factor moved his shop to the theatre district at 362 South Hill Street, 1919

He'd heard about "motion pictures." Maybe he could sell his wigs to moviemakers. Arriving in LA in 1908, he opened a shop at 1204 South Central Avenue, near the edge of downtown, offering wigs made from real human hair. Still barely able to read or write, Factor devoted long hours in his lab behind the shop, where he experimented with new forms of make-up for the movies. That's where he met Charlie Chaplin, Fatty Arbuckle, Buster Keaton and other one-reel comics who couldn't get enough of Factor's special concoction, "flexible greasepaint." Unlike thick stage make-up that created a mask, Factor's thin product was pliant, enabling these comics to give full facial expressions in close-up photography. There was nothing like it. When director Cecil B. DeMille discovered Factor's flexible greasepaint in a desperate moment, it would lead to Max Factor becoming one of Hollywood's first multimillionaires.

DeMille arrived in Hollywood with his troupe of New York actors to make the world's first feature film, *The Squaw Man*, a serious story about soldiers and Indians. But in 1913, there were no Native Americans left in LA. So, just like on Broadway, his actors applied greasepaint to look like

Native Americans; but unlike Broadway, the greasepaint dried and cracked outdoors in the California sun. DeMille's next step is immortalized in a song lyric by Johnny Mercer decades later:

> ... *To be an actor, see Mr. Factor.*
> *He'll make your kisser look good.*
> ... *Hooray for Hollywood!*

DeMille needed Factor's make-up, but his tight-fisted producer back in New York had no budget item for make-up, and no time for experiments. In the theater, actors provided their own make-up and applied it, too. Now DeMille was horrified when he peered through the lens. His actors looked comical, encrusted in stage make-up, wearing theatrical wigs made from wool and straw!

So Factor made a deal. The script required Indians. Factor, now the father of five, would provide his two young sons, painted as Indians, for the duration of the film shoot along with the much needed make-up. DeMille's payment to the young actors would include the cost of the flexible greasepaint supply.

Then Factor threw in another bargain: real human hair. Give up the phony stage wigs that were a distraction on film. Use the real wigs that Factor stitched himself. Again DeMille pleaded poverty; the producer wouldn't pay for Factor's authentic wigs. Their next decision set a Hollywood paradigm. Factor agreed to accept *rent* for his costly wigs (spawning an entire industry of rental products for filmmakers that still thrives a century later). With sons in the cast, the Factors kept an eye on their properties, and filming began. Upon its release, *The Squaw Man* was an immediate success, not just the first feature film in history, but also the first film to feature real hairpieces. From that day forward, Max Factor's hair department had all the business it could handle. His two sons would also be hired to play Indians in over one hundred Westerns!

Factor and Hollywood were in sync. As film technology advanced, Factor continued to innovate. As he later commented, "I realized that a new art of make-up must be created just as a new form of entertainment was being evolved." Years before the first color film, he devised a "Color Harmony" principle: Certain combinations of hair and eye colors looked best in make-up shades of the same color. By referring to his goods as *cosmetics*, not make-up, his products shed the tawdry, painted lady connotation. Instead, Factor convinced women that there was nothing wrong with embellishing one's physical gifts.

As new movie studios opened, everyone clamored for the pliant products that only Mr. Factor seemed to know how to make. Studios offered him full-time employment, but Factor wisely avoided favoritism; he sold cosmetics to everyone. He sold more cosmetics than all of his competitors combined! While his new wife and (now six) children ran the shop, Factor trained make-up artists to work at the studios, and continued to experiment with new products as demands from those studios increased.

For the 1925 version of *Ben Hur*, MGM ordered 600 *gallons* of Factor's flexible greasepaint. The invention of sensitive panchromatic film required an entire line of new products from Factor: a wider range of tints in an even thinner, more transparent application to make complexions look natural on the big screen. With each innovation, his fortune grew.

In 1928, Factor made the deal that almost single-handedly launched the retail cosmetics industry in America. He authorized Sales Builders Inc. to advertise and distribute his cosmetics in drug stores nationwide. Based on the Color Harmony principle, they put powder, rouge and lipstick in one

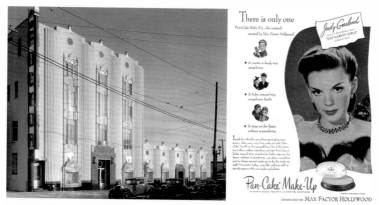

From left: Max Factor Building, the "Jewel Box of the Cosmetic World," 1660 North Highland Ave., Hollywood, c. 1930s; pancake makeup advertisement with Judy Garland, 1940s

At Max Factor's salon, 1935

package for every combination of hair and eye color. Moving away from greasepaint in tubes, his newest cosmetics came in a tiny pan. Inside was a little cake of make-up that was applied with a sponge. Factor's "pan-cake" make-up was revolutionary, giving birth to the industry we know today.

That same year, Factor made an even greater commitment to Hollywood. He purchased a building right off Hollywood Boulevard (1660 North Highland Avenue, it's today's Hollywood Museum) where his business expanded exponentially. It was the first building to feature mirrors ringed with lights to simulate the high intensity lighting on movie sets. There was an entire floor just for lipsticks (another Factor invention. Before Factor, lip color was a pomade applied from a little tin), a floor just for powders, and another just for wigs and hair care. Best of all, the ground floor featured Factor's Color Harmony rooms: Patrons were ushered into a blue, pink, peach or green room to determine the accurate shades that flattered them most.

For the grand opening of Max Factor's salon in November 1935, 3,500 were invited, but more than 10,000 well-wishers showed up! Seemingly, everyone in show business wanted to toast Max Factor, the Hollywood original. Every studio boss and movie star was in attendance. Klieg lights crisscrossed the night sky. Gossip columnists and newsreel cameras captured the proceedings, later proclaiming the event to be bigger than most movie premieres. That night, the former peasant became the prince of Hollywood.

Max Factor lived for another 10 years, with all members of his family participating in the family business. Upon his death in 1938, son Frank changed his name to Max Factor Jr. and continued the family's business and dynasty. Trust funds of five million dollars apiece were bequeathed to each of Max Factor's grandchildren. In 1973, his heirs sold the company for $500 million dollars.

Max Factor is remembered with a star on the Walk of Fame at 6922 Hollywood Boulevard. He is buried at Hillside Memorial Cemetery, at 6001 West Centinela Avenue.

IN THE MOVIES:

Max Factor's name appears in the credits for thousands of movies and television shows. Most often, it was actually Max Factor products applied by a Max Factor-trained make-up artist who was present for day-to-day filming.

The interior of the Max Factor building on Highland Avenue can be seen in *Beverly Hills Cop II* (1987).

THE FIRST SOUNDS: AL JOLSON AND THE WARNER BROTHERS

Harry, Sam, Albert and Jack Warner ran what was perceived to be a second-rate production company. Under contract, they had no outstanding comedian like Charlie Chaplin, no sweetheart like Mary Pickford; they had no money for an epic like *Birth of a Nation*. Their fortunes rested on one heroic dog: Rin Tin Tin. Their company was chronically low on cash. Drastic action was needed if the Warners were going to catapult their studio among the major players.

The fledgling movie industry inspired dreamers with all sorts of unique ideas to sell. More than one inventor attempted to sync a soundtrack to a movie, but each one failed to convince the studio chiefs that the expense was warranted. "Who the heck wants to hear actors talk?" was Harry Warner's famous retort when the idea was presented to the Warner brothers.

Younger brother Sam realized the sound gimmick was exactly the jolt their company needed. Don't want to hear actors talk? Then let them sing. Hollywood's first sound film would also be its first musical. Even Harry approved of that scheme.

The Jazz Singer was a hit show on Broadway starring George Jessel. Warner Brothers acquired the rights, but Jessel turned down the offer to act on film. The role went to Al Jolson, a wise choice, as his life mirrored some of the plot. In the movie, the son of a Jewish cantor wants to sing popular music, but his family wants him to be a cantor. In the dramatic conclusion, the young guy skips his Broadway opening to sing in the synagogue.

For the popular music sequences, Jolson performed parts of his stage routine. Right before launching into his big hit, "Toot, Toot, Tootsie," Jolson adlibbed, "Wait a minute . . . wait a minute.

From left: Sam, Harry, Jack and Albert Warner, 1926

First talking movie, *The Jazz Singer* at Warners' Theatre, 1927

You ain't heard nothin' yet!" The *talkies* were born.

The Warner brothers were all in: The project cost them half a million dollars, but their gamble on this new *Vitaphone* process from Western Electric catapulted them to the glory they sought. Their company pioneered the process for sound in the movies, paving the way for boundless innovation. *The Jazz Singer* would reap three million dollars that year, plus a place in history for the Warner brothers.

Opening night was scheduled for October 6, 1927 at the Warners' Theatre in New York City, but tragedy struck. Sam Warner, the brother who fostered the sound process, was overworked in the weeks leading up to the film's completion. An infection had spread through his body, unattended. On October 5, he was hospitalized. As surgeons attempted to remove a brain abscess complicated by pneumonia, Sam Warner died on the operating table. The mentor didn't live to see his success. In an eerie reenactment of their own movie, the Warner brothers skipped their big opening night on Broadway to mourn their loss in a synagogue. At the movie premiere, when "The End" flashed across the screen, the audience rose in wild applause. It

Al Jolson in *The Jazz Singer*

was Jolson, with tears in his eyes, who took a bow for all of them.

Five bigger movie studios controlled a majority of the nation's theaters. They attempted to block the expansion of talkies at first, but the Warner brothers were prepared. The studio released 12 talking pictures in 1928 alone. The overwhelming enthusiasm from the paying public informed all studios of the movie industry's inevitable future. Finally convinced that sound was here to stay, other studios made deals with Western Electric to make films with sound. An estimated 1000 movie theaters were wired for sound presentations by the end of 1928. At the very first Academy Awards ceremony, the Warner brothers were recognized for "revolutionizing the industry with sound."

At the studio, youngest brother Jack assumed control of operations, gaining notoriety for decisive actions and stern demeanor. By the 1930s, he had Warner Brothers producing more than 100 movies a year. His career continued for 45 years, outlasting every other studio mogul. Firing studio employees became one of his trademarks. In fact, in 1929, one of the first movie stars Jack fired was Rin Tin Tin. After all, who the heck wants to hear a dog bark?

ON THE WALK OF FAME:

Sam Warner:	6201 Hollywood Boulevard
Harry Warner:	6441 Hollywood Boulevard
Jack Warner:	6541 Hollywood Boulevard
Al Jolson:	6622 Hollywood Boulevard (for motion pictures)
	1716 Vine Street (for recordings)
	6201 Hollywood Boulevard (for radio)

THE FIRST ANIMATOR: WALT DISNEY

In Kansas City, Missouri, 18-year-old Walt Disney read a book by Edwin G. Lutz called *Animated Cartoons: How They Are Made, Their Origin and Development*. The high school dropout would do it by the book. Experimenting with his friend and fellow cartoonist Ub Iwerks, they borrowed a camera, then drew characters on transparent sheets of celluloid they then photographed frame-by-frame over a stationary background. Disney and Iwerks liked what they saw.

Soon they were business partners at *Iwerks-Disney Commercial Artists*, delivering a steady supply of *Laugh-O-Gram* cartoons to a Kansas City movie theater. The shorts were a success, but Disney and Iwerks were artists, not accountants. Their company soon went bankrupt.

Penniless, Walt Disney came to Los Angeles to visit his brother Roy, who was recuperating from tuberculosis in the veteran's hospital. Setting his sights on the fledgling film industry, Walt decided to stay. With Roy's help, he set up shop in a garage, then promptly made a deal to deliver *Alice's Wonderland*, his new cartoon, every month to New York distributor Margaret Winkler. He hired his good friend Ub Iwerks, who relocated his family to LA, and the two were in business again.

The *Alice* cartoons were such a success that they hired more artists, including Lillian Bounds, the future Mrs. Disney, and expanded the operation (on Hyperion Avenue in today's Silver

Disney Studio's staff, with Lois Hardwick who played the title character in the Alice Comedies. Top row: Walker Harman, Ub Iwerks, Lois Hardwick, Walt Disney, Rudolph Ising; bottom row: Friz Freleng, Roy O. Disney, Hugh Harman, 1927

From left: *Alice's Wonderland*, 1923; *Oswald the Lucky Rabbit-Trolley Troubles*, 1927

Lake neighborhood). Disney and Iwerks created another character: *Oswald the Lucky Rabbit*, also distributed by Margaret Winkler, which was an even bigger hit. Disney and Iwerks made 26 *Oswald* cartoons.

When Ms. Winkler got married, her husband promptly took charge of her affairs. He informed Disney that Universal Studios now controlled the rights to Oswald. Its animators could make the cartoons without Walt, so he'd have to take a pay cut or give up Oswald.

It was the turning point in Walt's career. Instead of working for others, he needed to work for himself, with a product that only he controlled and distributed. Reluctantly, he gave up the rabbit. He would start over. What he needed first was a new character. It would be a mouse.

It was October 1927; *The Jazz Singer* was being hailed as the first "talkie." Twenty-six year-old Disney understood the industry's rapid evolution; he jumped aboard. Disney's new mouse would be the first animated character with a soundtrack.

Iwerks made some final fixes to Disney's original sketch, and Mortimer Mouse was born. Lillian Disney thought that "Mortimer" sounded "too highfalutin" for a cartoon mouse, so at her suggestion Walt renamed his character "Mickey Mouse."

More artists joined the team to work on the new cartoon, always with a soundtrack in mind. To the beat of a metronome, one animator would play a harmonica while Disney and other cartoonists banged cowbells and tin plates, teaching themselves to sync sounds with images, inventing the first sound effects to be used in animation.

Mickey's film was called *Steamboat Willie*, the first cartoon with sound. He had no voice yet; there was no dialogue, but for the first time, recorded music and sound effects were synced to animated images. Premiering at the Colony Theater in New York (today's Broadway Theater) on November 18, 1928, it was an instant hit. From the *New York Times* to *Variety*, reviewers praised Disney's achievement and predicted Mickey's future potential. Over the next 18 months, Disney produced and distributed 31 cartoons starring Mickey Mouse, who promptly gained a voice, a wardrobe and millions of fans. He became more famous than living celebrities like Charlie Chaplin, providing Disney with the financial footing to build an empire.

ON THE WALK OF FAME:

Mickey Mouse:	6925 Hollywood Boulevard
Walt Disney:	7021 Hollywood Boulevard (for motion pictures)
	6747 Hollywood Boulevard (for television)

Mickey Mouse in *Steamboat Willie*, 1928

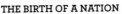

THE BIRTH OF A NATION

In 1915, D. W. Griffith delivered Hollywood's first film epic, *The Birth of a Nation*.

President Wilson hailed it as "writing history with lightening," the first film to be shown in the White House. "My only regret is that it is all so terribly true," he reportedly added.

African Americans and many film fans viewed it as a work of jaw-dropping racism, for the film depicts African-Americans (played by white actors in blackface) as lustful, lazy villains who are defeated when the Ku Klux Klan rescues White America.

LA's African American community was prohibited from working on the film in any capacity. The film they soon witnessed was a horror. (President Wilson later wrote that he disapproved of the "unfortunate production.")

The Birth of a Nation rekindled support for the Ku Klux Klan. Riots broke out in Boston and Philadelphia following the film's opening; the film's inflammatory images (it's a silent movie) provoked gangs of whites to attack black residents. The NAACP organized protests in some cities in advance, and succeeded in convincing theaters in Chicago, Minneapolis and elsewhere not to present the epic film.

Despite its repugnant politics, *The Birth of a Nation* represents an important achievement in film, still studied in film schools today. In an era of one-reel Charlie Chaplin comedies, here was a three-hour epic with a live orchestra and an intermission, an ambitious leap for the medium. *The Birth of a Nation* was the first to present film as an art form.

It was also the first to employ hundreds of extras for Civil War battle re-enactments (on LA's undeveloped acres), the first to depict historical figures (Lincoln's assassination) and the first to charge $2 per ticket (that's nearly $50 today!). Most importantly, it proved the power of film: its ability to affect an audience at a visceral level.

As a public *mea culpa*, director D.W. Griffith's next film was titled *Intolerance*.

RIN TIN TIN

Rin Tin Tin was one of Hollywood's most successful silent movie stars. True, he was a dog, but that didn't prevent him from earning $1,000 a week (that's about $14,000 a week today!) from Warner Brothers, the movie studio that kept him under contract.

Near the end of World War I, U.S. troops defended the French town of Saint-Mihiel. At a bombed-out dog kennel, U.S. Corporal Lee Duncan saved a newborn German shepherd puppy. Months later, when the war ended, Duncan returned to Los Angeles with his new best friend, Rin Tin Tin.

In LA, Duncan and Eugene Pallette, a friend who acted in silent movies, taught the young dog some tricks. They entered him in a dog show, where the first slow-motion camera captured Rin Tin Tin leaping to an extraordinary height of nearly 12 feet. Movie moguls who viewed the new camera technique were equally intrigued by the performing dog. With a shiny coat and deep, dark eyes, a star was born. Rin Tin Tin soon became Warner Brothers' most profitable star.

Because viewers everywhere could understand the actions of a dog, Rin Tin Tin was one of the world's first international stars, endearing to fans everywhere. He starred in 27 feature films and sired 48 puppies. Some of Rin Tin Tin's descendants performed in sound films, a television series, and dog food commercials.

The performing dog was so beloved that when the ballots went out in 1928 for the very first Academy Awards, Rin Tin Tin earned the largest number of votes for Best Actor. Fearing an unfortunate precedent, the Academy had to specify that only humans could qualify.

When Rin Tin Tin died in 1932, his body was returned to France, where he is interred at the famous *Cimetière des Chiens et Autres Animaux Domestiques* in a suburb of Paris.

In Hollywood, Rin Tin Tin's star on the Hollywood Walk of Fame is at 1627 Vine Street.

CHAPTER 10.

HOLLYWOODLAND
THE NEIGHBORHOOD BENEATH THE ICONIC SIGN

1923

Blame it on the unholy alliance of William Shakespeare and two streetcar tycoons.

The tycoons were Eli P. Clark and his brother-in-law, M. H. Sherman. They bought 640 rugged acres of Beechwood Canyon, a natural passageway through the Santa Monica Mountains, in 1905. Then, in honor of the Bard's 300th birthday in April 1916, silent movie star Douglas Fairbanks starred in Shakespeare's *Julius Caesar*, presented under the stars in that rugged terrain, featuring a cast of hundreds that even included the Hollywood High School football team. *Los Angeles Times* publisher Harry Chandler saw more than a play that night. He saw gold in those undeveloped hills.

Chandler formed a real estate partnership with Clark and Sherman at about the same time that the town was abuzz over the success of Windsor Square, a gorgeous new collection of costly mansions just a short distance down the hill. Chandler's son Norman bought a residence there, and now even wealthy celebrities like Ethel Barrymore were moving in. The partners wasted no time; they expanded their syndicate to include the talented

Harry Chandler

Windsor Square developers Tracy E. Shoults and S. H. Woodruff. Together, these partners envisioned a bright new future for their rugged canyon acreage. Forget about Shakespeare. They would call their new place: Hollywoodland.

The biggest expenses, they all knew, were bringing water, sewers and Mr. Edison's electricity into the undeveloped canyon. Lacking today's earth-moving equipment, there could be very little leveling of the rocky terrain. Instead, their houses would be built on top of little promontories or directly into the hillside itself, a radical new concept that was also its key selling feature. Unlike Windsor Square's flat terrain, where capacious homes baked all day in the California sun, these quaint Hollywoodland houses would be nestled directly into the shady foliage, protected from the summer heat. Living in the Hollywoodland Hills would be cool, naturally.

The streetcar tycoons provided the land; the acclaimed developers brought credibility, but Chandler? He was in charge of publicity. It was Harry Chandler's idea to build a sign 50-feet-high reading "HOLLYWOODLAND." Constructed of sheet metal, pipes, wires, telephone poles and 4,000 20-watt bulbs, the first sign cost $21,000 to construct. Mules were harnessed to haul the sign to its dramatic precipice, where it could be seen for miles in every direction. Just to make sure that everyone knew this new unusual development came with modern amenities like electricity, the sign blinked in segments: HOLLY ... WOOD ... LAND. Then all together, HOLLYWOODLAND.

Chandler continued the promotional drumbeat in print. When the Hollywoodland opening was announced in the March 31, 1923 edition of the *Los Angeles Times*, where it was publicized as the first hillside residential development in the United States, 120 buyers committed immediately. Subsequent ads stressed, "Give the kiddies a chance ... crowded boulevards, dangerous corners, unknown companions are an ever-present danger to the children of big cities. Come to Hollywoodland."

The allure was unbeatable. Here were the Windsor Square developers, offering their newest product at a fraction of Windsor Square's costs. Empty lots were available for sale, too, in Hollywoodland, starting at "$2,975 to $4,750 and up," though every construction on an empty lot required approval by a design review board. Styles were restricted to "French Normandy, English Tudor, Mediterranean or Spanish." Size was

Hollywoodland realty office. Developer S. H. Woodruff stands in the center, with bow tie, 1923

no concern; middle-class families lived beside wealthy ones throughout the canyon. Stones that were unearthed during construction were used to devise six communal staircases that connected some of the steepest streets. European stonemasons, who lived in tents in the canyon when they weren't at work, constructed massive retaining walls along some roadways to support the houses on the streets above. They erected two stone towers, now city landmarks, to designate the Hollywoodland entrance on Beechwood Drive.

But the good times couldn't last. When the Great Depression pummeled the partners' investments, they ceased all new construction. No additional roads were paved, and even the approved lots remained undeveloped. The giant sign became a constant nuisance. Never intended as a permanent fixture in the California landscape, its flimsy materials required frequent maintenance. A heavy storm or a broken branch meant hoisting the letters back into place and rewiring the electricity.

On the night of September 18, 1932, the Hollywoodland sign came to symbolize more than just the collection of houses assembled below it. Twenty-four-year-old actress Peg Entwistle was so distraught by the turns

From left: Hollywoodland sign, 1923; Peg Entwistle

in her career that she climbed the letter H with a workman's ladder and jumped to her death. Though Entwistle's suicide is largely forgotten, the sign was immortalized; it suddenly represented the dreams and nightmares associated with the entire entertainment industry in LA, a reputation the sign and the city have never shed. More iconic than the California sun or the Pacific beaches, the sign remains LA's most distinctive monument.

In 1949, the sign's ownership was transferred to the Hollywood Chamber of Commerce. Since it no longer promoted the sale of new Hollywoodland properties, the sign's final four letters were permanently removed. By then, vandals had destroyed or stolen every light bulb, the landscape was eroding and the original construction materials had deteriorated. Restoration of the Hollywood sign became a *cause célèbre* among movie stars with each passing decade. Actress Gloria Swanson spearheaded a makeover to coincide with the sign's 50th anniversary, but that repair didn't last for long. In 1978, when the sign nearly collapsed, another unholy alliance was formed to build a permanent new sign. This time, the disparate team comprised rockstar Alice Cooper, singing cowboy Gene Autry, easy-listening Andy Williams and Playboy founder Hugh Hefner, among many others who financed the sign's literal replacement. In 2000, Panasonic installed a state-of-the-art alarm system, and in 2010, another alliance including Tom Hanks, Norman Lear, Tiffany & Co., the Walt Disney Company, Hugh Hefner and others, pooled their resources to purchase the land behind the

Hollywood sign for $12,000,000, guaranteeing that no additional real estate development could encroach on the famous icon.

Today, stewardship of the sign is shared by three agencies: The City of Los Angeles owns the land, the Hollywood Chamber of Commerce controls the licensing rights and the Hollywood Sign Trust repairs and maintains its structure. The sign is now guarded, fenced and alarmed to make certain that no more suicides or publicity stunts mar the sign that is revered by so many.

Meanwhile, the value of Hollywoodland real estate soared. Over the decades, those quaint houses have been home to a Who's Who in the entertainment industry. A partial list includes Doris Day, Bela Lugosi, Humphrey Bogart, Bugsy Siegel, Anne Francis, Vincent Price, Richard Thomas, Edward Everett Horton, Ned Beatty, Connie Sellecca, bandleader Paul Whiteman, conductor André Kostelanetz, singer Melissa Manchester, author James Cain, even Peter Tork of The Monkees. Even the smallest houses routinely sell for a million dollars today.

The sign's fame ended the quaintness of Hollywoodland. Now, visitors come from around the world to hail the iconic site in Beechwood Canyon. Its lasting acclaim would surely persuade streetcar tycoons, Chandler, Fairbanks, Shakespeare, and probably even Julius Caesar to take a long, theatrical bow.

IN THE MOVIES: *Earthquake* (1974), *Day of the Locust* (1975), *Pretty Woman* (1990), *Bugsy* (1991), *The People vs. Larry Flynt* (1996), *Independence Day* (1996), *Hollywoodland* (2006), *Argo* (2012), *Gangster Squad* (2013), and dozens more.

Beechwood entrance to Hollywoodland subdivision, with S. H. Woodruff in foreground

CHAPTER 11.

SISTER AIMEE
LOS ANGELES GETS RELIGION
1922—1944

Los Angeles was one helluva party in the 1920s! Flappers and flivvers, bathtub gin, booming real estate, swimming pools, movie stars, movie moguls, movie studios; there was just one element missing. Los Angeles needed an evangelist to shout above the din and remind everyone they were on the road to eternal damnation.

Aimee Semple McPherson seized the opportunity. Arriving in LA in 1922 with two children and $100, Sister Aimee, as she was lovingly called, raked in more than one million dollars in three years (almost $13 million today) by praising the Lord at the Angelus Temple, her 5,300-seat auditorium that she filled three times a day. She called her Pentecostal enterprise the International Church of the Foursquare Gospel. As a theatrical production, it had no equal. Accompanied by one of the nation's largest theater organs, services included a brass band that mixed military pomp with the excitement of a circus, followed by a women's choir, and then radiant Sister Aimee herself, in flowing red tresses and a shimmering white gown. She raised the Good Book and promised redemption. She spoke of a loving God, with arms outstretched. The lower middle-class couldn't get enough of it.

Sister Aimee feared no risk. By the time she arrived in LA, she had already survived a colorful past. As teenaged Beth Kennedy from Ontario, Canada, she married missionary Robert Semple at the Salvation Army in 1908. They embarked on a mission to China in 1910 when the young missus was six months pregnant. Three months later, Robert Semple was dead from dysentery. Twenty-year-old Aimee buried Robert in Hong Kong, gave birth to Roberta Semple and returned to the Salvation Army in New York. That's where she met and married Harold McPherson in 1912. Their son

Aimee with her first love and spiritual mentor, Robert Semple

Rolf McPherson was born in 1913, but the marriage didn't last. Husband Harold was an accountant who soon wearied of life in the "Gospel Car" while Aimee evangelized in tents across America. His divorce, on grounds of "abandonment," was granted in 1921.

Now she was in LA, where shopkeepers, car mechanics, barbers and seamstresses flocked to the Angelus Temple not just for the sermons but for the network. It was a meeting place, literally, where Angelenos came to convene with people like themselves and find new friends from all over town. A visit to Sister Aimee was an affirmative experience that further strengthened everyone's bonds to her. And when Sister Aimee told her congregation that "faith heals," they threw down their crutches and walked. Sister Aimee's faith healing sessions reached such emotional highs, and such national notoriety, that she was investigated by the American Medical Association. Its verdict: Sister Aimee's healing was "genuine, beneficial and wonderful." Other documentation from the era confirms tens of thousands of very sick people came to Sister Aimee, blind, deaf and crippled. She would point to heaven, praise Christ the Great Healer, and take no credit for the results. Witnesses reported the lame walked; maybe it was temporary for some, but others were healed forever.

An astute businesswoman, Sister Aimee promptly franchised. She opened a school that graduated new missionaries; they eventually expanded her

Foursquare Gospel to 450 branch churches in the U.S. and nearly 200 overseas. She established a nursery for the many abandoned babies left on the Angelus doorstep. She reached out to migrant workers, and welcomed Spanish speakers into the fold. When she built radio station KFSG in 1924, Sister Aimee became the second woman in history to be granted a broadcast license. Her gospel programs were soon heard around the world.

Production values increased, packing the Angelus Temple beyond capacity. The Red Car Line added more trolleys; extra police were needed to direct the traffic around Sister Aimee's theatrical church. In staged vignettes, she could be costumed as a police officer sounding a siren on speeding sinners, or as a football star that would "carry the ball for the Foursquare Church." The lavish presentations frequently involved animals, even a live camel. Then out came the collection baskets, and Sister Aimee would chide, "No coins, please."

Though she seemed to radiate purity, this divorced mother of two yearned for a carnal life, too. When she attempted a respite from the spotlight, it ended badly.

On May 18, 1926, Sister Aimee went swimming at Ocean Park Beach in Venice, California. When she didn't come back up for air, everyone thought that Sister Aimee had drowned, and her body swept out to sea. As search teams scanned the ocean, thousands flocked to the Venice beach, dropped to their knees and prayed for Aimee's return or her entrance into heaven. William Randolph Hearst's newspaper The *Los Angeles Examiner* mourned

From left: The Angelus Temple, c. 1920s and Sister Aimee's service at the temple

Crowds at a train station awaiting the return of
Aimee Semple McPherson from Douglas AZ, 1926

the tragedy by publishing a poem by Upton Sinclair. Aimee's mother took over at the Angelus Temple, ending her sermons with, "Sister is with Jesus," reducing the parishioners to tears.

Then on June 23, 1926, Sister Aimee stumbled out of the desert in Agua Prieta, a town in northern Mexico. She claimed that she had been kidnapped, chloroformed and tortured; she escaped by walking for 13 hours across the desert.

What followed next was surreal. Embarking from Douglas, Arizona, Sister Aimee, perfectly coiffed and attired in a radiant white gown, traveled by train back to Union Station in LA. Planes flew overhead, dropping flowers on the rails as the train approached LA. A carpet of red roses marked Aimee's path on the station platform, where an estimated crowd of 50,000 awaited. The brass band from the Angelus Temple led a parade in their snappy white uniforms for Sister's triumphant return to LA. Airplanes dropped flower petals on the parade route, while politicians tripped over each other to welcome Aimee back home. White-robed flower girls surrounded her, two dozen cowboys escorted her, and the Los Angeles Fire Department donned their dress parade uniforms to welcome her. Bigger than any movie star or politician, the newspapers would report that the delirious crowd attending Sister Aimee's homecoming set a record for the largest gathering in the history of LA.

Then the newspapermen studied her alibi more closely. Evidence told another story: Sister Aimee spent the month in Carmel-by-the-Sea in a beach shack with a former radio announcer she had hired. Newspapers pounced, writing wild and lurid conjectures of what really happened, with no disclaimers or retractions. The clergy pounced, incensed that Aimee's theatrics had reduced the Christian bible into a series of vaudeville sketches. Then the politicians pounced. Sister Aimee was arrested and charged with providing false information designed to hinder the due process of law. She faced 42 years in prison.

The legal wrangling dragged on for two years. Sister Aimee took to the airwaves to defend herself, while the Christian clergy collected petitions and passed resolutions condemning her, and the newspapers published whatever sold copies. In the end, charges were dropped; the government conceded that there was insufficient evidence to prosecute. What was the crime? Nobody goes to jail for adultery, especially in Hollywood.

Sister Aimee with KFSG radio engineer Kenneth Ormiston, with whom she was rumored to have engaged in a scandalous affair

Sister Aimee resumed her services at the Angelus Temple. With the alleged hoax unresolved, she was mocked in the media for years, but the scandal did not diminish her popularity. The trial's judge was impeached instead. In January 1927, Sister Aimee traveled America on a "Vindication Tour," continuing her spiritual work. During the Great Depression, she opened a commissary that fed an estimated 1.5 million people. She convinced doctors, dentists and nurses to donate their services for free at her Angelus clinic. Mahatma Gandhi honored her with a sari. Then, on September 27, 1944, an accidental overdose of sleeping pills killed Aimee Semple McPherson at age 53. Though the Foursquare Gospel Church was worth millions at the time, when Sister Aimee's estate was sorted out, she had just $10,000 to her name.

Her body lay in state at the Angelus Temple for three days while approximately 45,000 worshippers waited in line for hours to file past her casket. Cars were double parked on every street within a one-and-a-half-mile radius. Eleven trucks were needed to transport all the flowers to Forest Lawn Cemetery, where Sister Aimee was laid to rest.

Rolf McPherson took charge of the Angelus Temple, presiding there for 44 years, until he finally retired in 1988. As the progenitor of America's mega-churches, the Angelus Temple was inducted into the National Register of Historic Places in 1992.

CHAPTER 12.

GREYSTONE MANSION
DOHENY AND THE TEAPOT
DOME SCANDAL

1921—1929

Penniless when he arrived in Los Angeles in 1891, Edward L. Doheny was the wealthiest oilman in the world by 1920. But, when the prosperous Doheny built a 55-room limestone mansion in Beverly Hills as a gift to his son, the world witnessed his dynasty's epic collapse. That gift, the sad but beautiful Greystone Mansion, is a national landmark today, an empty reminder of the scandals and murders committed there.

Even before prosperity arrived, Doheny's private life in LA was overwrought with drama. Just weeks before he struck oil, his seven-year-old daughter died of heart failure. Barely one year later, his still inconsolable wife gave birth to "Ned," Edward L. Doheny Jr., on November 6, 1893. Frustrated by her husband's long absences in pursuit of more oil, she abruptly ended the marriage in 1899, taking Ned to live in San Francisco. Despite his Catholic faith that forbid it, Doheny agreed to a divorce. Then he fell in love with the voice of the telephone operator who placed his long-distance business calls. On August 22, 1900, just three months after their first acquaintance, Edward Doheny married Estelle Betzhold in a splendid, new railroad car that would serve as their first home. Four weeks after the wedding, the ex-Mrs. Doheny

Ned Doheny, Jr., Mrs. Estelle Doheny, and Edward L. Doheny, Sr., leaving the Federal Court in Los Angeles, after being tried in an oil scandal, 1924.

swallowed battery acid and killed herself. Doheny regained custody of Ned, buried his ex-wife beside his dead daughter in LA's Evergreen Cemetery, and the new Mrs. Doheny became the delighted mother to an equally delighted seven-year-old son. The family relocated to 8 Chester Place, an exclusive enclave of 14 mansions; their neighbors were the power elite of the West. For the rest of their lives, Edward and Ned Doheny would infer that Estelle was Ned's birth mother, but on Memorial Day each year, Estelle returned to Evergreen Cemetery to place flowers on Ned's mother's grave.

Doheny had lofty plans for young Ned following his graduation from the University of Southern California. World War I had just ended; big oil companies now dominated American politics. When President Harding took office in 1921, he filled his Cabinet with officers from Gulf Oil, Standard Oil and Sinclair Oil, and he appointed Doheny's longtime friend (and by now, former senator) Albert B. Fall as the new Secretary of the Interior. Though Democrats derisively dubbed them "the Oil Cabinet," Doheny saw no conflict; he was thrilled when Secretary Fall arranged a meeting with President Harding. This cozy relationship between government and oil tycoons would lead to Doheny's downfall, though he failed to heed the warnings. Instead, he viewed this easy access as an opportunity for Ned to advance the Doheny name to political prominence.

That opportunity arrived promptly. Although conservationists denounced the Harding administration for its backroom deals with oilmen who reaped private profits from public land, that didn't stop Secretary Fall or President Harding. They offered Doheny access to two oil-rich federal reserves: in Kern County, California, and Teapot Dome, Wyoming, named for the shape of its unique rock formation. Doheny readily accepted. He didn't own the land, but he would pay the U.S. government 35 percent of the value of the crude oil his company extracted. The balance covered overhead and provided Doheny a hefty profit.

Then, Secretary Fall asked Doheny for "a personal loan" of $100,000. It seems he had lost a fortune on copper mines; his property taxes in New Mexico were 10 years in arrears. Doheny complied. In fact, he saw this as Ned's chance to become acquainted with American politics. He directed Ned to withdraw $100,000 in cash from a New York bank, then deliver it personally to Secretary Fall in Washington, D.C. ($100,000 cash in 1921 would be nearly $1.3 million today.)

Ned Doheny employed Hugh Plunkett as his personal secretary and confidante for the past seven years, a salaried friend who oversaw many tasks and remained knowledgeable about private matters. Hugh accompanied Ned by train from LA to New York to deliver the loan to Secretary Fall. They withdrew the cash and hand-carried it on another train to Washington, D.C. Secretary Fall received the cash from the two young men in exchange for a Promissory Note.

Edward Doheny knew that there was a social caste system among the wealthiest Americans: Catholics and Jews were not welcomed within the rarified strata. To demonstrate that he was no one's inferior, Doheny spent liberally. One by one, he acquired the 13 remaining mansions on Chester Place until he owned the entire gated compound. For his philanthropy within the Catholic Church, bishops and church officials held Doheny in the highest esteem. Now Doheny focused his attention on a new kind of investment: conferring prestige on his scion. When Ned married Lucy Smith, Doheny acquired 400 acres in Beverly Hills. The exclusive new subdivision

A postcard of the Fairbankses at home paddling in their swimming pool.

had already earned its reputation among LA's wealthiest residents; famous movie stars like Mary Pickford and Douglas Fairbanks led glamorous lives there. Doheny reserved 12.5 acres on a hilltop for Ned and Lucy, where he planned to build Beverly Hills' most splendid mansion, establishing the next generation of Dohenys in Los Angeles society.

The three-foot-thick limestone facade earned the Greystone Mansion its name. Resembling a baronial castle, the main residence would sprawl more than 46,000 square feet, plus stables that occupied nearly 16,000 square feet, a two-bedroom gatehouse, an enormous garage with its own gas pumps and machine shop; even its own fire station. The mansion was filled with outlandish amenities like a walk-in vault for furs and jewels; a room for cutting flowers; a room for wrapping presents; a room for Ned's guns; a movie theater; a bowling alley; and (since this was during Prohibition) a retractable bar that disappeared with the push of a button. Outdoor features included a 60-foot swimming pool, terraces, tennis courts, kennels, riding trails and formal gardens. Maintaining a residence of this scale required not just cooks, maids and gatekeepers, but also 10 gardeners, four chauffeurs and two telephone operators to run the internal switchboards. Ned's friend Hugh Plunkett oversaw many of these details during construction. When moving day finally arrived, Ned was a 35-year-old father with five children.

Meanwhile, back in Washington, D.C., the Senate demanded a Congressional investigation into the use of federally-owned land for private profit. All fingers pointed to Secretary Fall, who admitted that he awarded the oil production rights to Doheny without

A 1924 cartoon depicts Washington officials racing down an oil-slicked road to the White House, trying to outpace the Teapot Dome scandal of President Warren G. Harding's administration

soliciting a single competing bid. On March 4, 1923, Fall was forced to resign from office. Even more shocking, weeks later, President Harding suffered a stroke and died. The new Calvin Coolidge administration was far less cozy with America's oilmen, especially with a Congressional investigation under way.

Edward L. Doheny (second from right) testifying before the Senate Committee investigating the Teapot Dome Scandal, 1924

Next, an unexpected blow: The *Albuquerque Morning Journal* reported that Albert Fall had suddenly paid off ten years' worth of taxes and even purchased additional property. Again the former Secretary of the Interior faced the congressional committee, this time to explain the source of his sudden wealth. Doheny was summoned, too. He confirmed that he furnished an interest-free loan to Fall with "my own money, and it did not belong in whole or in part to any oil company with which I am connected." When asked for evidence of the cash withdrawal, Doheny disclosed that Ned and Hugh withdrew the cash from an account in New York.

Doheny was indicted for bribery; Albert Fall became the first U.S. Cabinet member to be sent to prison. As a result, a new Act of Congress stated plainly that federal lands cannot be used for private profits. Doheny's legal battles with Congress dragged on for years as the government now pursued him for conspiracy. He liquidated some assets to pay legal fees and wisely transferred much of his wealth to trust funds for his grandchildren. Still, this new investigation ratcheted up the tension in the Greystone Mansion because this time Congress demanded that Ned and Hugh testify, too.

Unaccustomed to such high-profile scrutiny, and in fear of a jail sentence for delivering the cash, Hugh Plunkett panicked. In the Greystone Mansion on Christmas Eve 1928, Plunkett collapsed. Doheny's doctor diagnosed the incident as "a nervous breakdown." Then Plunkett's condition worsened. At 9:30 p.m. on February 16, 1929, after Ned dressed for bed, Plunkett arrived in a suit and tie. They convened in a guest room for a private discussion over drinks and cigarettes, but as Plunkett grew increasingly agitated, the discussion degenerated into an argument. Ned phoned the doctor who cared for Plunkett during his breakdown, then suddenly Lucy heard "a loud noise." As Lucy and the doctor approached the guest room, Plunkett slammed the door. Next, they heard two gunshots. The doctor barged into the guest room and saw Plunkett lying dead on the floor with blood oozing from his skull. Ned was shot but still breathing, with blood seeping from both sides of his head. The bullet passed straight through his cranium and embedded in the wall. Lucy phoned her family for help while the doctor attempted to clear Ned's breathing passages by turning him on his side. Lucy returned to see Ned die, too. She wailed uncontrollably as pandemonium ensued in the Greystone Mansion. Relatives descended; servants awoke. Doheny raced to the mansion, stared in silence at his dead son, then crumpled to the floor and wept.

Hours later, Lucy's brother-in-law finally called for the police. A detective and the investigator for the District Attorney arrived at around 2:00 a.m. They took down statements from the doctor and others present, then closely scrutinized the crime scene. The gun was too hot for a discharge that occurred hours earlier, and it had been wiped clean of all fingerprints. Had someone heated the gun to mislead the investigation? Powder burns surrounded the bullet holes in Ned's head, indicating that the gun was held at extremely close range, but no such powder appeared on Plunkett's

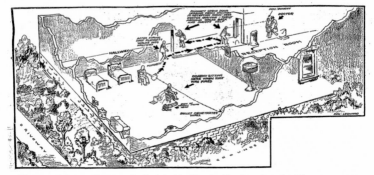

Diagram retraces the events that led to the deaths, *Los Angeles Times*, February 18, 1929

From left: "Father Crumpled When Told of Tragedy" *Los Angeles Examiner*, 1929; Lucy Smith Doheny, 1918

wounds. Further, the angle of Ned's wounds implied a very awkward position if Plunkett had been Ned's assassin, especially since Plunkett was holding a cigarette in one hand. It was apparent that the crime scene had been tampered and statements rehearsed. Under questioning, the doctor admitted that he moved Ned's body. Detectives could not determine whether this was a murder and suicide perpetrated by Ned or by Plunkett.

Less than 36 hours later, the chief investigator announced that the case was closed. Plunkett had gone berserk and shot Ned, then taken his own life. The investigator reversed the facts regarding the powder residue, now claiming that it appeared on Plunkett's cranium instead. Newspapers pandered to the case's uncertainties. The *Los Angeles Examiner*, Randolph Hearst's paper, screamed: "Bullet-Torn Bodies Found in Oil Man's Home." The *Los Angeles Times* published an interview with the doctor, who confided that Plunkett "was nervous, very nervous and irritable too. Mr. Doheny always treated him with the utmost consideration." International speculation kept the story alive long after the coroners and detectives closed the case.

To bury Ned, Doheny purchased a rare Italian marble mausoleum from the second century, in which Ned's unmarked sarcophagus was installed at Forest Lawn Memorial Park in Glendale, CA. Weeks later, Doheny had the bodies of Ned's birth mother and young sister exhumed from Evergreen and installed in the mausoleum so that all three might rest in peace together. On the day after Ned's burial, Hugh Plunkett was interred about 30 feet from Ned's mausoleum, with two of Lucy's brothers serving as pallbearers in a display of unity between both families.

Thirteen months later, the federal investigation rested: Doheny was exonerated of all charges. The relief arrived too late; Doheny was already a broken man. Months earlier, the stock market crashed, triggering the Great Depression. When he died in 1935 at age 79, Doheny's estate was worth a fraction of its previous glory. In their final years, Edward and Estelle Doheny found solace in their Catholic faith, bequeathing many of their remaining possessions to the Church, which the Church eventually liquidated. Today, the Chester Place compound is Mount Saint Mary's College. Doheny's copy of the Gutenberg Bible is now in the collection of Bill Gates.

Lucy remained in the Greystone Mansion for 26 more years. She remarried and lived to be 100 years old, dying in 1993. The acreage surrounding the Greystone Mansion is known today as the Trousdale Estates, some of the toniest real estate in Beverly Hills. A library on the campus of USC commemorates Ned Doheny, and Doheny State Beach is an eight-mile gift to California from Edward Doheny. Estelle devoted her final days to developing the Doheny Eye Institute, a foundation that thrives today.

The Greystone Mansion is now owned and maintained by the City of Beverly Hills, where its park-like grounds are open for free to all visitors year-round.

GREYSTONE MANSION IN THE MOVIES

The 18 acres of parkland surrounding Greystone Mansion are open to the public (no charge) . . . when it's not in use as a film set! Since 1955, the Greystone Mansion has appeared in more than 50 feature films, plus countless music videos, television episodes and some incredible private events. Some popular films shot on location at the Greystone Mansion include:

Title	Starring
The Disorderly Orderly (1964)	Jerry Lewis
Dead Ringer (1964)	Bette Davis, Karl Malden
The Loved One (1965)	Robert Morse, Jonathan Winters
The Trouble With Angels (1966)	Hayley Mills, Rosalind Russell
The Dirty Dozen (1967)	Ernest Borgnine, Charles Bronson
Phantom of the Paradise (1974)	Brian De Palma, Director
Eraserhead (1977)	David Lynch, Director
Winter Kills (1979)	Jeff Bridges, Elizabeth Taylor
Stripes (1981)	Bill Murray
All of Me (1984)	Lily Tomlin, Steve Martin
The Golden Child (1986)	Eddie Murphy
Jumpin' Jack Flash (1986)	Whoopi Goldberg
The Witches of Eastwick (1987)	Michelle Pfeiffer, Susan Sarandon
Ghostbusters II (1989)	Dan Aykroyd, Bill Murray
Death Becomes Her (1992)	Meryl Streep, Goldie Hawn
The Bodyguard (1992)	Whitney Houston, Kevin Costner
Indecent Proposal (1993)	Robert Redford, Demi Moore
Batman & Robin (1997)	George Clooney, Arnold Schwarzenegger
Rush Hour (1998)	Jackie Chan, Chris Tucker
The Big Lebowski (1998)	Jeff Bridges, John Goodman
What Women Want (2000)	Mel Gibson, Helen Hunt
X-Men (2000)	Hugh Jackman, Patrick Stewart
Rock Star (2001)	Mark Wahlberg, Jennifer Aniston
Spider-Man I, II & III (2002)	Tobey Maguire
Garfield II (2006)	Bill Murray
The Prestige (2006)	Hugh Jackman, Christian Bale
There Will Be Blood (2007)	Daniel Day-Lewis
The Social Network (2010)	Jesse Eisenberg, Justin Timberlake
The Muppets (2011)	Chris Cooper, Jason Segel

The entrance to the Greystone Mansion is located at:
905 Loma Vista Drive, Beverly Hills, CA 90210

Exterior areas are open to the public. Interiors are shown by appointment only. Enjoy a stroll through the Greystone's elaborate gardens.
See: www.greystonemansion.org

CHAPTER 13.

SUNSET STRIP UNINCORPORATED

MICKEY COHEN'S TERRITORY, A.K.A. WEST HOLLYWOOD

1925–Present

Thanks to Huntington's Red Cars, new communities popped up all around Los Angeles County. Property owners in places like Venice and Hollywood were eager to see their neighborhoods incorporated into Los Angeles, where they could benefit from the city's schools, police, paved roads and fire protection. A few neighborhoods, however, like Beverly Hills and Santa Monica, made the opposite choice. Though technically located within LA's city limits, these communities preferred to be self-sufficient. They incorporated independently. To this day, Beverly Hills and Santa Monica are self-contained cities that do not elect LA's mayor; they've got their own, thanks, as well as police, schools, libraries and (better) paved streets.

But there was a third, unexpected option: Do *nothing*. Don't support the LA city government and don't support an independent one, either. Remain *un*incorporated. That was the defiant decision made by residents in one of LA County's primest locations, the roughly two square miles between Hollywood and Beverly Hills. Why? Less scrutiny. In the twentieth century, that notorious stretch of land, dubbed West Hollywood by the local realty board in 1925, provided a safe haven for two distinctly different groups of

From left: Mickey Cohen (second from the left) and cohorts await booking in the LA County Jail, 1948; Michael's Exclusive Haberdashery, 8804 Sunset Boulevard

lawbreakers who preferred life under the radar.

The laws of LA County, not the city, governed all activities in unincorporated territory, and that was just fine with professional crooks like Benjamin "Bugsy" Siegel and his pal Mickey Cohen. They could fleece half the town in the time it took for a County Sheriff to respond to a police call. Meyer Lansky, Siegel's boss back in New York, controlled "the wire," a phenomenally profitable service that relayed the racing results, plus prizefights and sporting events, to off-track bookies. Lansky sent Siegel to oversee the West Coast operations, where he teamed up with Cohen, a scrappy featherweight boxer with a Star-of-David on his trunks, reputed to be LA's most prominent bookie. It was Cohen who really ran their day-to-day bookmaking business in LA, especially when Siegel took over the Flamingo Hotel construction project in Las Vegas and then got shot for mismanaging it.

The stretch of Sunset Boulevard between Beverly Hills and Hollywood was the ideal place for everything illicit. Since those two communities already zoned Sunset Boulevard for commerce, the unincorporated Strip between them was a ready-made commercial playground where the cops had no jurisdiction. During Prohibition, nightclubs set up business there because they could get away with bootleg liquor sales. That's when Cohen concealed his illegal bookmaking business beside the fashionable clubs. His first front was an expensive men's store at 8804 Sunset Boulevard that he named Michael's Exclusive Haberdashery; Cohen managed bookies in three counties from its basement. Business was so good that he needed more space, so he opened an adjacent store called Courtley's Exclusive Jewelry; then he set up a custom-made shirt shop that was actually a front for wholesale narcotics distribution. In a fourth storefront, he installed a former NYPD detective to keep an eye on the rackets at all times, and an attorney with a successful record of representing underworld crime figures to keep the operation out of trouble. In the used car dealership nearby, Cohen housed an exact replica of a police car, along with a fleet of customized navy-blue Cadillacs with hidden compartments to stow guns and cash, used by Cohen's nattily-dressed seven-man team to transact business.

Mickey Cohen and his bulletproof car

What business? Cohen learned an effective swindle from Bugsy Siegel: Using oblique threats of blackmail or violence, he simply told local merchants that he wanted "a loan" that he never intended to repay. His team (known as the "Seven Dwarfs" to law enforcement) collected that cash, plus the winnings from an estimated network of 500 bookmakers in the area; they delivered supplies to local drug dealers, and escorted beautiful women for big-money sex and blackmail schemes.

Next, Cohen entered the publishing industry to establish a network of contacts with the press and the movie studios. *Hollywood Nite Life* was a scandal sheet (with the name of Frank Sinatra's manager appearing atop its masthead) that was delivered to every studio boss and producer. Its intimate disclosures sent shock waves through Hollywood. Then, Cohen's well-tailored team (now poised as "salesmen") would follow up to extort cash from the celebrities who might appear in the next issue, threatening to turn their indiscretions into career-crashing exposés. Judy Garland allegedly paid off Cohen four times to keep her troubles out of the press. Even Sinatra paid to hide his extramarital affair with Ava Gardner. When movie star

From left: Judy Garland and Humphrey Bogart at Ciro's, 1955; Robert Mitchum in jail in 1949; Frank Sinatra and Ava Gardner

Robert Mitchum was arrested at "a marijuana party" and sent to jail in 1948, the scandal was published around the world. Not noticed: the other guy at that party, Sir Charles Hubbard, a wealthy Englishman who paid Cohen $85,000 (that's about *$800,000* today) in hush money. The Englishman's arrest went completely unnoticed thanks to Cohen's muscle with the rest of Hollywood's publishers.

This couldn't go on forever. Cohen was squeezed from every direction. The Italian Mafia tried to seize control of the wire racket; law enforcement bugged his house on Moreno Drive; a New York Mafioso bombed the house with 35 sticks of dynamite, and the IRS finally closed in with warrants for tax evasion. Cohen went to Alcatraz, then Atlanta Federal Penitentiary. Released in 1972, he died of stomach cancer in 1976 and was buried in LA's Hillside Memorial Cemetery (as Meyer H. Cohen, in a wall crypt beside Moe Howard from *The Three Stooges*).

And those fancy nightclubs on the Sunset Strip? They were no competition for America's new pastime: television. The Strip fell into decline for years, only to be reconfigured in the 1960s for rock bands like The Doors at the Whiskey a Go-Go and Hugh Hefner's Playboy Club at 8560 Sunset Boulevard. As the Strip turned into LA's site for love-ins and anti-war protests, traces of Mickey Cohen's gang faded fast.

There was another group of outlaws that needed to remain under the radar in West Hollywood: gay men and lesbians. Unincorporated West Hollywood provided a relatively safe haven in the decades when having a gay orientation was a crime. With little surveillance on the residential side streets, gays and lesbians could cohabit and commingle without fear of entrapment, blackmail and the brutality that often came from policemen and detectives.

In 1950, neighborhood activist Harry Hay founded the Mattachine Society, the first-known gay rights group in the U.S. The underground movement gained tremendous support when member Dale Jennings was arrested for "lewd and dissolute behavior" in February 1952. Jennings took the courageous action of acknowledging his homosexuality in court, then pleaded innocent to the charges against him. His precedent forced authorities to draw a distinction between being guilty of illegal activities or simply being a homosexual. When the district attorney's office dropped all charges, the event drew great (though quiet) support, and national membership in the Mattachine Society grew by several thousand in the succeeding weeks.

At about the same time, just a few short blocks from the Sunset Strip, cars and buses were replacing the antiquated Red Cars on Santa Monica Boulevard. When the giant depot in the heart of West Hollywood was finally closed, and the tracks were paved over that stretch of famous Route 66, Santa Monica Boulevard assumed a new prominence. Although the Sunset Strip was a destination for many, Santa Monica Boulevard became the new main street for residents in the expanding "WeHo" neighborhood. An even bigger change awaited.

In the 1970s, as gays and lesbians asserted their

Members of the Mattachine Society: Harry Hay (upper left), then (left to right) Konrad Stevens, Dale Jennings, Rudi Gernreich, Stan Witt, Bob Hull, Chuck Rowland (in glasses), Paul Bernard

rights across America, they found more than safety in West Hollywood; they discovered a welcoming *community*. Still governed by Los Angeles County, the neighborhood was densely populated by renters. When LA County announced plans to end its rent control provisions, many locals feared that rapid rent increases would price them out of the community they helped to build. Amazingly, gay activists who were once viewed as outlaws became the leaders who finally brought legitimacy to the neighborhood. They successfully incorporated the City of West Hollywood in 1984, then promptly enacted one of the strongest rent control laws in the nation. More importantly, they made headlines around the world by proclaiming West Hollywood to be "America's first gay city."

In an era when there were nearly no openly gay elected officials anywhere on earth, the West Hollywood City Council was the first in the nation with a gay majority. Valerie Terrigno, the city's first mayor, was a lesbian. Not surprisingly, one of the City Council's first acts was an ordinance banning discrimination against homosexuals. With scores of gay men battling the AIDS epidemic, the young city government launched one of the first AIDS education campaigns in the nation.

Since then, Santa Monica Boulevard in West Hollywood has been the site of AIDS vigils, gay rights protests and political celebrations. It hosts the largest annual Halloween celebration in America. Its annual Gay Pride Parade and the vibrant nightlife scene along Santa Monica Boulevard prompt many to refer to today's West Hollywood as "Boystown." (The census confirms: Almost 90 percent of gay residents are male.) The rainbow flag, representing the gay community around the world, is flown beside the American flag in traffic islands; it is paved into the crosswalks, and its rainbow colors are embedded in the city's logo.

The gay elected officials proved to be effective legislators. West Hollywood operates in the black while the City of Los Angeles (like most major cities) struggles to get out of the red. It is home to many power players in entertainment, and some of the most celebrated restaurants in Southern California. WeHo remains a hip address thanks to new construction that augments the classic supply of rent-controlled apartments. And it is one of the few urban environments in LA where people actually walk to shops and businesses.

Just like the gay community, the neighborhood continues to evolve. In addition to the prolific nightclub scene, West Hollywood is also a place for gay residents to get married and raise children. In fact, it's one of California's most popular destinations for gay weddings. Still, activism remains the unifying force in West Hollywood. One large and popular club prohibits "every legislator in any state that supports discrimination against LGBT people," and provides headshots of those legislators to the club's security guards.

Santa Monica Boulevard, West Hollywood

Although West Hollywood has transitioned greatly from the days of gangsters, bookies and blackmail, its bohemian culture remains intact. In the twenty-first century, there's no reason to remain under the radar.

IN THE MOVIES:

West Hollywood is one of the most frequently seen neighborhoods in films and television. Some popular titles include *The Blue Dahlia* (1946), *Sunset Boulevard* (1950), *Chinatown* (1974), *Annie Hall* (1977), *Scarface* (1983), *Beverly Hills Cop* (1984), *The Doors* (1991), *LA Confidential* (1997), *The Big Lebowski* (1998), *The Hangover* (2009) and many more.

CHAPTER 14.

PENTIMENTO
THE CONTROVERSIAL ART OF DAVID SIQUEIROS

1932

With more than 1,500 murals glowing in the Left Coast sunshine, Los Angeles holds the distinction of displaying more public art than any other city. (No city sprawls over so many streets either.) These bursts of color on LA street corners and freeways also mark eras in the city's history, like the additions for the 1932 and 1984 Summer Olympics, and the images in Hollywood that celebrate a century of memorable actors.

Muralist David Alfaro Siqueiros imagined public walls as sites to encourage debate. Renowned today along with Diego Rivera and José Clemente Orozco, the *Tres Grandes* advanced the idea that art in a public forum should provoke and educate. The concept wins them respect now, but their convictions forced them to lead confrontational lives. Siqueiros was apparently the firebrand: President of the Communist Party of Mexico, he was jailed in Mexico, deported from Argentina, and he was even arrested for attempting to assassinate Leon Trotsky. Siqueiros the artist lived like a warrior.

Tres Grandes—David Alfaro Siqueiros, José Clemente Orozco and Diego Rivera, 1949

In 1932, he was commissioned to install a mural on a second floor façade near the historic Plaza. He was teaching fresco painting at the Chouinard School (now the California Institute of the Arts) at the time. F. K. Ferenz, the director of the Plaza Art Center, sponsored the project where, true to his communist convictions, Siqueiros could employ twenty workers, his students. Ferenz got to pick the title and, hence, its theme: *América Tropical*.

The second-story wall extends for 82 feet, straddling Main and Olvera Streets. Since the mural would be seen primarily from street level, Siqueiros drew clever shadows that accommodated the visual range of pedestrians from either parallel street. As he put it, the mural "must conform to the normal transit of a spectator." His workers applied new sciences to their art, working quickly on wet cement instead of conventional plaster. *América Tropical* is one of the first murals to be created with electrical equipment: They worked at night, tracing the mural from a projected image, then painted it with car enamel loaded into a spray gun, the first air brush. The work was completed in two weeks, and its unveiling was scheduled for October 9, 1932.

Fortunately, it rained. If a larger crowd had been present, Siqueiros might have been bloodied, for the artwork he unveiled was a brazen, anti-American affront, an embarrassment to Ferenz and a finger in the face of the art elite assembled. Ferenz got his *América Tropical*, with lush sinewy branches of a tropical forest. But at the top of this forest is an American eagle with its wings spread, hovering over a crucified, spread-eagled peon that is the focal point of the mural. In one corner, stealthy revolutionaries sight their rifles at the eagle, aiming to shoot down imperialism.

Siqueiros was deported five weeks later. The stealthy revolutionaries were covered within weeks and, in 1938, *América Tropical* was whitewashed into oblivion.

Or was it? When an artist brings a new creation into the world, it can never vanish completely, even if it only survives in memories. For centuries, artists recycled their canvases by painting over earlier artworks that fell out of favor. Eventually, the paint from that lowest level bleeds to the surface, exposing the history underneath, a process called *pentimento*. In the twenty-first century, you could say that pentimento transfused new life into *América Tropical*.

It wasn't a romantic masterwork oozing to the surface. It was merely whitewash that cracked and peeled after decades of sunny neglect, revealing hints of the angry artwork pulsating underneath. Siqueiros was world famous and dead for decades when a new generation of City officials pondered whether to resurrect the only outdoor mural Siqueiros created in the U.S. The Getty Conservation Institute signed on to oversee the restoration and cover part of its costs, but also to give Siqueiros his public dialogue, addressing two questions posed by *América Tropical*:

If there is a line between art and propaganda, on which side does *América Tropical* fall? Answer: Instead of propaganda, *América Tropical* earned its reputation as a symbol of suppression, censored by the same imperialists Siqueiros suggested in his painting.

And, are government officials ever justified in censoring an artist's work if they don't like the message? Not on the Left Coast! Championed by

The mural portion visible from Olvera Street was promptly whitewashed; eventually the entire mural was hidden under white paint.

Colorized rendering of David Alfaro Siqueiros' *América Tropical*, 1932

Mayor Antonio Villaraigosa, the City invested $5 million to make things right with Siqueiros. On October 9, 2012, 80 years to the day after *América Tropical* was first unveiled, a new art elite assembled for the unveiling of its restoration, now a symbol for free speech, *pentimento* no more.

América Tropical is on display, for free, six days a week. Enter through the *América Tropical* Interpretive Center on Olvera Street, in the Pueblo de Los Angeles Historic Monument.

See: www.americatropical.org

THE WINDSHIELD PERSPECTIVE

Siqueiros spawned generations of artists who turned today's Los Angeles into the mural capital of the world. "Outdoor walls are the new gallery space. We live through our windshields in this city," explains one contemporary muralist. And he's right. More than 1,500 works of art, spanning decades, are registered with the Mural Conservancy of Los Angeles, with more permits issued every year.

The Conservancy also enforces the rules that every artist knows: no guns, no drugs, no nudes. With those basic guidelines, a vast array of styles emerged over the years. Here's a selective sampling.

Murals (detail) in Los Angeles (clockwise from top left): *Dolores del Rio* (Hudson Ave. and Hollywood Blvd.), Alfredo de Batuc, 1990; *You are the Star* (Wilcox Ave. & Hollywood Blvd.), Thomas Suriya, 1983; *We Are Not A Minority* (3217 W. Olympic Blvd.), Mario Torero, 1978; *Venice Reconstituted* (25 Windward Ave., Venice Beach), Rip Cronk, 1989

WATTS TOWERS

Simon Rodia

As Calvin Trillin explained in the *New Yorker* in 1965, "If a man who has not labeled himself an artist happens to produce a work of art, he is likely to cause a lot of confusion and inconvenience." Simon Rodia was that artisan. His sculpture, known today as the *Watts Towers of Simon Rodia*, is an American Naïve masterpiece, reminding visitors that art can be created anywhere, and by anyone.

On a small triangular lot that he purchased in Watts, a neighborhood in East Los Angeles, the barely solvent Italian immigrant fulfilled his passion on weeknights and weekends, building a tribute to his adopted country that he lovingly named *Nuestro Pueblo*, or "our town."

For 34 years, from 1921 to 1954, Rodia constructed a cluster of 17 lacy columns made of scrap rebar that he twisted into gigantic spirals. He encrusted the framework with mortar and embedded it with a pop-culture mosaic of found objects: more than 70,000 seashells, pebbles and discarded artifacts like chunks of broken pottery, broken bottles and beads. Working alone without scaffolds, bolts, rivets or power tools, Rodia relied on his own ingenuity and the simple hand tools of his trade—plus a window-washer's belt and buckle for safety when he scaled the Towers' heights. With no predetermined design, he slowly and painstakingly created the whimsical, multi-colored towers that sparkle in the California sun, even including a gazebo and three birdbaths. The tallest tower stands 99-and-a-half feet high.

The neighbors *absolutely* didn't get it. They frequently vandalized Rodia's work and made him feel unwelcome. Some locals even rumored that the Towers were antennae communicating with enemy forces during World War II. Despite the disrespect, Rodia persevered.

The city's administration didn't get it, either. The Department of Building and Safety eventually ordered the Towers to be demolished. At age 75, weary of defending his efforts, Rodia deeded the property to a neighbor. He turned away from his 34-year obsession and never returned. Hounded out of the neighborhood in 1954, he relocated nearly 400 miles away in Martinez, California, north of Berkeley, where he died, still penniless, in 1965. As he stated before he departed, "I had it in mind to do something big, and I did it."

To save the structure, a group of concerned citizens collected signatures and money to battle the Buildings Department. They convinced the city to perform a stress test before dismissing the work as unsafe. With live TV news cameras rolling, Rodia's construction resisted the strain of steel cables pulled by a tractor. That was the turning point in the Towers' survival, finally winning overdue recognition. The property was eventually deeded to the State of California, which created the Watts Towers of Simon Rodia State Historic Park.

Today the Towers are a National Historic Landmark, a California Historic Park and a City of Los Angeles Historic-Cultural Monument. Now supported by a half-million dollar grant, the Los Angeles County Museum of Art conserves and promotes the Watts Towers.

No longer a work of "confusion and inconvenience," Rodia's single-handed labors capture the imaginations of students and visitors all year long. It's also the site of the annual Simon Rodia Watts Towers Jazz Festival and the Watts Towers Day of the Drum Festival. The Towers can be viewed from behind its protective fence at any hour, and tours are offered through the adjacent arts center on sunny days.

The *Watts Towers of Simon Rodia* are located at 1765 East 107th Street.

IN THE MOVIES:

The Towers can be seen in *Colors* (1988), *Ricochet* (1991), *Hit Man* (1972), and on television in *Six Feet Under* (third season, 2004) and animated on *The Simpsons* (season 22, episode 14).

CHAPTER 15.

THE LEFT COAST
REINVENTING THE DEMOCRATIC PARTY
1934

Upton Sinclair was the first celebrity to run for governor of California. His book *The Jungle* was a national sensation, earning him a Pulitzer Prize. It even prompted federal regulations for the meatpacking industry it exposed. (His book *Oil!* was the basis for the Oscar winner *There Will Be Blood*.) Sinclair was a prolific writer, but also an outspoken Socialist who frequently made news. He founded the California chapter of the American Civil Liberties Union, wrote a screenplay for Charlie Chaplin once, ran for Congress twice and landed on the cover of *Time* magazine. Witnessing the desperation of many Californians during the Great Depression, Sinclair devised EPIC, End Poverty In California, his campaign platform for governor in 1934. His brutal defeat at the polls changed American politics forever.

Ever since California became a state, Los Angeles was a center for conservative thinking. Republicans outnumbered Democrats three to one in California; its newspapers vied fiercely for Republican readership. William Randolph Hearst, owner of the largest newspaper chain in America (later depicted in the movie *Citizen Kane*), was so aggressive in his pursuit of

readers that his publications gave birth to yellow journalism (referring to a yellow cartoon character that ran in Hearst magazines). Webster's dictionary defines yellow journalism as "the use of cheaply sensational or unscrupulous methods in newspapers to attract or influence readers." A Democrat in name only, when the Great Depression hit in 1929, Hearst ran salacious headlines and outright lies in his *Los Angeles Examiner* to attract conservative readers. Meanwhile, East Coast Democrats, swept into office with President Franklin D. Roosevelt, were shaping a liberal agenda much like Upton Sinclair in LA.

Hearst's *Examiner* needed those eye-grabbing headlines because his publication was locked in a daily battle with its Republican rival, the *Los Angeles Times*. The fiercely conservative Harry Chandler had recently inherited the *Times*, and his siblings were determined to retain control of their Republican base in Los Angeles. Some even wanted the family's paper to espouse the far right-wing ideals of the John Birch Society. When notorious Socialist Upton Sinclair won the Democratic Primary, California had a new Democrat in name only, a political challenge that the Chandlers eyed with relish, for they knew that yet another major force would join them in the fray.

For the first time in history, a political consulting firm was founded in 1933. Campaigns Inc., headed by Clem Whitaker and his future wife Leone Baxter, specialized in running political campaigns for businesses. During the Depression, big businesses were just as interested in advancing a

political agenda as they were in selling a product or service. To monopolies like Standard Oil and DuPont, who hired advertising agencies to promote legislation that favored big business, the ingenuity of Campaigns Inc. was a dream come true. Pacific Gas and Electric was so impressed that its executives put

Upton Sinclair broadcasts a speech during his campaign for governor of California, 1934

From left: Governor Frank Merriam (center); Leone Baxter and Clem Whitaker, 1933

Campaigns Inc. on retainer.

Like most California Republicans, Whitaker and Baxter were horrified at the prospect of Sinclair taking charge as governor. Working for incumbent Republican Governor Frank Merriam, they formed the California League Against Sinclairism, not to promote Merriam but simply to destroy Sinclair and EPIC.

If the Los Angeles press was guilty of yellow journalism before, Campaigns Inc. would now take journalism to a vibrant shade of ochre. Locking themselves in a room for three days with many of Sinclair's books, Whitaker and Baxter scoured Sinclair's writings for quotes they could attribute to him out of context, a ploy that worked spectacularly well. As the Sinclair campaign rolled out, Campaigns Inc. furnished the *LA Times* with quotes from Sinclair novels, but cited as fact. The *Times* featured those quotes in boxes on the front page daily. Voters in 1934 fell for it, though the statements are so over-the-top that readers today will laugh:

SINCLAIR ON DISABLED WAR VETERANS: "The lecture was delivered before a lot of good-for-nothing soldiers in some hall."

SINCLAIR ON MARRIAGE: "The sanctity of marriage . . . I have had such a belief . . . I have it no longer."

Sinclair lacked the staff and the funds to refute the *LA Times* distraction on a daily basis; he was trying to run a statewide campaign. Then, William

From left: William Randolph Hearst, 1934; Anti-Sinclair cartoon from the *Los Angeles Examiner*

Randolph Hearst raised the stakes. He warned his friend Louis B. Mayer at MGM, who was also the Republican Chairman for California, that union organizers under a Sinclair administration would overtake Hollywood. Another precedent: In 1934, Hollywood and politics discovered each other. For the first time ever, movie studios would produce propaganda, newsreels that exploited a political position just like Hearst's newspapers. Funds were deducted directly from studio employees' paychecks to support Campaigns Inc. and Governor Merriam. Studio heads threatened to move the industry to Florida if Sinclair won the election. Even Aimee Semple McPherson raised her voice to sermonize against the threat of Sinclair's socialism.

Eleven days before the election, *The Hollywood Reporter* editorialized, "This campaign against Upton Sinclair is DYNAMITE. It is the most effective piece of political humdingery that has ever been effected . . . It will undoubtedly give the bigwigs in Washington and politicians all over the country an idea of the real POWER that is in the hands of the picture industry."

Just what was Sinclair saying that put so many titans in a lather?

He pointed out that Republicans occupied every seat in the State Senate and Assembly, and that unemployment stood at 29 percent. There were one and a quarter million people relying on charities (Social Security wasn't invented yet), while large companies paid little or no tax to support them. Denouncing the manipulations of big businesses, Sinclair tried to speak for the little guy. He advocated "Production for use, not production for profit," his way of calling attention to the unfair distribution of wealth in America. His plan to end poverty called for the state to take control of factories and farms that were idled by the Depression, then hire unemployed workers to run those factories and farms as self-sufficient, worker-run co-operatives. President Roosevelt would soon create the W.P.A. (Work Projects Administration) as part of his New Deal, implementing much of this idea on a national scale.

Sinclair also said it was time to tax the rich. EPIC called for the implementation of California's first state income tax, a progressive scale that demanded 30 percent from the wealthiest Californians. (Roosevelt later implemented that one too, proposing a progressive tax on all businesses in 1935.) Of course the wealthiest people balked, but the backlash they provoked is still heard today, as Californians decry the small number of individuals who control the vast supply of U.S. wealth.

To the relief of many, Sinclair went down in defeat on Election Day, but it was no landslide. He won 879,000 votes (spectacular for a Socialist!) versus incumbent Governor Merriam's 1,138,000. With nearly two thousand Democratic clubs supporting Sinclair's candidacy, 24 Democratic candidates won state elections, making California's legislature a two-party system again. Among the new officials was LA lawyer Culbert Olson, who would be elected governor just four years later, the first Democrat to hold that office in 40 years. Sinclair's candidacy reinvented the Democratic Party in California, taking a sharp turn to the left, earning California its moniker, The Left Coast.

EPILOGUE

Whitaker, Baxter and Campaigns Inc. changed the political landscape forever. They flourished as political consultants for Eisenhower, Nixon and many others, giving birth to an industry. Political consultants of all stripes raced into competition. As President Kennedy observed decades later, they made political consultancy the new Arms Race in American politics.

The propaganda mechanism at the movie studios turned out to be good training for the war effort that was to follow. Hitler was in the news every week in 1934; newsreels continued to follow the story directly into World

War II. Just seven years after the invention of talkies, movies had grown up. Observers recognized film's ability to influence our culture, not just reflect it.

President Roosevelt signs Social Security Act on August 14, 1935

The *Los Angeles Examiner* flourished during Hearst's lifetime, but a decade-long labor strike scared off its biggest advertisers. It ceased publication in 1989.

The *Los Angeles Times* changed its voice under fourth generation Otis Chandler, earning respect for its objective reporting. It won four Pulitzer Prizes during Chandler's leadership, and dozens more since then.

Upton Sinclair died in a New Jersey nursing home in 1968, author of 88 novels, plus plays, autobiography and non-fiction writing. Eight of his stories were made into films. He was heartened by the youth culture in the 1960s espousing his views, and enraged that Richard Nixon (who lost the election for governor of California) became president! Sinclair never ran for political office again.

Days after Sinclair's defeat in 1934, he received a letter from fellow-leftist Albert Einstein. It ends, "You have done more than any other person. You can in good conscience hand over to men with tougher hands and nerves." Apparently, it worked, for the number of liberals in state office has increased steadily ever since.

IN THE MOVIES:

Stories by Upton Sinclair: *The Jungle* (1914), *The Adventurer* (1917), *The Money Changers* (1920), *Jimmie Higgins* (1928), *The Wet Parade* (1932), *Damaged Goods* (1937), *The Gnome-Mobile* (1967), *There Will Be Blood* (2007)

Toward Los Angeles, California, Dorothea Lange, 1937: Two migrants walking on a deserted road towards Los Angeles during the Depression

CHAPTER 16.

THE PARTY IN LITTLE TOKYO
DANCING IN THE FACE OF HARDSHIP

1934–Present

Each summer, the whole world is invited to a party in Little Tokyo. Nisei Week is a Japanese American festival held every August, so eventful that it now spans most of the month, attracting revelers from around the world. Since the 1930s, Nisei Week has involved everyone from beauty queens to politicians, the LA Dodgers and even Charlie Chaplin. Born out of heartbreak, its success is a testament to the resilience of the Japanese community in LA.

An early wave of Japanese men arrived in Los Angeles, forcibly, in 1903, when the newly unionized workforce at the Pacific Electric Railway went on strike. Owner Henry Huntington imported thousands of Japanese immigrants from San Francisco to run the railroad in Los Angeles and break the union. Instead, a community was born. In 1900, there were fewer than two hundred Japanese people in Los Angeles. By 1904, there were nearly 3,000, though less than two hundred of them were women and children. Thousands of men, known as *Issei*, the first generation to immigrate to America, brought their dreams to Los Angeles.

They were wise not to rely too heavily on employment from the Anglos. The Chinese, 50 years earlier, tried to work side-by-side with Anglos, only to be called "cheap labor" and then lynched. Instead, the Japanese community created its own economy by remaining insular.

Grand Parade at First and San Pedro Streets, 1951

Shopkeepers in Little Tokyo rarely solicited customers beyond the Japanese community.

Meanwhile, millions of acres of undeveloped farmland, the former cattle ranchos, glistened in the California sunshine. Japanese immigrants couldn't buy farmland, but they knew enough about vegetables to take their chances as tenant farmers instead.

By 1910, Japanese farms held an important position in the Los Angeles economy; by 1920, their acreage had expanded sevenfold. Industrious Japanese farmers gained near monopolies on the lettuce, celery, strawberry and tomato markets. Their industry supported a whole network of Japanese retail shops around First Street at San Pedro Street, today's Little Tokyo. Export businesses flourished too, distributing California produce. The railroad opened the market wide, delivering Japanese farmers' produce across the west.

The Issei became comfortable with their roles in America. They gave birth to *Nisei*, first generation Americans who were second-generation Japanese. In the 1920s, the Japanese population was the largest minority group in California. But in 1924, relations became contentious. When some Issei attempted to buy their farmland, the California government stopped them by enforcing the Alien Land Law, reminding the Issei that they were prevented from owning property.

The news got worse. The Supreme Court upheld the Naturalization Acts that empowered "free, white persons" and later "persons of African descent" to become U.S. citizens, but Issei were "aliens ineligible for citizenship" because of their race. The Immigration Act of 1924 prevented any more Asians from entering the country. Nisei were treated like foreigners too, overlooked for job opportunities even though they were educated, American-born citizens.

From these grim prospects, an adventurous idea was launched during the Great Depression. The Nisei would throw a party, a multi-day mardi gras that would coincide with the traditional Japanese Obon Festival. Little Tokyo would celebrate the accomplishments of their Issei parents, thereby putting the Nisei experience on display. A beauty pageant and a baby contest would show the American-ness of Nisei life, culminating with a final parade and outdoor dance to display their respect for a long and rich culture. Most radically, Little Tokyo merchants would seek to capitalize on the Anglo tourist trade, a dramatic turnaround from decades of business practices.

Rehearsals began. Chiye Nagano, LA's first Japanese dance instructor, choreographed several contingents within the big parade. She simplified the traditional *ondo* dance steps to attract as many Issei and Nisei as possible, and soon had them dancing side by side. She held extra practices, and even advised the seamstresses on costume designs. Floats were built; farmers decorated their tractors. The community united around a cause.

Japanese Americans evacuate from Little Tokyo under the U.S. Army's war emergency order: from left; sign on Japanese-owned shop in Little Tokyo; Japanese Americans sent to camp at Owens Valley gather around baggage car at the old Santa Fe Station. Lee Russell, 1942

Manzanar War Relocation Center, the mess line at noon. Ansel Adams, 1943

The first Nisei Week celebration in 1934 was the success that everyone wanted. When Charlie Chaplin showed up to observe the final night's *ondo*, the outdoor Japanese folk dance, nearly 1,000 kimono-clad young people were excited to see the screen idol during their performance. Chaplin's presence was the validation that the community sought. The template, the precedent was established. Nisei Week became an annual event, celebrating the uniqueness of being Japanese Americans.

In 1941, however, there was little to celebrate. That August, the *Los Angeles Times* urged its readers to attend Nisei Week because Japanese Americans "had no part in and no responsibility for causing war clouds to gather in the Orient." Los Angeles Mayor Fletcher Bowron was the honored speaker who kicked off Nisei Week that year. He echoed the statement, adding, "We know you are loyal." Four months later, when Japanese bombs dropped on Pearl Harbor, Mayor Bowron was one of the first to point a condemning finger. "Right here in our own city," he warned, "are those who may spring into action at an appointed time in accordance with a prearranged plan."

Such anti-Japanese hysteria was everywhere, especially in Los Angeles, home to one of the largest Japanese enclaves outside of Japan. When the federal government declared an immediate military action, all people of Japanese ancestry were rounded up and moved with force. Many were incarcerated in the Manzanar War Relocation Center more than 200 miles away. More than two-thirds of those incarcerated—who committed no crimes, who faced no trials—were American-born citizens. Their elders were prohibited from citizenship by federal law.

Most in the community survived the indignities of living behind barbed wire for years, in desert heat, where they stood in lines for everything from food rations to latrine trips. They faced another harsh reality in 1945 when they returned to Los Angeles: Since Japanese farmers were not allowed to own property, they were renters, now unable to reclaim their farms. It was the moment that Nisei children assumed control, acquiring property in their names for their Issei parents.

Meanwhile, Americans were not quick to forgive the Japanese enemy. The Nisei were still distrusted; they hadn't been seen in Los Angeles for years. Japanese were refused service in public places; they couldn't join trade unions, they were hassled over housing. It was time for the Japanese community to reinvent itself once more. What could they do?

Defiantly, they danced! In 1949, Nisei Week burst back into life in red, white and blue. *Ondo* dancers paraded through the streets of the old Japanese quarter once more. "Look, we've come through," seemed to be the message, both a reassurance to Japanese Americans and a newsflash to the rest of the world. Nisei Week organizers maintained a positive

Japanese girls in kimonos dancing down the street for the Nisei Week celebration, 1951

Nisei Week Queen contestants, 1966

image: Beauty contestants visited Nisei servicemen at the Veteran's Administration hospital; a souvenir booklet commemorated the Nisei war dead. The community returned, stronger and more resolved than ever.

American attitudes toward the Japanese softened. Fletcher Bowron, still LA's mayor, testified before the U.S. Congress that Japanese internees must be compensated for their economic losses. Those who could actually prove their losses were partially compensated, but many claims were denied due to lack of evidence. Instead, Issei and Nisei focused on the future, more determined than ever to restore the old community of Little Tokyo as the spiritual center of Japanese Los Angeles. Congress rescinded the laws that barred Issei from citizenship and prevented Japanese immigration in 1952. Finally, there was no legal basis to anti-Japanese discrimination.

In 1970, the city government partnered with community leaders to form the Little Tokyo Redevelopment Project. It funded housing, retail and office development, including the Japanese American Cultural and Community Center in 1980 and the Japanese American National Museum in 1992. These new nonprofits have grown in vitality, helping to make Nisei Week an exciting cultural festival for the entire city. And finally, in 1995, Little Tokyo was declared a National Historic Landmark District.

And that's why the Japanese dance in the LA streets every August.

IN THE MOVIES:

The Bodyguard (1992), *Showdown in Little Tokyo* (1991), *Brother* (2000), *The Crimson Kimono* (1959) and many television episodes.

You're invited to join the fun, too, starting with Japanese American Night at Dodger Stadium, plus beauties, babies, gyoza-eating contests, and the closing night's *ondo* dancers. Visit: www.niseiweek.org for details.

CHAPTER 17.

ON THE AVENUE
JAZZ NIGHTS AT THE DUNBAR
1928—1948

In the early twentieth century, opportunities seemed to be boundless in LA, and those opportunities extended to the African American community, too. On the faraway island of Jamaica, John Somerville dreamed of pursuing California's opportunities. He relocated to LA in 1902, then made history in 1907 as the first African American student to graduate from the University of Southern California. After earning his degree in dentistry, Dr. Somerville addressed the needs of the black community with another enduring accomplishment: He built one of the most celebrated hotels in America. It's a National Landmark today, and Dr. Somerville is remembered as one of LA's African American pioneers.

Unlike Dr. Somerville, African Americans came late to the party in LA. Fifty years after the Emancipation Proclamation freed the slaves, most blacks still remained in the South. Hundreds of thousands found their way to Los Angeles after World War II, but the real pioneers of black Los Angeles were the daring souls who ventured to California before 1920. Nearly half of the state's African Americans lived in Los Angeles then, though they were fewer than 20,000 people, just two percent of LA's total population. They

From left: Dr. John Somerville; Jazz musicians "Common Sense" Ross, Albertine Pickens, Jelly Roll Morton, Ada "Bricktop" Smith, Eddie Rucker and Mabel Watts outside the Cadillac Café, c. 1917

established a genuine black middle class; 36 percent were homeowners in 1910, the highest in the nation.

LA outlawed segregation, but "restricted" neighborhoods for whites only proliferated anyway, effectively segregating the small black community (with people from Japan, China and Mexico, too). In downtown LA, the black neighborhood began where the Japanese neighborhood ended, on Central Avenue. Poor folks lived down in Mud Flats, the two-square-mile neighborhood called Watts today, but the upscale scene for black Los Angeles was on Central Avenue.

That's where Jelly Roll Morton, the father of stride piano, came to town in 1917, introducing jazz to Los Angeles at the Cadillac Café on the corner of 5th Street. Kid Ory and his Original Creole Jazz Band soon followed, as did their friends the Spikes Brothers from New Orleans, who opened a music store that flourished for decades on the corner of 12th Street, a major intersection for connecting streetcars. 12th and Central became the unofficial town square for the black community: a hub to buy music, meet a date, hear some gossip and change trains amid the shouts from newsboys and hotdog vendors who greeted every streetcar.

There were job opportunities for African American men in LA. They laid the tracks for the constantly expanding Pacific Electric streetcars, served as Pullman porters and cooks on the Southern Pacific Railroad, or became entrepreneurs who added new shops along Central Avenue. But the black community soon faced the same indignities in California that they faced in the South. Whites streaming into Los Angeles from Jim Crow states convinced the local government to enforce new restrictions. Even the Pacific Ocean was off limits. Blacks couldn't frolic along the Santa Monica Pier; they were permitted into the "Ink Well," the half-mile stretch of beach between Pico and Ocean Park Boulevards, and even that was challenged in court as the beach population swelled. Closer to Central Avenue, LA's public swimming pools were restricted, too. Under pressure by voters in 1925, LA's Playground Commission segregated the pools that were originally open to the public. Instead, one day a week was reserved for "International Day," when non-whites were permitted to use the public pools—then the pools were drained.

Meanwhile, there was a Harlem Renaissance going on back East, uniting black authors, artists and musicians with a new political voice. Harvard-educated W.E.B. DuBois founded the National Association for the Advancement of Colored People (NAACP) as a watchdog group on a national scale. Observing the West Coast scene, DuBois chose Los Angeles as the site for the 1928 NAACP Convention. Delegates from East Coast cities would cross America to see the West for the very first time; it would be the largest gathering of African Americans LA had ever seen.

Dr. Somerville was ecstatic! As a founder and board member of the local NAACP branch, he hoped to focus a national spotlight on LA's restrictions, but the local board members soon confronted a more immediate problem those restrictions caused. In a sprawling city dotted with restricted neighborhoods and restricted hotels, where would all those black delegates sleep? Central Avenue needed a grand hotel.

To Dr. Somerville, the challenge was an opportunity. Through the NAACP branch, he kept company with LA's small, black elite: the lawyers, doctors and professionals regarded as community leaders. Though not exactly wealthy, they were accepted as reliable references. Somerville secured a bank loan for $100,000 and assumed the responsibility for constructing a hotel in advance of the delegates' arrival.

He knew that the hotel had to be on Central Avenue, but he also knew that

Dunbar (Somerville) Hotel on Central Avenue, c. 1930

he couldn't afford to put it on 12th Street. The Hotel Somerville was built far afield on a large empty lot at 42nd Street. Employing black contractors, laborers and craftsmen, the Somerville Hotel was completed just two weeks before the start of the NAACP Convention. When the conventioneers arrived, some were even moved to tears.

Nobody had ever constructed an upscale residence for African Americans before. As Somerville put it, his clientele "did not have to wait for white people to wear off the newness." The hotel was a knockout; not just new, but elegant. The lobby soared two stories high with a massive Art Deco chandelier. Decorated in the Mediterranean style that was popular throughout LA, the 115-room hotel featured a Spanish-style courtyard, decorative arches and tilework, plus wrought-iron staircases that ascended to a mezzanine level. DuBois was stunned, calling the hotel "a jewel done with loving hands." He added, "We were prepared for, well, something that didn't leak. Instead . . . we entered a beautiful inn with soul." The Somerville Hotel was front-page news in African American publications across the country.

The convention was newsworthy, too. Thirty-five hundred delegates from 44 states packed Philharmonic Auditorium to hear (white, Republican) Mayor George Cryer swallow hard as he welcomed this rare delegation to Los Angeles for seven days of consciousness-raising discussions. DuBois was thrilled by its success. "The boulevards of Los Angeles grip me with nameless ecstasy," he wrote in the NAACP newsletter. It was an invitation for African Americans to head west.

Suddenly, 12th and Central was off the radar. Somerville's hotel became the new hub for black Los Angeles. More than a personal triumph, Somerville's efforts reshaped the boundaries of the black community. Within six months, every empty lot between 12th Street and 42nd Street was occupied along Central Avenue. The Club Alabam opened next door to the hotel, bringing jazz (with chorus girls) to the new neighborhood. Even wealthy whites from the west side, seeking the authentic new music that could only be found in the black part of town, found their way to the new clubs that opened near 42nd and Central, which was soon simply known as "The Avenue."

Heartbreak followed. The Great Depression destroyed the black middle class. Somerville went bankrupt. His hotel, once a symbol of black achievement in America, was foreclosed and sold to white investors. They renamed it the Dunbar Hotel, in honor of poet Paul Lawrence Dunbar, the name that remains on the building today.

The white owners were shrewd: They secured a cabaret license for the

From left: the Dunbar lobby in earlier times; the mezzanine of the hotel, where many of the top jazz performers of the day could be seen, 1928

The Club Alabam, 1945

dining room. Though the cabaret experiment lasted for just a few months, it cleared the way for something far more magical. As racial tensions escalated in the 1930s and '40s, glamorous Hollywood movie stars wanted to dance to jazz bands in restricted clubs like the Cocoanut Grove at the Ambassador Hotel. Black bandleaders like Duke Ellington and Cab Calloway earned a fortune for those nightclubs, but when closing time came, black musicians were ushered out the back door. There was no room for them in those fancy hotels. Instead, they stayed at the Dunbar. Every black celebrity from Billie Holliday to Lena Horne, every jazz luminary from Louis Armstrong to Count Basie, checked into the Dunbar when they performed in Los Angeles. Then, in the wee hours after places like the Cocoanut Grove had closed, those musicians slipped into the empty dining room at the Dunbar for spontaneous jazz sessions. Some of the most inspired jazz emerged from their impromptu gatherings at the Dunbar. There were no tickets and there were no patrons, just friends who jammed, establishing an unforgettable legacy at the Dunbar. Thanks to that cabaret license, even the mezzanine was used as a rehearsal space for Duke Ellington, as witnessed by the celebrities who stayed in the classy hotel on The Avenue.

Then it all faded away. When the Supreme Court invalidated all the racially restrictive covenants in 1948, African Americans no longer needed to cluster along The Avenue; there were so many unrestricted parts of Los Angeles to explore (now including the Pacific Ocean!). The Dunbar was sold to a black gambler, but as barriers slowly toppled, his Dunbar fell into disrepair; African American visitors could check into hotels all over town. Dr. Somerville recovered his finances and continued his political activism, but never pursued the hotel again. He became California's first African American delegate to the Democratic Convention; he died in 1973 at age 91. During those years, LA County's black population exploded, from 63,000 in 1940 to 763,000 in 1970.

The Dunbar was added to the National Register of Historic Places in 1976. The city's Housing Authority combined the Dunbar with adjacent new construction to create 82 apartments in 2013, a $30 million restoration. No longer open to the public, the once-grand hotel is now a private residence for fixed-income senior citizens. Recalling the hotel's heyday, they revel in the legacy of Dr. Somerville's opportunity.

Making a night of it at the Club Alabam, c. 1945

IN THE MOVIES:

Central Avenue can be seen in *The Magnificent Ambersons* (1942), *A Place in the Sun* (1951), *Hit Man* (1972). The Dunbar Hotel is shown in *Dolemite* (1975) and *The Human Tornado* (1976). Central Avenue and the Dunbar Hotel of the 1940s are recreated in *Devil in a Blue Dress* (1995), actually filmed inside the Ambassador Hotel and along South Main Street in LA.

CHAPTER 18.

LOVE ON THE LOT
ROMANCES AT THE STUDIOS DURING HOLLYWOOD'S GOLDEN AGE

1930s—1950s

Fame has its consequences. As movies filled the studios' coffers, movie stars' careers rose. Their successes also spawned a publishing industry: *The Hollywood Reporter* and a slew of fan magazines highlighted movie stars' activities (even though the studios' publicity departments planted some of those stories and photos in an attempt to control or fictionalize the lives of stars under contract). Privacy was impossible for even remotely successful actors. The press and the fans were everywhere.

In that claustrophobic environment, where could an eligible young movie star meet a potential mate? The studio lot. Countless actors and actresses found romance within the studio walls while working together on a new movie. They might eventually step out in public, at a place like the Cocoanut Grove or Chasen's in Beverly Hills, where rival gossip columnists like Hedda Hopper and Louella Parsons pounced, quick to publish the news about Hollywood's newest couple, regardless of the truth. Here are some memorable Hollywood romances that started on a studio lot.

Humphrey Bogart's career was on the upswing when he met his third wife,

Mayo Methot while filming *Marked Woman* in 1937. She was already an established star on both coasts, having appeared in Broadway musicals with George M. Cohan, introducing the classic ballad "More Than You Know" on Broadway, and now under contract at Warner Brothers. And, like Bogart, she loved to smoke and drink. The couple wed one year after the film's release.

The press dubbed them "the battling Bogarts." Mayo Methot was charming when sober, but violent when drunk. She stabbed Bogart with a knife, pointed a pistol at him during a party, and even set the house on fire, always in a jealous rage. Bogart humored the press by saying "I wouldn't give you two cents for a dame without a temper," but this relationship couldn't last. To keep the peace at home, when Bogart filmed *Casablanca* in 1942, he barely spoke to his co-star Ingrid Bergman. "I kissed him, but I never knew him," is how Bergman dismissed their classic romance on screen.

The Bogarts separated and reconciled several times during their seven-year marriage. During their separation in 1943, Bogart filmed *To Have and Have Not* on the Warner Brothers lot, where he fell head-over-heels in love with his dazzling, 19-year-old co-star Lauren Bacall. Methot filed for divorce in Las Vegas on May 10, 1945—Bogart wed Bacall on May 21.

To Have and Have Not, Humphrey Bogart and Lauren Bacall, 1943

Bogart and Bacall's romance became a Hollywood legend; and their onscreen chemistry was palpable. They made four films together, and Bacall gave birth to a son and a daughter. Cigarettes brought the romance to a crashing end. After twelve years of marriage, Bogart died of esophageal cancer at age 57. Bacall was 33. Her later work earned her a Golden Globe, a Tony Award and an honorary Oscar. Mayo

Methot's career never recovered. She died of acute alcoholism at age 47, six years after divorcing Bogart. A forgotten movie star, her dead body wasn't discovered for days.

Clark Gable first married his acting coach 15 years his senior. When that didn't work out, he married a Texas socialite who was even older. When he made the film *No Man of Her Own* in 1932, he met beautiful Carole Lombard. He was so confused, he didn't speak to her for four years. She thought he was a "stuffed shirt." He was put off by her boisterous humor and unladylike talk. But when he saw her again in a chic white gown at a formal affair in 1936, Gable was smitten. In white tie and tails, he invited her to dance by reciting a line from their movie: "I go for you, Ma," to which Lombard replied on cue: "I go for you too, Pa," the first spark of their romance together.

Separately, they were already regarded as Hollywood royalty. He had an Oscar for Best Actor in *It Happened One Night*. Lombard would soon earn a Best Actress nomination for her role in the screwball comedy *My Man Godfrey*. Her annual salary of $150,000 (during the Great Depression) made Lombard one of the highest-paid women in the world. In private, when these actors stopped acting, their vulnerabilities were exposed. Gable was shy. Lombard talked tough to avoid the politics of the casting couch. Each had a tenth-grade education, then quit school to take a chance on show biz. Together, Gable and Lombard were a perfect fit; each one's strength complemented the other partner's soft spot.

Aware of Gable's love for fancy cars, Lombard bought a jalopy for $15. For Valentine's Day, she had it painted with big red hearts, then it was delivered to Gable at MGM where he was filming *San Francisco*. He laughed and invited her to dance at the Trocadero that night. With her stunning figure wrapped in a beaded gown, her jaw dropped when Gable came to pick her up, not in his shiny Duesenberg, but in the painted jalopy! Chugging their way down the Sunset Strip 15 miles-per-hour, the jalopy introduced Hollywood's newest couple.

Their affair lasted 39 months while Gable's second wife wrangled over money and property. Gable eventually paid nearly a half-million dollars to free himself; a chunk of that money was advanced from MGM, locking Gable into a new contract. When the divorce was issued in March 1939 while

Gable filmed *Gone With the Wind*, the lovers eloped. With press agent Otto Winkler acting as driver, witness and best man, Gable and Lombard were married in Kingman, Arizona, 400 miles from the Hollywood spotlights.

When the U.S. entered World War II, many movie stars joined the Hollywood Victory Committee to promote the war effort through the sale of U.S. Defense Bonds. Gable was elected committee chairman. Lombard recommended that Gable enlist in the army, but MGM wouldn't risk one of its most lucrative stars. Instead, Gable suggested that Lombard use her celebrity in her native Indiana to launch that state's campaign, a life-changing decision he would regret forever. Traveling by train with her mother and Otto Winkler, they rallied support and raised money in Salt Lake City, Chicago, and Indianapolis. Aiming to raise $500,000 on January 15, 1942, Lombard's appearance in Indiana that day set a record, bringing in more than two million dollars. In a last-minute decision, she canceled her final stops in Kansas City and Albuquerque to fly home and surprise Gable. The plane crashed into Table Rock Mountain near Las Vegas. Everyone aboard was killed.

Gable was inconsolable; the entire nation mourned. President Roosevelt awarded a posthumous medal to Lombard: "the first woman to be killed in action in the defense of her country." All movie productions ceased on January 19 in tribute, as Taps was played at every studio. Gable buried Lombard in Forest Lawn Cemetery. When he died of a heart attack in 1960, he was buried beside his beloved wife.

Not all Hollywood romances were the stuff of legends. To some performers, seeking your next date in the studio lot was like being locked in a candy store. Consider this messy scandal that unraveled for decades:

Eddie Fisher was a heartthrob and pop crooner with his own television show at age 25. That's when he met Debbie Reynolds, whose performance in *Singing in the Rain* made her a rising star at MGM. The cute couple married in 1955 and starred together in the movie musical *Bundle of Joy* in 1956, also produced by Fisher. Billed as "their first movie together," it was also their last. The couple gave birth to Carrie Fisher (Reynolds was pregnant while filming *Bundle of Joy*) and Todd Fisher, but a seemingly unrelated tragedy suddenly impacted their lives.

Fisher was a best friend to Oscar-winning producer Mike Todd, who was married to actress Elizabeth Taylor, regarded as the most beautiful woman in the world. The two couples were such good friends that the Fishers even named their son in Mike Todd's honor. Tragically, in 1958, Mike Todd died in a plane crash. Claiming to "console" the bereaved Elizabeth Taylor, Eddie Fisher struck up an affair with her while still married to 26-year-old Reynolds, an embarrassment to her that made national headlines. Within 14 months, Fisher managed to romance Taylor, divorce Reynolds, and then marry Taylor. A year after the wedding, Fisher was on the lot at MGM, filming the drama *Butterfield 8* with his wife, the performance that earned Taylor her first Oscar. It was their first film together, but once again, it was also their last.

This time, Taylor dumped Fisher. Cast as the lead in *Cleopatra*, Taylor played love scenes opposite Richard Burton as Mark Antony. While filming in England and Italy, the two began an affair that made international headlines since both were married to others. Production stopped when Taylor fell ill. Fisher flew overseas to his wife's aid (and every reporter's delight). Though Taylor professed devotion to her husband, the romance with Burton continued, generating more bad publicity for the troubled

Cleopatra, Richard Burton, Elizabeth Taylor, 1963

The Long, Hot Summer, Paul
Newman, Joanne Woodward, 1958

production. Even the Vatican weighed in, denouncing the affair as "erotic vagrancy." While filming the epic sequence in which Cleopatra makes a triumphant entrance into Rome, Taylor genuinely feared for her life, she admitted later. Thousands of Italian extras turned against the couple in moral outrage over their scandalous romance. That didn't stop the couple though. *Cleopatra* opened in July 1963. Within months Taylor divorced Fisher, who was now washed-up as a singer and actor. Nine days after the divorce, she married Burton.

Taylor and Burton were married for ten years and appeared in eleven movies together. They were not without their conflicts, and in 1974, they divorced. Their separation lasted 16 months, during which Burton again wooed Taylor; they remarried in 1975 but separated again, and were redivorced in 1976.

Years later, Debbie Reynolds traveled on the ocean liner *Queen Elizabeth* at the same time as Elizabeth Taylor. As Reynolds explained on the *Oprah Winfrey Show* in 2011, she invited Taylor to dinner, to aright their former friendship. The two reconciled, and as Reynolds remembers: ". . . we had a wonderful evening with a lot of laughs." Reynolds' daughter Carrie Fisher wrote *These Old Broads*, a script for television in which Taylor and Reynolds performed together. It was Taylor's final performance; the show aired just five weeks before her death in 2011.

Perhaps Paul Newman and Joanne Woodward set the best example for love on a studio lot. They were married in Las Vegas in 1958 after filming *The Long, Hot Summer* at 20th Century Fox. They had three daughters, they performed together in 10 feature films, and Woodward starred in five more films that Newman directed or produced. Their relationship lasted 50 years until Newman's death from lung cancer in 2008. When asked about the secret of their long, successful marriage, Newman replied candidly: "You don't fool around with hamburger at the studio when there's steak for you at home."

AFTER ELVIS

After kissing Elvis Presley on the big screen, what does a young actress do? She checks in to a convent!

That's what Dolores Hart did. She was the first girl to be kissed by Elvis in *Loving You,* in 1957. Hart paired with Elvis again in 1958's *King Creole;* then she went to Broadway, where she was nominated for a Tony Award for her performance in the romantic comedy *The Pleasure of His Company* in 1959. Her career won the admiration (and the envy) of many.

But Dolores Hart's heart was not in show biz. During her Broadway run, she visited the Regina Laudis Abbey in Bethlehem, Connecticut. She said that she left with a "sense of peace."

Hart then starred in MGM's cult classic *Where The Boys Are* in 1960. Contract offers poured in, but in 1963, she broke off her wedding engagement and entered the Benedictine Abbey in Connecticut. She has led a cloistered life there ever since.

In 2012, the Reverend Mother Dolores was interviewed for a documentary, *God Is The Bigger Elvis,* about her path from Hollywood to the convent. When the film was nominated for an Academy Award, she was in the spotlight once more.

At a press briefing prior to the Oscars, the 74-year-old Hart was asked, "What was it like to be kissed by Elvis Presley?" The Reverend Mother replied, "I think the limit for a screen kiss back then was something like 15 seconds. That one has lasted 40 years."

Loving You, Dolores Hart and Elvis Presley, 1957

From left: Dodger manager Walter Alston and owner Walter O'Malley, 1953; The Dodgers assemble at Ebbets Field, 1955

go were the New York Giants. In May 1957, National League club owners granted permission for the ballclub to depart from the polo grounds in Queens; they became the San Francisco Giants. Likewise, O'Malley met with eager officials in Los Angeles, but his demands were steep; never again would the Dodgers be beholden to the whims of bureaucrats like Robert Moses. The ballclub must own its stadium and the land beneath it.

"No problem," assured the LA officials. Los Angeles had the ideal site, though it came with a murky history: a large tract of vacant land in a central location called Chavez Ravine.

Before statehood, when Los Angeles was still part of Mexico, 36-year-old Julian Chavez petitioned the *ayuntamiento* (similar to a City Council) for permission to take possession of the unoccupied tract. He was granted title to some hopelessly steep acres that the earliest settlers avoided. A few years later, when California became a state, Chavez was elected to public office, where he remained for decades; he did next to nothing with his undeveloped land. For the next century, impoverished Mexicans built ramshackle houses and fostered a closely-knit, self-sustaining farm community. Goats, sheep, pigs and even peacocks roamed the wild Chavez hills and unpaved roads. Horse-drawn plows tilled the hillsides that were planted with corn and sugar cane. The unpaved commune resembled a rural Mexican village, though it was barely three miles from urban downtown Los Angeles.

In 1949, President Truman introduced the Fair Deal. As a result, ramshackle housing was to be demolished and replaced with modern public housing for thousands of low-income families. To Los Angeles officials, Chavez Ravine was an eyesore: more than three hundred barely occupied acres that were ripe for demolition, where the government could build 10,000 new public housing units in a central location. With the best intentions, the city planned to clear the site through eminent domain, pave new roads and apply for federal funds to construct public housing. Current residents of the Ravine were granted the first option to return when construction was completed.

The Ravine residents were given a few thousand dollars each for their properties and their moving expenses in 1951. Architect Richard Neutra designed 24 towers and many more low-rise buildings that would provide thousands of subsidized apartments on the site. He incorporated Chavez Ravine's rugged terrain into the design for garden apartments on terraced slopes, separated by landscaped promenades for privacy.

A bizarre, seemingly unrelated conflict permanently halted public housing construction in Chavez Ravine. The U.S. Congress was on a witch-hunt. In Washington, D.C., Republican Senator Joe McCarthy shrieked that Communists were lurking everywhere, especially in Los Angeles, where he accused filmmakers of manipulating the minds of unsuspecting viewers in a plot to overthrow democracy. Some filmmakers were defiant; others were so scared that they turned against their friends. Los Angeles was at war with itself as Angelenos dodged the accusations from right-wing fanatics to save their careers. Sharpening their focus, a public interest group called Citizens Against Socialist Housing (CASH) exacerbated the Cold War fears. They condemned the housing plan at Chavez Ravine as part of a socialist plot. The city fathers caved. Although construction plans were already approved, the housing authority returned the site to the city, with the

Hillside view of Chavez Ravine, 1951

Chavez Ravine eviction, 1959

caveat that the land must be used for public purposes only. Chavez Ravine sat fallow for years. It was offered to Walt Disney as the site for the original Disneyland, but he turned it down.

Some of the displaced residents returned to their old homes, labeling themselves *los desterrados* ("the uprooted"). More accurately, since they accepted payments for their properties, they were squatters on city-owned land, paying no taxes.

Now it was 1957; with the National League's blessing, the City of Los Angeles moved aggressively to attract a major league baseball franchise. O'Malley and his Brooklyn Dodgers were offered all 315 acres of Chavez Ravine. The Dodgers would own the land and the stadium just as O'Malley stipulated.

An angry political brawl ensued. The deal with O'Malley violated the city's agreement to use Chavez Ravine for public purposes. In June 1958, Angelenos went to the ballot box and approved a referendum that transferred the public land to the Dodgers' private ownership. To *los desterrados*, the vote was one insulting slap. They sold their way of life to benefit the public, then saw their land sit idle for nearly a decade. They were offered first access to housing that now would not be built. Now the broken promise was sanctioned by voters who chose to welcome a baseball team instead. The California Supreme Court slapped *los desterrados* again by upholding the agreement.

Back in New York, Robert Moses and Mayor Wagner looked like fools. They had called O'Malley's bluff and lost (again) to the Left Coast. New York was the only city in America that went from three major league teams to one (the New York Yankees). Robert Moses groveled, offering O'Malley a piece of the World's Fair Ground in Queens, but since the Dodgers wouldn't own the fairgrounds or the stadium, his proposal was dead on arrival. New York politicians drove away one of their city's most lucrative and iconic assets. "Dem Bums!" the Brooklyn fans wailed as the Dodgers boarded a plane and headed for the palm trees.

The City of Los Angeles still needed to evict the final holdouts in Chavez Ravine. When bulldozers and deputies arrived to enforce the eviction orders, television cameras were there to capture the ugly confrontation. Men in uniform dragged the remaining 20 families from the properties. Women kicked and scratched as they were forcibly removed. Public sympathy was aroused but it promptly ebbed when the newspaper reported that one televised family actually owned 11 other residences in LA. Hypocrisy brought an end to the battle of Chavez Ravine.

The earth was graded, and construction began on the hillcrest for one of America's most beautiful stadiums. Slopes were terraced, canyons filled and new access roads were carved through adjacent neighborhoods. The Dodgers set up temporary headquarters at the Coliseum that was built for the 1934 Summer Olympics. Then something magical happened.

The Los Angeles Dodgers won the 1959 World Series. The city with no baseball franchise suddenly discovered that it had the nation's biggest winners. As City Councilwoman Roz Wyman recalls, "It was the first time in Los Angeles that this town pulled together for something. The Dodgers brought the city together."

Groundbreaking for Dodger Stadium on Sept. 16, 1959 as 3,000 fans watched

Angelenos suddenly loved their Dodgers, along with the legitimacy of hosting a major league ballclub. When the stadium opened in 1962, they had even more to celebrate. Dodgers Stadium (one of the oldest in America) is perfect. Built at the top of the tallest hill, it provides shimmering views of downtown LA, plus palm trees bending in the Pacific breeze, in a climate where ballgames almost never get rained out.

The Dodgers are welcomed with a parade, 1958

On May 1, 2012, the Dodgers were sold to the Guggenheim Partners, a group of investors including movie producer Peter Guber (*Rain Man, Batman, The Color Purple*) and fronted by former LA Lakers star Magic Johnson. The price tag for the Los Angeles Dodgers: $2.15 billion in cash (including the stadium). It was by far the largest purchase price in history for a professional sports team. The Los Angeles Dodgers are great at setting records.

Dodgers Stadium, at 1000 Elysian Park Avenue, is fewer than three miles from Union Station. On game days, take the subway to Union Station, or park there, then hop onto one of the frequent shuttle buses that run before, during and after the game.

IN THE MOVIES:
Dodger Stadium can be seen in *Star Trek* (2009), *Transformers* (2007), *Superman Returns* (2006), *The Fast and the Furious* (2001), *The Naked Gun* (1988) and many more.

Aerial view of downtown LA and Dodgers Stadium, built in 1962 on the former Chavez Ravine

CHAPTER 20.

SURF CITY

FREETH, KAHANAMOKU, BLAKE, GIDGET, DORA AND THE BEACH BOYS

1907—1964

A tan, athletic surfer catches a wave as it crests toward the Pacific coast: Is any image of Los Angeles more iconic than that?

Despite all claims to the contrary, surfing was *not* invented in Los Angeles. However, without the perfect collusion of sun, surf and show business (of course!), surfing might still be just a quaint Hawaiian novelty instead of the multi-*billion* dollar industry it is today. That's LA's contribution.

On an expedition through the South Pacific in 1778, Captain James Cook was apparently the first westerner to witness the phenomenon of humans riding a wooden plank on the crest of a wave. In the South Pacific, surfboard riding was even linked to a place in society. The royals used their prowess on a surfboard to display their cunning in battle; commoners gained fame (or notoriety) by the way they handled the waves. Anthropologists estimate that Polynesians may have surfed for 800 years.

Then the Americans arrived. In 1907, bestselling author Jack London (*The Call of the Wild* is one of his classics) visited Hawaii, where he met George

A sketch of the Polynesians wave riding when Captain Cook arrived on the scene

Freeth, a 23-year-old local who explained the art of surfing. In *Royal Sport: Surfing in Waikiki*, London wrote of Freeth, "I saw him standing upright with his board carelessly poised, a young god bronzed with sunburn. In his heels is the swiftness of the sea." Within weeks, the mainland onslaught began.

First came Henry Huntington. His Pacific Electric Railway was laying trolley tracks in every direction to connect his real estate offerings. As a gimmick to get buyers to distant Huntington Beach, he brought George Freeth to LA, giving him a train schedule and instructions to mount that surfboard every time a streetcar came into view. As Huntington's trolleys clacked past the ocean on their way to Huntington Beach, astonished passengers who had never seen such a feat were sold. Freeth was dubbed "the first man to surf in California."

Again on Waikiki Beach, Jack London wrote of a powerful young swimmer named Duke Kahanamoku, who would soon represent the U.S. at the 1912 Olympics in Stockholm. Muscular and trim, Kahanamoku was a dazzling surfer, too. On his way to the Olympics, he stopped at the beach in Santa Monica for a surfboard demonstration, creating an even greater sensation than Freeth. When he won Olympic gold, Kahanamoku was touted as "the fastest swimmer alive." Then he returned to the Olympics in 1920 and won a silver medal beside Johnny Weissmuller's gold. Hollywood was hooked. They were both offered careers in the movies. Weissmuller became famous as *Tarzan* (in 12 feature films) and Kahanamoku, always cast as the exotic Aztec chief or Hindu prince, appears in over a dozen feature films, from *Lord Jim* to *Mister Roberts*. On the days when he wasn't filming, Kahanamoku took his board and his Hollywood pals to the LA beaches, where he introduced them to the sport of surfing. Suddenly, there was something to do in the Pacific Ocean besides swim or float! Industries were born: Music, fashion and manufacturing surfboards, of course, were opportunities for American entrepreneurs to serve a new niche market.

Surfing put men's swimwear in the spotlight. In 1933, Weissmuller was hired to model BVD underwear at about the same time that the American Association of Park Superintendents relaxed its beachwear restrictions. Men went topless at the beach for the very first time, just like Tarzan. Weissmuller and Kahanamoku were willing participants (everyone was topless in Hawaii); the papers were willing advocates as well, giving birth to LA's iconic surfer boys. By 1940, men bared their chests at every beach and pool in America.

The science of surfing evolved rapidly in LA. Kahanamoku's disciple, Tom Blake, was a devoted surfer, the first to photograph the sport from the water. He also devised a hollow board with a redwood veneer that sent him soaring past the other surfers on old-fashioned planks. By adding a fin for navigation, Blake made daring new feats possible on lighter boards. Thrill-seeking Angelenos bought them up and headed to the ocean, plying their skills along the LA coast, where the sun shines 300 days a year. Communities of surfers invented their own lingo for board maneuvers and the characters who performed them. On uncrowded beaches, LA's first generation of surfers enjoyed these idyllic years of discovery.

From left: George Freeth; Johnny Weissmuller and Duke Kahanamoku at the 1924 Paris Olympics

Duke Kahanamoku tandem surfing, 1920s

Tom Blake organized the Pacific Coast Surf Riding Championships, attracting the best surfers from California in an annual wave-riding competition for trophies and a place in the news. Miki Dora won acclaim for his speed and agility: He perfected the stance of keeping his arms below his waist while balancing on the lightweight board. With no extraneous movements in Dora's turns and cutbacks, he earned the reputation as California's greatest surfer.

It took a teenage girl, however, to set off the biggest surfing revolution. Kathy Kohner was a spunky 16-year-old who loved to hang out with the surfers on Malibu Beach. The guys even devised a slang name for her—Gidget: part girl, part midget. When Kathy gushed to her father, screenwriter Frederick Kohner, about those colorful characters and their escapades on Malibu beach, Dad got an idea. He'd write a girl's coming-of-age story, and he'd call it *Gidget*. He even eavesdropped on his daughter's phone conversations to get the lingo right. Kohner's book was a best seller in 1957, then a screenplay for Columbia Pictures. Heartthrob Cliff Robertson and pop singer James Darren were cast as the surfer dudes; the role of perky, young Gidget would make a star of 15-year-old Sandra Dee.

The problem: In 1959, surfing was still new. Few actors had surfboard experience. Cliff Robertson practiced with the locals and performed his own stunts in the movie, but James Darren? He could barely swim. Columbia Pictures spied an inexpensive solution. Hire Kathy Kohner's beach friends to play themselves in the movie. Miki Dora, California's greatest surfer, was cast as James Darren's stunt double for the surfing sequences. Getting paid to surf on Leo Carillo State Beach in Malibu, the beach bums were in bliss, unaware of the changing tide they were witnessing. What follows next is a tsunami of commerce.

Gidget was a terrific success; it spawned several sequels and countless knockoffs that kept Miki Dora and his friends employed for years. Millions of moviegoers were first exposed to surfing through *Gidget*, a scrubbed-up version of Kathy Kohner's friends. Now, beachgoers everywhere wanted to ride the waves. Each movie endorsed a bohemian beach life while increasing demand for commercial products. Surfboard manufacturers raced into business, aloha shirts seen on Duke Kahanamoku became a fashion staple, and movie soundtracks sold millions of vinyl platters.

The rising popularity of surfing mirrored the rising popularity of rock 'n' roll. Surf music was a new genre, all reverb-heavy instrumentals; it had no lyrics, just music made by surfers for surfers. When groups like the Surfaris went from LA's dance clubs to movie soundstages and finally to network television, surfing suddenly had fans in places nowhere near an ocean. Vocalists came next. Brothers Jan and Dean, and, of course, The Beach Boys grew up on LA beaches. Their appearances on the *Ed Sullivan Show* in 1964 established LA's surfer style as part of American popular culture.

Miki Dora was appalled at the commercialization, unable to see that he was partially responsible for its genesis. With each successive paycheck, Dora and his friends effectively ended the lives they depicted in the movies. Their success crowded the beaches now; they had to compete for waves packed with wannabes swept up in a fad. They resented how their bohemian lives had been co-opted and packaged into frivolous movies that didn't resemble reality. While beachgoers were dancing barefoot in LA, The Beach Boys were performing on television in matching neckties. Miki Dora's achievements were now just statistics among the tournaments, movies, records,

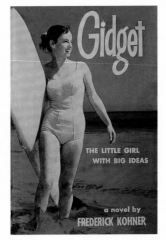

Kathy Kohner on the cover of the *Gidget* first edition, 1957

surfin' safari
THE BEACH BOYS
SURFIN' SAFARI • 409 • SURFIN' • SUMMERTIME BLUES • COUNTY FAIR
HEADS YOU WIN • TAILS I LOSE • CUCKOO CLOCK • MOON DAWG
THE SHIFT • TEN LITTLE INDIANS • CHUG-A-LUG • LITTLE MISS AMERICA

Beach Boys debut album, *Surfin' Safari,* 1961

fashions, lotions, postcards and paraphernalia that were part of surfing lore. Dora snapped at the 1967 Malibu Invitational Surf Classic. During his competition heat, he spun around on his surfboard, pulled down his trunks and mooned the judges. It ended Dora's career in the movies, of course, and his invitation to future tournaments. A vagabond for the rest of his life, Dora died of cancer in 2004.

Other pioneers ebbed more gracefully as massive new waves crashed in. Today there are nearly two million surfers in the U.S., and about 23 million globally. Surfing industry revenue tops six billion dollars a year. Surfboards begat *sidewalk* surfboards, the multi-billion dollar skateboard industry, and the X Games competitions.

The surfing pioneers found a new way to make their voices heard: the ballot box. In 2009, the surfing community elected Zuma Jay, proprietor of a prominent surfboard manufacturing company, to be the mayor of Malibu, California. That classic surfer in today's promotions is not the lovable goof from a beach blanket movie, but a sharp Los Angeles businessman with political influence fueled by global commerce.

Ever since George Freeth surfed on Huntington Beach, the surfing industry found exponential growth in Southern California. It's so completely integrated into Los Angeles culture that some locals refuse to believe that the surfboard was *not* invented in Los Angeles.

IN THE MOVIES:
Leo Carrillo State Beach, where *Gidget* was filmed in Malibu, is the site for
more than one thousand movies and television episodes. Other notable
films include *Inception* (2010), *Point Break* (1991), *The Karate Kid* (1984),
American Gigolo (1980), *10* (1979), *Grease* (1978), *Easy Rider* (1969), *Valley
of the Dolls* (1967), *Muscle Beach Party* (1964), *Mildred Pierce* (1945), *Citizen
Kane* (1941).

ON THE WALK OF FAME:
| Johnny Weissmuller | 6541 Hollywood Boulevard |
| Cliff Robertson | 6801 Hollywood Boulevard |

Gidget, from left: Cliff Robertson, Sandra
Dee, James Darren, 1959

CHAPTER 21.

BOBBY KENNEDY AT THE AMBASSADOR
A NATIONAL TRAGEDY
1968

In 1968, while the Vietnam War raged overseas, it raged in the U.S. too. Thousands of young Americans protested on Los Angeles streets and campuses while young soldiers continued to die. The generational conflict over the war's continuation tore American families apart. 1968 was also a national election year; no presidential candidate was more aggressive in his opposition to the war than Democratic candidate Robert F. Kennedy. He demanded the war's end immediately, insisting that the divisive conflict was not what his slain brother, President John F. Kennedy, intended when the first "advisors" were sent to Vietnam in 1963.

Angelenos not only embraced Bobby Kennedy's message, they embraced Bobby Kennedy, the man. Returning the kindness, Kennedy insisted on little protection as he pressed flesh with well-wishers during his campaign spins through LA. On June 4, it all came to a climax when Kennedy won the California Primary. The populous state earned him the largest bloc of candidates to the upcoming Democratic Convention. Euphoria was in the air, as many Americans anticipated an end to the divisive war. Kennedy would make his acceptance speech late that night at the Ambassador Hotel

RACING RESULTS-ENTRIES

Los Angeles Times

LARGEST CIRCULATION IN THE WEST, MORE THAN 950,000 DAILY; MORE THAN 1,230,000 SUNDAY.

VOL. LXXXVII   FIVE PARTS—PART ONE   WEDNESDAY MORNING, JUNE 5, 1968   104 PAGES   Copyright © 1968 Los Angeles Times   DAILY 10c

KENNEDY SHOT

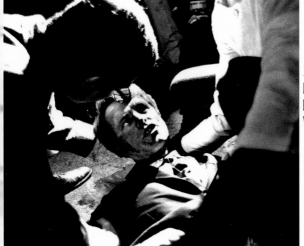

MOMENTS AFTER SHOOTING — Sen. Robert F. Kennedy lies on the floor of the Ambassador moments after he was struck down by bullets.
Times photo by Boris Yaro

Critically Wounded in Head at Victory Fete

BY DARYL E. LEMBKE
Times Staff Writer

Sen. Robert F. Kennedy was shot in the right ear early this morning in a kitchen of the Ambassador only a few moments after he had made a victory statement after capturing the California Democratic presidential primary.

The New York senator's condition was listed as critical at Good Samaritan Hospital, where he was in the intensive care unit.

A suspect in the shooting was arrested minutes after the shots were fired and was taken to the police administration building downtown under heavy guard. The suspect was not identified.

Inspector Robert Rock of the Los Angeles police said that only one suspect was involved. Rock said there was no reason to believe more than one person was involved.

The police also have the gun that fired the shots, Rock said.

Witnesses nearby said Kennedy's head was covered with blood and a

Additional photos of Kennedy on Pages 2 and 3.

woman standing nearby was also splattered with blood.

Also shot was Paul Schrade, UAW official. The extent of his injuries was not known.

The shooting occurred at 12:20 a.m.

Shouts and screams filled the packed hall as the call went out over the public address system for a doctor. Three came to Kennedy's aid as his campaign assistants pleaded for his supporters to be calm and clear the hall.

The senator appeared to be in great pain, but conscious.

As he was lifted into the police ambulance, Kennedy was heard to say:

"Oh, no! No! Don't . . .!"

Mrs. Kennedy whispered to him, apparently trying to comfort and reassure her husband. Then she entered the ambulance, doors were closed behind them and the vehicle sped away.

Kennedy was taken first to Central Receiving Hospital, then was transferred to Good Samaritan, his head wrapped in bandages.

Silence and Shock

Back in the hotel, shocked and silent members of the Kennedy party gathered in small groups around television sets, attempting to clarify their own memories of the event.

Others left in tears.

Kennedy was leaving the Ambassador to attend a party at the Factory in the aftermath of his victory in the Democratic primary.

His path through the kitchen was taken on the spur of the moment.

The assailant fired at the senator at close range and began spraying bullets around the kitchen, witnesses said.

William Barry, a former FBI agent, who is Kennedy's bodyguard, grabbed the gun from the man and wrestled him to the floor.

Roosevelt Grier, the football player, then sat on the assailant while police officers arrived

Please Turn to Page 23, Col. 8

Kennedy Wins Race; Rafferty Apparent Victor Over Kuchel

BY RICHARD BERGHOLZ
Times Political Writer

A late surge of votes from Mexican-American and Negro precincts—particularly in Los Angeles County—made Sen. Robert F. Kennedy the winner in California's Democratic Presidential primary battle Tuesday.

Sen. Eugene McCarthy of Minnesota, Kennedy's major rival in the key primary contest, said he was "reconciled" to a Kennedy triumph. But he said he intended to keep fighting for the party nomination at the Chicago convention Aug. 26.

On the Republican ballot, Sen. Max Rafferty, state superintendent of public instruction, appeared to have ended the political reign of Sen. Thomas H. Kuchel of Anaheim.

The Senate GOP whip and a veteran of 15 years on Capitol Hill ran up leads in Northern and Central California.

Rafferty Vote Projection

But the late surge of votes from Southern California wiped out the Kuchel margin and, on the basis of vote projections, appeared to have swept the conservative Rafferty to an impressive victory.

NBC analysts said their projection of the vote showed Rafferty would get 52% of the Republican vote, and Kuchel would get 45% with the balance going to lesser-known candidates.

The Democratic race for the U.S. Senate nomination was never in doubt.

Former State Controller Alan Cranston easily outdistanced four lesser-known opponents from the very start of the vote-count. For Cranston, it was a political comeback after his defeat two years ago by the current state controller, Republican Houston I. Flournoy.

Tried for Senate in 1964

Cranston had tried for the Democratic nomination for U.S. senator in 1964 but was defeated by Pierre Salinger, who then lost to Republican George Murphy in the finals.

Returns were badly delayed in Los Angeles County, where the old-style paper ballot voting system was changed this year to the IBM-Votomatic punchcard system.

Delays in transporting the punchcard ballots from the precincts to the 93 collection centers and then to the computer counters were blamed for the breakdown in tabulations.

And in Fresno County, a programming error in comp l ters was blamed for a breakdown that made their returns lag far behind the rest of the state.

Even before the breakdowns in

'FIRED AT POINT-BLANK RANGE'

Witness Describes Shooting, Says, 'He Didn't Have Chance'

BY DICK MAIN
Times Staff Writer

"The gunman started firing at point-blank range and Sen. Kennedy didn't have a chance."

Times photographer-reporter Boris Yaro, who was standing only three feet away from the shooting in the kitchen corridor at the Ambassador, fought back tears as he gave this graphic description of the shooting:

"I was getting ready to shoot a picture and I thought the shots were firecrackers going off.

"Kennedy backed up against the kitchen freezers as the gunman fired at him at point-blank range.

"He cringed and threw his hands up over his face.

"I think five shots were fired.

Moved Close to Kennedy

"The gunman was a short, dark-complexioned man. He moved closer toward the senator, holding a short-barrel revolver.

"Three or four people grabbed him but by then it was too late.

"I turned around and saw Sen. Kennedy lying on the floor. Blood seemed to be pouring out of a wound in his head or ear.

"It seemed as though he was trying to say something but you couldn't hear him."

"The gunman who pinned against the freezer and the gun was knocked from his hand.

"People were shouting, 'He's been

a minute after Sen. Kennedy stepped off the stage at the Embassy Room. He walked behind the stage through a foyer and into a hotel kitchen corridor.

"He stopped to shake the hand of a bus boy or a waiter who was wearing a white coat.

"Then he moved to shake someone else's hand when the shots rang out."

Karl Uecker, assistant maitre d' at the hotel, helped disarm the gunman. He also witnessed the shooting.

"I heard six shots," he said. "They sounded like Chinese firecrackers."

Please Turn to Page 23, Col. 6

FEATURE INDEX

BOOK REVIEW, Page 9, Part 4.
BRIDGE, Page 11, Part 4.
CLASSIFIED, Pages 1-20, Part 5.
COMICS, Page 7, Part 2.
CROSSWORD, Page 7, Part 2.
EDITORIALS, COLUMNS, Pages 4, 5. Part 2.
ENTERTAINMENT, SOCIETY, Pages 1-21, Part 4.
FINANCIAL, Pages 9-15, Part 3.
METROPOLITAN NEWS, Part 2.
MOTION PICTURES, Pages 15-19, Part 4.
SPORTS, Pages 1-8, Part 3.
TV-RADIO, Pages 20, 21, Part 4.

THE WEATHER

Light smog today. Heavy night and morning low cloudiness with partial afternoon clearing today and Thursday. High today and Thursday near 73. Low

L.A. COUNTY RETURNS

PRESIDENTIAL DELEGATION

Democratic

1,805 out of 6,924 Precincts		
Kennedy	147,110	30%
McCarthy	115,974	39
Lynch	31,332	11

Republican

1,805 out of 6,924 Precincts		
Reagan	123,301	100%

STATEWIDE RETURNS

PRESIDENTIAL DELEGATION

Democratic

7,186 out of 21,201 Precincts		
Kennedy	444,120	45%
McCarthy	400,323	42
Lynch	117,928	12

Republican

6,597 out of 21,301 Precincts		
Reagan	292,593	100%

U.S. SENATE

Democratic

7,226 out of 21,301 Precincts		
Cranston	474,222	59%
Beilenson	173,545	22
Bennett	60,259	9
Buchanan	50,518	7
Crail	23,818	3

Republican

7,267 out of 21,301 Precincts		
Kuchel	204,703	52%
Rafferty		

U.S. SENATE

Democratic

1,805 out of 6,924 Precincts		
Cranston	145,685	54%
Beilenson	77,739	29
Buchanan	19,681	7
Bennett	16,337	6
Crail	8,338	3

Republican

1,805 out of 6,924 Precincts		
Rafferty	109,740	59%
Kuchel	73,888	39
Ware	2,225	1
Jones	1,545	1
Cammack	1,473	1

CONGRESS

13th DISTRICT

Democratic

6 out of 33 Precincts		
Horwitz	264	41%
Schenbaum	277	40
Cole	134	19

13th DISTRICT

Republican

6 out of 33 Precincts		
Teague (inc.)	720	100%

17th DISTRICT

Democratic

22 out of 394 Precincts		
Anderson	1,430	32%
Tucker	1,167	25
Gibson	860	18
Hayward	425	9
Frantz	377	8
Griffin	187	4
Pipersky	70	2
Van Petten	67	1

17th DISTRICT

Republican

22 out of 394 Precincts		
Howard	443	34%
Blatchford	419	32
Sciarrotta	255	20

The Ambassador Hotel

in Los Angeles, the city's grandest and most storied gathering place.

Since the 1920s, the Ambassador was also home to the Cocoanut Grove, the glittering nightclub where Hollywood royalty cavorted nightly. Decades later, here was Kennedy, surrounded by an equally celebrated entourage of boosters, including singer Andy Williams, football star Rosey Grier, Olympic champ Rafer Johnson, movie producer Budd Schulberg, astronaut John Glenn and many others. They assembled at the Ambassador to witness Kennedy's acceptance speech.

Hundreds of flashbulbs popped as Kennedy entered the Embassy Ballroom; a sea of arms reached for congratulatory handshakes. His speech reiterated the commitments he articulated during his campaign, including grateful thanks to voters and the campaign volunteers who made this big win possible. Kennedy's momentum going into the presidential primary now seemed unbeatable.

Balloons, confetti and near-deafening cheers filled the air. In the confusion on the crowded platform, Bobby Kennedy was separated from his aides. The Ambassador's assistant maître d' hotel took his hand and led him behind the gold drapes, off the platform and into the kitchen pantry corridor. Mrs. Kennedy and the aides struggled through the crowd to reach him.

Kennedy stopped by the large ice-making machine to shake hands with members of the kitchen staff. Boxed in by the arms of animated supporters who continued to cheer "We want Bobby!" his eyes searched the crowd for Mrs. Kennedy.

Then, witnesses report, they heard a single soft pop, followed by a rapid volley of pops. As hotel employee Jesus Perez later testified before the grand jury, "I was shaking hands with him, and then he let go and fell to the floor."

The unthinkable: An assassin's bullets felled Robert Kennedy less than five years after his brother, President John F. Kennedy, was assassinated by gunfire in Dallas.

This night on Wilshire Boulevard changed the course of American history. Kennedy's killer, Sirhan Bishara Sirhan, was the first terrorist to bring the Middle East conflict onto U.S. soil. This date, June 5, 1968, marked the first anniversary of the Six-Day War, when Israel won a decisive victory, capturing the Gaza Strip from Egypt, the West Bank from Jordan and the Golan Heights from Syria. A Jordanian citizen, Sirhan stated at his arrest, "I did it for my country."

Robert Kennedy, the Senator from New York, was a strong supporter of Israel. On the campaign trail, he pledged that, as president, he would send 50 bomber jets as U.S. aid to Israel, a pledge that Sirhan was determined to prevent. As Sirhan would later state, he stalked Kennedy because of "his deliberate attempt to send those 50 bombers to Israel to obviously do harm to the Palestinians."

Kennedy's hands flew up toward his face as he collapsed by the ice machine. Rosey Grier and Rafer Johnson pinned down Sirhan, whose bullets struck five additional people in the crowd (none mortally). At Good Samaritan Hospital in Los Angeles, Robert Kennedy's brain activity ceased on June

From left: Robert Kennedy, Mrs. John F. Kennedy and her children depart the Capitol building, 1963; Sirhan Sirhan is detained after the assassination of Robert Kennedy

Robert F. Kennedy, speaking at the Ambassador Hotel in Los Angeles in the early morning hours of June 5, 1968

5 at 6:30 p.m., then his body followed at 1:44 a.m. on June 6, 1968, nearly twenty-six hours after the shooting. His body was interred in Arlington National Cemetery beside his brother, President John F. Kennedy, on June 8, 1968. Robert Kennedy was 42 years old.

America was bluntly reminded of its involvement in other global conflicts besides Vietnam. Hubert Humphrey won the Democratic Primary but lost the election to Richard Nixon, paving a path for decades of Republican dominance in the White House. The war in Vietnam raged for another five years.

Los Angeles was left with a heartbreaking eyesore. The once grand Ambassador Hotel went on a steady decline for decades, as hotel guests and Hollywood stars avoided the somber memories lurking there. When the hotel finally closed in 1989, preservationists lobbied to save the historic building. But, when Robert F. Kennedy Jr. finally recommended its demolition, the 24-acre site was cleared to become the home of the new Robert F. Kennedy Community Schools that opened in 2010. The schools are closed to the public.

In true LA fashion, the stretch of Wilshire Boulevard where the Ambassador once stood is now renamed the Robert F. Kennedy Parkway.

IN THE MOVIES:

The Graduate, *Pretty Woman*, *The Wedding Singer*, *Apollo 13*, *Forrest Gump*, and many more have scenes at the Ambassador; Emilio Estevez's film *Bobby* was filmed on the actual site of Kennedy's assassination while the Ambassador was undergoing demolition.

BARRYMORES AT THE COCOANUT GROVE

Since its opening on New Year's Day 1921, the Ambassador Hotel on Wilshire Boulevard was considered LA's most elegant inn. Its sprawling grounds were also home to the Cocoanut Grove, a famous nightclub that sparkled nightly for decades.

In the early years of filmmaking, when stars and producers didn't have the opulent homes they have today, the Cocoanut Grove was the official place for movie stars to entertain in style, to be seen by the press, to find their next love, or cause a scene with an ex on the dance floor. It was twice the site of the Academy Awards ceremonies, where Howard Hughes wooed Katharine Hepburn, and where Mickey Rooney met his first wife, Ava Gardner. These actors under contract had demanding diets and early schedules on Hollywood movie sets. The Cocoanut Grove proprietors understood; their parties started early, too. The management at the Cocoanut Grove accommodated just about anything. One anecdote they confided:

John Barrymore and his beloved pet monkey, Clementine

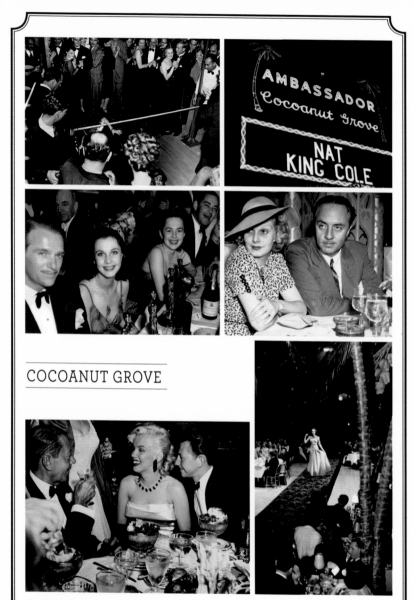

COCOANUT GROVE

Clockwise from top left: Limbo dance contest, 1939; Nat King Cole show, 1961; Jean Harlow and William Powell; fashion show, 1938; Marilyn Monroe, Donald O'Connor and Cole Porter, 1953; Douglas Fairbanks Jr., Vivien Leigh, Olivia de Havilland at the Oscars, 1940

Eccentric movie star John Barrymore frequented the swanky nightclub with his pet monkey. He'd release the live monkey inside the club to climb the famous palm trees that were salvaged from Rudolph Valentino's famous film *The Sheik*. He'd tussle with the stuffed monkeys to the delight of the glitterati below. Determined to upstage his showboating brother, Lionel Barrymore arrived at the Cocoanut Grove one night with *seven* live monkeys. When the monkeys started swinging from tree to tree, the club went a little crazy. Patrons on the dance floor mimicked the monkeys in an effort to attract them. As the band played loud and fast, a dance called The Monkey was born.

Is there a nightclub in any other American city that would admit *live monkeys* into the dining room?

CHAPTER 22.

NEW VIEW

LA'S ARCHITECTURAL INNOVATIONS

1921—2003

LA was a boomtown in the early 20th century. Newspaper magnates, railroad tycoons, oil barons and movie moguls earned fortunes with breathtaking speed. Where should they live with their newfound wealth? They looked to European gentry for the answer—in castles, of course. Faux chateaus, English Tudor and Italian Renaissance-styled mansions sprang up in LA's toniest enclaves simply because LA's *nouveau riche* knew of no other options.

Then modern architects discovered LA's open spaces. They experimented with contemporary styles that exploited LA's unique landscape, attempting dramatic new architectural feats. In the twentieth century, Los Angeles earned its reputation as a center for daring new architecture, setting trends that would be copied around the world. Here are three groundbreaking styles, born in LA, spanning three generations and nearly one hundred years.

EARLY 20TH: FRANK LLOYD WRIGHT AND FRIENDS

In Europe, architects were embracing a new look in the early twentieth

From left: Frank Lloyd Wright, 1926; living room of the Hollyhock House

century, too. Known as the International style, designers returned to basic forms that "dared to be simple." The logic: By stripping an interior of its busy ornamentation, there was a stronger focus on the humans within it. Architects everywhere eschewed the "gingerbread" to rediscover the straight line, the arch, the cube and the circle. Flat-roofed buildings became the rage.

In America, architect Frank Lloyd Wright understood all that, but he was reluctant to remove all ornamentation. Instead, he made his ornamentation functional. By embedding a textured pattern onto precast concrete blocks that were stacked and repeated again and again for dramatic effect, the decorations actually held up the roof. Already renowned for his free-flowing Prairie-style houses in Arizona, Wright's expansive designs were a natural fit for horizontal LA. When he landed his first LA commission in 1917, Wright stated that buildings in Los Angeles should "grow right out of the soil." His Hollyhock House, completed in 1921, incorporates that California soil so ingeniously in its landscaped courtyard and patios that Wright's first California residence is a National Landmark today.

Wright's Hollyhock House, and four more houses in the area, all incorporate his pre-cast concrete block construction system. His designs made vivid use of the topography and climate, with an interior fireplace always prominent as the central congregating point. More than just luxurious homes, Wright's modern lines were a radical break that encouraged occupants to embrace a new, free-flowing lifestyle that was determined by the open floorplans.

196

While Wright's residences were under construction in Los Angeles, he was also engrossed in an elaborate hotel project in Japan. During his frequent, lengthy absences from LA, Wright hired his son Lloyd Wright and Viennese architect Rudolph Schindler to supervise construction of the Hollyhock House. Both Schindler and young Wright later embarked on impressive careers of their own.

Schindler's first work was revolutionary, not just for Los Angeles, but for all of America. In 1921, in today's West Hollywood, Schindler built one of the nation's first, and severest applications of the International style. Like Wright, the Schindler House is constructed of concrete, but unlike Wright, the building is shockingly simple inside, for Schindler redefined the concepts of public and private spaces within a residence. The house has no conventional living room, dining room or bedrooms, but makes clever use of several L-shaped areas instead, credited as the first live/work design in America. Unappreciated at first, the building later became an inspiration and a reference point for a generation of architects worldwide. Today, the Schindler House is a National Landmark.

Schindler encouraged fellow Austrian architect Richard Neutra to explore opportunities in Los Angeles, too. Neutra designed the pergola at the Hollyhock House complex, collaborated with Schindler on a beach house, and then literally stopped traffic when the beach house owners asked him to create a house above Griffith Park, in the Los Feliz neighborhood. The Lovell residence, completed in 1929 at 4616 Dundee Drive, is a National Landmark today, too. Constructed on a platform that is perched on a dramatic cliff overlooking the park, Neutra introduced industrial design into residential living, a hallmark of the International style. In place of Wright's repeating concrete blocks, Neutra made repetitive use of factory windows. Ford Model-A headlights illuminate the main

First floor plan of Schindler House

stairwell. The modern look was so radical when juxtaposed beside traditional homes in the area that it attracted hordes of sightseers, earning an international reputation for Neutra. The Lovell House is recognized as a turning point in architectural history: the first residence in the U.S. to be built with a steel frame, and one of the first to use Gunite, sprayed-on concrete, in its construction. Despite numerous LA earthquakes, the residence remains stable, while other constructions in less precarious settings have toppled.

The Lovell House, with Richard J. Neutra, c. 1931

These creative architects pushed the borders of modernism, winning Los Angeles its reputation as a testing ground for innovative architecture that continues to this day.

IN THE MOVIES:

The Schindler House is seen in *Twilight* (1998). The Lovell House is seen in *L.A. Confidential* (1997) and *Beginners* (2010).

MID 20TH: LLOYD WRIGHT GOES GOOGIE

When modernists broke away from the rigidity of traditional architecture to give LA its exciting new façades, another element emerged: whimsy.

That whimsy was expressed in Googie architecture—flashy, futuristic structures that imagined Space Age design years before America (or any nation) put a man into space. Although the style had its genesis in Los

Angeles, it was soon franchised across the country, usually in coffee shops, bowling alleys, motels and other public structures. The word comes from Googie's, an archetypal coffee shop on the Sunset Strip (that is long gone), designed by architect John Lautner. These ultramodern buildings beckoned with bright lights and cantilevered roofs, attempting to proclaim to us what the feel-good future would look like.

The form actually started with Lloyd Wright in 1928, decades before the style had a name. He designed the Yucca-Vine drive-in store, a precursor to the drive-in restaurants that would soon be ubiquitous in LA. With its upswept corrugated roof and pylon that jutted into the skyline, making it visible from all directions, Wright's building was the first to address an important functional issue. Los Angeles was becoming a car-oriented society. Yucca-Vine was the first urban strip architecture, a spatial concept with the car and driver, not the pedestrian, in mind. The building was a polygon with folding doors that completely exposed the market's wares to the street and the parking spaces nearby.

Architects ran with the idea for the next three decades. Near the oil wells and tar pits on Wilshire Boulevard, Wayne McAllister designed Simon's drive-in, the first circular restaurant with parking spaces in lieu of tables. (There were exactly 12 stools inside.) Cars were organized around the building like spokes in a wheel, making all vehicles equally accessible to the central kitchen and the carhops waiting under a canopy outdoors. Like Wright's building, Simon's had a pylon jutting into the sky too, but this one was illuminated in neon, lighting up the night sky with a giant exclamation point. Simon's drive-in

Yucca-Vine drive-in store

Theme building at Los Angeles airport, 1961

never closed, literally; it had no doors!

McAllister designed several more Simon's, as well as many of its competitors. In the process, he established illumination as an integral Googie element. To make these relatively small buildings visible, the entire structure must be conceived as a sign to attract customers.

America's prosperity after World War II put more cars on the road, and not just in Los Angeles. The expanding car culture turned all roadside businesses into a growth industry, including motels, drive-in movies, shopping centers, supermarkets and, yes, snazzier drive-in restaurants that were not always circular. A roadside vernacular took hold; drivers learned to discern the services they sought from the highways. The bright orange roofs on Howard Johnson's coffee shops pioneered that roadside architecture, bringing Googie style to countless locations across the nation. Angles were emphasized, and chevrons and wings—anything to lure passing motorists into the imaginary future.

By 1961, when the restaurant at the center of the Los Angeles International Airport opened for business (a designated city landmark today), Googie style reached its exuberant crest. A perfect storm was stirring in the 1960s. Americans soon witnessed the hard realities of the real future, and they were not whimsical. The assassination of John F. Kennedy; the Russians' first man in space; the Vietnam War; the British invasion of music, fashion and film; then hippies, yippies and recreational drugs all steered culture in a different direction. Googie was no longer fun; it was tired. It was someone else's fantasy, now left behind. One by one, as the paint wore thin, the buildings were demolished. Today, just a few are protected by landmark status. Instead, recreations of the now-retro style can be found at Universal Studios and Disneyland.

LATE 2OTH: POST-MODERN FRANK GEHRY

Architect Frank Gehry moved to LA in 1949. He witnessed the artistry of Schindler and Neutra as it happened. He studied architecture at the University of Southern California during Googie's most prolific years, then watched the construction of the Music Center, LA's proper theaters for opera, dance and drama. That knowledge, both formal and assimilated, served Gehry well in 1987, when Lillian Disney, Walt Disney's widow, donated $50 million from her personal fortune to add one more theater to the Music Center complex: a dedicated hall for the LA Philharmonic. It was the largest single gift in U.S. history for a cultural building. Local architect Frank Gehry won the competition to build the Walt Disney Concert Hall in honor of Walt Disney.

The instructions were plain: "a single purpose hall, a space where musicians and concertgoers will feel at home and the audience will embrace the performers, with acoustics that are rich, clear and warm." Seeing that proscenium arches separated players from listeners, and that balconies and boxes reinforced a social hierarchy, Gehry and his team restarted from scratch. Starting with its interior, they created a more democratic auditorium where the audience surrounds the orchestra and faces each other on all sides.

Seventy years earlier, Frank Lloyd Wright had it easy: He only had to appease one wealthy client at a time. For Gehry, on the cusp of the twentieth century, things were different. Los Angeles was a sprawling and populous city, regulations were in place, and a committee that was frequently in disagreement oversaw the development of this very public building. Thankfully, the tense collaboration between Gehry and the committee is what produced LA's most iconic structure, an edifice hailed today to be as important as the Eiffel Tower and the Sydney Opera House.

From the start, Mrs. Disney's generosity was woefully inadequate. Had everyone rallied behind the project and raised the necessary funds, the project could have been completed by 1993, but the hall would have fallen far short of the acoustic and aesthetic masterpiece that finally opened in 2003. A chronic lack of funds forced the committee to demand changes. Switching the surface to stainless steel saved a purported $10 million over

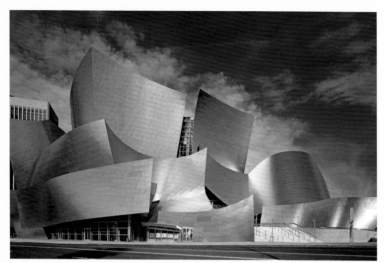

The Walt Disney Concert Hall

the stone in Gehry's earlier design; that new surface freed Gehry to reinvent its shape once again. Employing a new software product called CATIA, Computer-Aided Three-dimensional Interactive Application, Gehry devised the exuberant curves and daring contours that were inconceivable to earlier generations of architects.

He also recognized that no matter how spectacular the exterior was, "if the hall didn't work acoustically, it would be judged a failure." To achieve warmth and intimacy for the audience, the interior walls were covered in wooden panels of Douglas fir, but they are merely decorative. Working with acoustician Yasuhisa Toyota, the sound is actually enhanced by four inches of plaster beneath the wooden panels. As the outer surface took on its dramatic shape, Gehry and LA Philharmonic conductor Esa-Pekka Salonen climbed to the back of the empty auditorium while first violinist Martin Chalifour stood onstage. Upon hearing the first notes from the violinist, Gehry grabbed Salonen's hand . . . and the two of them wept. After a few minutes, Salonen whispered, "This is the best sound I've *ever* heard in a hall." From that magic moment, Gehry knew that the 16 painful years he invested in Walt Disney Concert Hall were not in vain. Disney Hall is the defining achievement of his career, and best of all it's in his hometown!

"an intellectual Disneyland." Loudest of all was the *LA Times* critic, who labeled the Villa "Pompeii on the Pacific," and a monument to "aggressive bad taste." The public, however, was delighted. A few Sundays after the opening, the line of cars waiting to get in stretched for two full miles along Pacific Coast Highway. Just seven weeks later, the Villa recorded its 100,000th visitor: one hundred times the *annual* attendance of the old museum. The Getty Villa was an immediate success. Perhaps in scale with the wealth of its benefactor, monumental transitions soon followed.

The Villa's earliest curators shared a disdain for their stingy benefactor. Over the years, they presented countless opportunities for Getty to acquire important works for the collection, only to see those rarities land elsewhere when the boss couldn't hustle a satisfactory bargain in the process. Early in 1976, they were notified that Getty was diagnosed with prostate cancer. There would be no further communication, as Getty retreated from the world for medical treatment. Expense requests and even telephone calls went unanswered. In June 1976, 83-year-old J. Paul Getty died in England. He never saw his new ancient Villa or its employees. When the Villa's chief curator was summoned downtown to the LA County Courthouse for the reading of Getty's will, many suspected that they would soon be seeking employment elsewhere. What happened next changed the art world forever.

Getty had already provided for his three surviving sons through a family trust and was estranged from all of them. He supported no particular charities. Where would his money go? "I give, devise and bequeath all the rest, residue and remainder of my estate . . . to the Trustees of the J. Paul Getty Museum, to be added to the Endowment Fund of said Museum." The Villa suddenly owned 11 percent of the Getty Oil Company, catapulting the tiny museum in Malibu into the wealthiest art institution on the planet.

The Getty Villa in Malibu

The curator raced back to Malibu, broke the jaw-dropping news to the Villa's 30 employees, and then the champagne flowed! Taking turns toasting the dear, beneficent old man, they hailed the bright new horizon, and envisioned the untold acquisitions that such wealth could confer. Clearly, they were going to need a bigger building.

Not so fast. There were more immediate concerns. To maintain the museum's tax-exempt status, the Getty was *required* to spend 4.25 percent of its endowment's value annually. By 1981, when the oilman's heirs finally exhausted their various disputes over the will, Getty's bequest had swelled to more than one billion dollars. That meant the museum had to spend more than *50 million dollars* a year. (By contrast, the enormous Metropolitan Museum of Art in New York had to spend just *two*.) How often does museum-quality art find its way to the marketplace to make such expenditures possible? How could any museum even plan for such unknowns?

The problem escalated as competing oil companies wrangled for a takeover of Getty Oil, knowing that no deal could be consummated without the bizarre twist of gaining approval from an *art museum*. A showdown between Pennzoil and Texaco eventually yielded another $1.165 billion for the museum's endowment from Texaco. Thanks to wild fluctuations in the oil market, by 1987 the museum's endowment had ballooned to $3 billion dollars, increasing the required expenditure to over $140 million annually. Meanwhile, jealousies within the art world stoked wild accusations: The Getty invested in fakes; the Getty was trading in contraband. The museum needed to change global opinions in a hurry.

Harold M. Williams, former chairman of the Security and Exchange Commission (SEC) under President Jimmy Carter, accepted the job as the Getty's chief executive officer. He devised a visionary plan for the Getty's wealth: create a Trust. The Getty would not merely collect art and display it like a conventional museum, it would operate five independent but related programs. To fulfill the late benefactor's interest in science, the Trust would sponsor a Conservation Institute to restore damaged objects, sending experts throughout the world to save cultural monuments that were deteriorating. The Trust would launch an Education Institute to bolster art studies in the public schools, along with an Art History Information Program. It would create a Research Institute to build a common database for art historians everywhere, and expand its philanthropic reach through the Getty Foundation. And yes, now was the time to erect a new campus to achieve these goals. Antiquities would remain on display in the Getty Villa in Malibu, while the rest of the vast collection of paintings, sculptures, rare books and decorative arts would be shown on the new campus.

Williams and the Board of Directors selected a 750-acre site on an undeveloped hilltop above Sunset Boulevard in Los Angeles, with unrivaled views that spanned from downtown skyscrapers to the Pacific Ocean. The design by architect Richard Meier & Partners, a stunning work of art itself, was selected to become The Getty Center, which the locals soon dubbed The Acropolis.

After three years of designs, discussions and approvals, construction began in 1987. The Getty even acquired a stone quarry in Italy to guarantee a steady supply of matching marble for the construction of all buildings. Richard Meier lived in a cottage on the site for years, overseeing construction details to completion. The magnificent Getty Center was opened to the public—for free—in December 1997.

The Getty Center

Panoramic view of Los Angeles from the Getty Center

There was one last delicious twist. The Getty collection is almost exclusively European art. In the weeks prior to the public unveiling, curators and critics from everywhere were invited to view the Getty Center privately. Jaded Europeans descended, prepared to sneer at another intellectual Disneyland, but what they witnessed this time made them gush with superlatives. In a city famous for its three hundred days of constant sunshine, Meier's clever architecture makes maximum use of natural light, with louvered skylights (and protective filters) in every gallery. Never had Europeans seen European art look so . . . fresh! From the most somber *Pietá* to Van Gogh's vibrant *Irises*, the Getty's dazzling display beneath the California sun made other museums look musty by comparison, as art critics quickly proclaimed.

Today, the Getty Center is hailed for the masterpieces in its collection, along with the masterful design of its presentation. The Getty Conservation Institute is involved in almost every major archaeological dig in the world; the Foundation and the Research Institute underwrite projects everywhere; and through Getty's Open Content program, thousands of images are available to art lovers and historians royalty-free. At the Getty Center, the notorious miser is finally exonerated through one simple truth: When amassing great wealth, be remembered for your generosity.

IN THE MOVIES:
The Getty Center can be seen in *Star Trek Into Darkness* (2013) and *Thor* (2011).

Irises, Vincent van Gogh, 1889

CHAPTER 24.

LAST STOP HOLLYWOOD
WHERE FAME RESTS IN PEACE
1946—2012

Lots of towns in America can point with pride to the birthplace of someone special.

Los Angeles, however, holds another distinction. It's the place where many of those special people point with pride when it's time to expire. **George Harrison** of The Beatles fame will be remembered forever as a great British musician, but he picked Los Angeles for his final days. Harrison's body was cremated at Hollywood Forever Cemetery; his international, interdenominational memorial was held at the Lake Shrine on Sunset Boulevard in 2001.

Of course, most folks don't have the luxury of planning their final hours; sometimes that's the consequence of being a bad boy in LA. Consider these much-loved personalities who took their opportunities too far, then paid the ultimate price.

Bugsy Siegel – In 1946, the Flamingo in Las Vegas was the most expensive hotel ever constructed. Financed with mob money, it was operating in the

From left: George Harrison, 1974; the Lake Shrine's picturesque windmill and Meditation Garden, below the interfaith chapel where Harrison's memorial was held in 2001

red due to Bugsy Siegel's inexperience. The investors were not pleased. While Siegel read the *Los Angeles Times* near the undraped front window of his girlfriend's living room at 810 Linden Drive in Beverly Hills, a gunman hiding behind a rose bush in the front yard fired nine shots through the window. The marksman hit Siegel twice in the heart and twice in the head. The impact was so great that it blew Siegel's left eye out of its socket. Benjamin "Bugsy" Siegel, the gangster from New York, died in Beverly Hills on June 20, 1947 at age 41. He is buried at Hollywood Forever.

Janis Joplin – The rocker came to Los Angeles in August 1970 to record with her group Full Tilt Boogie at Columbia Records. On October 4, 1970, her road manager John Cooke found Joplin dead in her motel room at 7047 Franklin Avenue, with needle marks on her arms, plus open bottles of tequila, vodka and wine. He believes Joplin accidentally overdosed on heroin that was more potent than usual, since other customers overdosed that week, too. Official cause of death: heroin overdose possibly combined with the effects of alcohol. Joplin's song "Mercedes Benz," recorded in one take just three days before her death, is her final performance and her most profitable recording, certified quadruple platinum by the Recording Industry Association of America.

John Belushi – While his wife stayed at home in New York, comedian John Belushi checked into Bungalow #3 at the Chateau Marmont hotel to finish writing a screenplay. Instead, dozens of celebrities showed up for one continuous, drug-fueled party, including drug dealer Cathy Smith.

After partying all night, Smith administered one last speedball to Belushi, a combination of heroin and cocaine, on March 5, 1982. When she returned with groceries, Belushi was dead. Smith went to prison; Belushi got a star on the Walk of Fame, at 6355 Hollywood Boulevard.

Marvin Gaye – The Grammy-award-winning singer was shot to death on April 1, 1984 by his father, the minister Marvin Gaye Sr., during an argument in their home, just a few blocks from the LA mayor's mansion. Rev. Gaye pleaded guilty to voluntary manslaughter. His son Marvin Gaye is remembered today with a star on the Walk of Fame at 1500 Vine Street. Cremated at Forest Lawn Hollywood Hills, his ashes were scattered in the Pacific Ocean.

River Phoenix – The Oscar nominee was all set to party on the Sunset Strip at Johnny Depp's throbbing rock club, The Viper Room. But the recreational drugs in his system triggered a drug-induced heart failure, causing Phoenix to collapse outside the club. He was pronounced dead at Cedars-Sinai Medical Center in Beverly Hills on October 31, 1993.

Phil Hartman – The Emmy-winning comedian from *SNL* and *The Simpsons* was married to a drug addict. After taking cocaine at 3 a.m., Brynn Hartman shot Phil with a .38 caliber handgun as he slept. She confessed the killing to friends, who didn't believe her, and then she shot herself. Phil and Brynn Hartman died on May 28, 1998.

From left: Benjamin "Bugsy" Siegel; Janis Joplin, 1970; John Belushi as Samurai Futaba, 1977

Foreground: Johnny Ramone's grave at Hollywood Forever Cemetery; background: the tomb of LA Philharmonic founder William A. Clark, Jr.

Richard Pryor — The comedian famously set himself on fire when he fumbled with a lighter while freebasing cocaine, then tried to douse the flame with the alcohol he was drinking. But that didn't kill him; multiple sclerosis did. Pryor died on December 10, 2005, after making more than 40 films, pioneering humor during the civil rights struggle and reaping countless awards. Richard Pryor is remembered with a star on the Walk of Fame at 6438 Hollywood Boulevard.

Michael Jackson — Will we ever know the real story? The King of Pop suffered cardiac arrest in his bedroom at 100 North Carolwood Drive in the Holmby Hills section of LA while in rehearsals for a stage show to be titled *This Is It*. When he died on June 25, 2009, the LA Coroner's office reported that Jackson had at least five medications in his system and weighed a skeletal 112 pounds. Michael Jackson is remembered with a star on the Walk of Fame at 6927 Hollywood Boulevard. He is buried at Forest Lawn Glendale.

Whitney Houston — The powerhouse singer was in LA for the 54th Grammy Awards. She checked in to the Beverly Hilton Hotel, where her friend and producer Clive Davis planned a giant pre-Grammy bash. But on party night, February 11, 2012, Whitney was a no-show. She was found dead in her hotel room bathtub. Houston's death was pronounced "accidental" when toxicology reports indicated a combination of cocaine and four other drugs that caused her heart to fail in the hot bath. The next night at the Grammy Awards stunned performers remembered Houston in their remarks. Jennifer Hudson performed in tribute while the audience sobbed.

Want to hang with celebrities in Los Angeles? Visit them at these seven popular cemeteries.

Graveyards are a booming business in Los Angeles, even rented out as sites for private parties and movie screenings. Los Angeles cemeteries employ real estate brokers to show plots to shoppers and discuss the neighbors, like Hugh Hefner, who paid $75,000 for the crypt next to Marilyn Monroe. More recently, the crypt *above* Marilyn was auctioned for $4.6 million.

As one Beverly Hills socialite describes her cemetery visits, "It's all the fun people. Everyone you haven't seen for a while, that's where they are!"

Hollywood Forever (6000 Santa Monica Boulevard) is the power cemetery, the graveyard with more stars than any other, reputed to be the most costly burial site. It's also the only cemetery to offer guided tours (cemeterytour. com). Famous residents include Vampira, Johnny Ramone, Cecil B. DeMille, Rudolph Valentino, Faye Wray, Jayne Mansfield, Benjamin "Bugsy" Siegel and even Charlie Chaplin's mother.

Forest Lawn Glendale (1712 S. Glendale Avenue), the largest cemetery, also features an art museum on its pastoral acreage, and the chapel in which Ronald Reagan married Jane Wyman. Its famous residents include Michael Jackson, Elizabeth Taylor, Walt Disney, Clark Gable, Nat King Cole, Sammy Davis Jr., Aimee Semple McPherson and L. Frank Baum, author of the *Wonderful Wizard of Oz.*

Forest Lawn Hollywood Hills (6300 Forest Lawn Drive) is also a park, featuring a replica of the Old North Church made famous in Paul Revere's ride, a copy of the Liberty Bell, and a giant mosaic: The *Birth of Liberty*, the largest in the United States. Prior to becoming a cemetery, this land can be seen in the Civil War battles depicted in Cecil B. DeMille's *Birth of a Nation.* Notable residents here include Liberace, Lucille Ball, Bette Davis, David

Carradine, John Ritter, Godfrey Cambridge, Andy Gibb, Stan Laurel, Telly Savalas, Annette Funicello; and Ozzie, Harriet and Ricky Nelson.

Hillside Memorial Park (6001 West Centinela Avenue) Though many celebrated individuals are buried here, no one commands attention quite like Al Jolson, ensconced in a monument with a cascading waterfall, plus Jolson's likeness cast in bronze, forever on one knee. Other residents include Max Factor, Nell Carter, Dinah Shore, Jack Benny, Shelley Winters, George Jessel, Eddie Cantor, Milton Berle, Aaron Spelling and the Sunset Strip's favorite gangster, Mickey Cohen.

Westwood Memorial Park (1218 Glendon Avenue) is hard to find. Enter from Glendon Avenue, just south of Wilshire Boulevard, to see one of LA's most intimate and star-studded cemeteries. Joe DiMaggio picked this site to bury Marilyn Monroe because her childhood babysitter was already buried here. Since then, many celebrated names have checked in, including Natalie Wood, Billy Wilder, Jack Lemmon, Walter Matthau, Burt Lancaster, Fannie Brice, Minnie Riperton, author Truman Capote and Beach Boy Carl Wilson.

Mount Sinai Memorial Park (5950 Forest Lawn Drive) is a cemetery exclusively for Jews. (Non-Jewish relatives are buried to avoid splitting up families.) The cemetery features a memorial to the six million European Holocaust victims, and an enormous mosaic that depicts Jews in America. Celebrated residents include "Mama" Cass Elliot, Bonnie Franklin, Totie Fields, Jack Klugman, Lee J. Cobb, Pinky Lee, Phil Silvers and Hillel Slovak, guitarist for the Red Hot Chili Peppers.

Angelus-Rosedale Cemetery (1831 West Washington Boulevard) is integrated. For decades in Los Angeles, "whites only" cemeteries prevailed. Hattie McDaniel, the first African American to win an Academy Award, wanted to be buried in Hollywood Forever cemetery, but that was not permitted. Her body landed here, instead. Other people of color include Anna May Wong, the first Chinese American movie star; Andy Razaf, the lyricist for *Ain't Misbehavin'* and *Honeysuckle Rose*; Fernando Lamas, the Argentinean-born actor; and many more. One of LA's oldest graveyards, this is also the final resting place for many of LA's prominent founders, including three mayors and one California governor.

Marilyn Monroe and Jane Russell putting hand prints in wet concrete at Grauman's Chinese Theatre, 1953

LOS ANGELES
DRIVING & WALKING TOURS

Visit the Places Where History Really Happened

① **TOUR ONE**....... El Pueblo and Chinatown 222

② **TOUR TWO**....... Bunker Hill. 230

③ **TOUR THREE**.. Hollywood 242

④ **TOUR FOUR**..... Hollywood Heights. 254

⑤ **TOUR FIVE**...... Sunset Strip and Beverly Hills 270

⑥ **TOUR SIX**......... Santa Monica and Venice Beach 284

Los Angeles

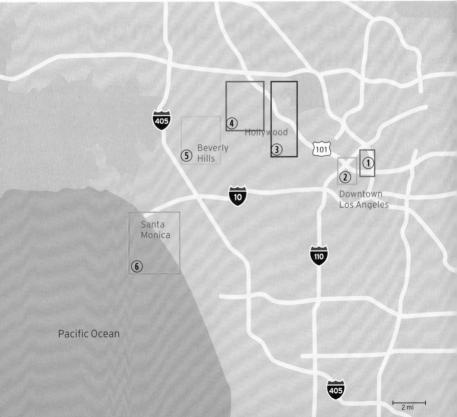

405

① Hollywood

④

Beverly
Hills
⑤

③

101

②

①

Downtown
Los Angeles

10

Santa
Monica

⑥

110

Pacific Ocean

405

2 mi

EL PUEBLO AND CHINATOWN WALKING TOUR

No car required! Take the Red Line (the underground LA Metro) to Union Station for a visit to the center of Los Angeles in its days as the Mexican capital of *Alta California*. Then, just a short stroll from the historic Pueblo, the tour continues through Chinatown, with its colorful shops, restaurants and bakeries. There's plenty to see, and all of it's free.

EL PUEBLO

1. Union Station
2. El Pueblo
3. Tribute to Antonio Aguilar
4. The Plaza
5. Olvera Street
6. Avila Adobe
7. América Tropical Interpretive Center
8. Sepulveda House
9. The Old Firehouse
10. Chinese American Museum
11. Our Lady, Queen of the Angels Catholic Church

CHINATOWN

12. Twin Dragon Gateway
13. Chinatown Central Plaza
14. Phoenix Bakery
15. Chinatown Station

Bamboo Ln ⑭

Gin Ling Way ⑬

Lei Min Way

W College St.

Cleveland St

Yale St.

N Hill St.

N Broadway

CHINATOWN

Alpine St.

N Spring St

N Spring St

N Main St

⑮

Ord St.

N Hill St.

N Broadway

New High St

N Spring St

N Alameda St

Bauchet St.

Fort Moore Pioneer Memorial

⑫

W Cesar E Chavez Ave

N Main St

Olvera St

⑧

⑪

⑤ ⑥ ⑦

Plaza Park

③ ②

④

Union Station

①

⑨

Arcadia St.

N Spring St.

N Los Angeles St

W Aliso St.

101

250 ft

START:
Union Station

END:
Metro: Chinatown
Station

TOUR TIME:
About 3 hours

CHAPTERS:
1, 2, 3, 4, 5, 14

Bring your appetite! Consider an authentic Mexican lunch in the Pueblo or dim sum in Chinatown. The tour covers a few miles, mostly flat. Wear walking shoes, sunscreen and a hat.

❧

1. Start at **Union Station**, the historic terminal that united the Southern Pacific, Union Pacific and Santa Fe railroads. It connected LA's Southern Pacific to the Transcontinental Railroad, opening the orange groves to a national market. The passenger terminal opened in 1939. Interiors of Union Station are favorites with filmmakers. Today, it's used by travelers on Amtrak and Metrolink, plus underground passengers on the LA Metro.

NOTABLE FILMS SHOT HERE:
Blade Runner (1982), *Catch Me If You Can* (2002), *500 Days of Summer* (2011), *Pearl Harbor* (2001), *Bugsy* (1991), *The Hustler* (1961), *The Way We Were* (1973) and many television shows.

Exit through the front doors. You'll face the promenade that leads to El Pueblo National Historic Monument.

2. El Pueblo—the birthplace of Los Angeles, home to the *pobladores*, the first Mexican settlers—is open, for free, seven days a week.

Go up ramp to the left or the steps to the right.

Union Station

Station's 1939 opening

Promenade

3. The steps lead to a tribute to **Antonio Aguilar**, a singer and actor who slept on benches in El Pueblo prior to achieving fame in Mexico. He recorded more than 160 albums and performed in more than 100 films before his death in 2007 at age 88.

El Pueblo

4. A short walk to the left is **the Plaza**. Free events take place here. See elpueblo.lacity.org

Before California became the 31st state, LA was the final capital of the Mexican state of *Alta California*. To your left is an early administrative building. To the right, the hotel owned by Pio Pico, the last governor of *Alta California*.

Tribute to Antonio Aguilar

Ahead is the Catholic Church Our Lady, Queen of the Angels. Visit the church last. First, walk to the center of the Plaza, where you'll see a plaque that lists the original *pobladores*, the 11 families that founded Los Angeles. The circle surrounding the Plaza is embedded with commemorative plaques detailing each of the founding families.

The Plaza

There are three exhibits in the Plaza. The first continues the early Pueblo's Mexican heritage.

The Plaza, c. 1862

5. To the right of the church is the entrance to **Olvera Street**. Continue into the Olvera Street market. You'll find handmade and unique surprises in the stalls.

6. Ahead, you'll spy the **Avila Adobe** on the right, the house of the former *alcalde*, or mayor. The house of Francisco José Avila, built in 1818, is the oldest standing residence in LA, now a

Olvera Street

Avila Adobe

América Tropical Center

América Tropical mural

Sepulveda House

The Old Plaza Firehouse

museum. Turn right to enter the house. In the courtyard you'll find a self-guided tour about life in *El Pueblo de los Angeles* in the 1820s. The exit from the house circles back into the courtyard.

7. Across the street from the Avila Adobe (on the other side of the stalls down the center of Olvera Street), visit ***América Tropical Interpretive Center***. A free museum explains the history of *América Tropical*, the mural that is viewed, via elevator, on the floor above.

Muralist David Alfaro Siqueiros saw public walls as sites to encourage debate, but city officials disagreed with Siqueiros' message. His artwork was whitewashed into oblivion. *América Tropical* became a symbol for suppression and government censorship. In 2012, 80 years after its unveiling, *América Tropical* was unveiled once more.

8. Next, view the **Sepulveda House** exhibit in the adjacent doorway. It's the back entrance to an old boarding house.

Turn right down the ramp to Olvera Street. On Olvera Street, turn right, back toward the Plaza.

9. On the far side of the Plaza (southeast) stands the **Old Plaza Firehouse**, dating back to 1884. The museum displays equipment from LA's early firehouses, photos, and firefighting memorabilia.

Next, turn left, toward the church, as you exit. Turn left again, for a detour into the Chinese American Museum.

10. The **Chinese American Museum** is free. See treasures from the earliest Chinatown, and artifacts from the Chinese pioneers of LA. (This exhibit adds context to today's Chinatown, where this tour heads soon.)

Chinese American Museum

Upon exiting, turn right, back toward the Plaza, then turn left, toward **Our Lady, Queen of the Angels Catholic Church**.

11. Dedicated in 1822, the church was rebuilt and expanded in 1861 using elements from the original building, but little of the original edifice remains. The historic church is reserved for special occasions. A larger church was annexed; parishioners enter the church from the other side of the building.

Queen of the Angels Church

To get there, go through the courtyard. Proceed to the right of the church, then walk left toward the other side of the building. Or, bypass the courtyard by continuing to the right. Walk around the side of the building, where you'll see the mosaic of *Our Lady, Queen of the Angels*.

Mosaic, Our Lady, Queen of Angels

Continue west, toward the church entrance. *La Placita*, as the chapel is nicknamed, was the first American parish for many Catholic immigrants arriving in LA. In the 1980s, it was a sanctuary for refugees threatened with deportation to El Salvador.

La Placita Chapel

Next, turn right (north) on Spring Street. Continue to the end of the block, where Spring Street meets Cesar Chavez Avenue. Turn left, uphill along the outskirts of Chinatown.

Plaza and the Church, c. 1873

Route 66 sign

Twin Dragon Gateway

Chinatown Central Plaza

Gin Ling Way

Chinatown, 1974

Today's Cesar Chavez Avenue (formerly a section of Sunset Boulevard) is part of Route 66, the road that links Chicago, Illinois, to the Pacific Ocean. It travels through eight states to end in Santa Monica. Route 66 was immortalized for younger generations in Pixar's animated film *Cars* (2006).

Travel on Route 66 for one block. At North Broadway, turn right, heading into Chinatown.

12. You're welcomed by the **Twin Dragon Gateway**. Installed in July 2001, the dragons symbolize luck, prosperity and longevity. Follow the sidewalk that crosses underneath the dragons. This is North Broadway, the main commercial street for modern-day Chinatown. Architecture adheres to tiled roofs with pagoda references in the rooflines.

Continue on North Broadway for three blocks, to the Central Plaza of New Chinatown, which boasts a variety of shops, restaurants and businesses.

13. You'll spot the entrance to the **Chinatown Central Plaza** before you arrive at 947 North Broadway. Completed in 1938, the Central Plaza is the first modern American Chinatown, owned and planned by Chinese residents.

Stroll across Gin Ling Way, the main thoroughfare, or wander down side streets to discover delightful restaurants and shops. Chinatown is a favorite location for filmmakers.

NOTABLE FILMS SHOT HERE:
Chinatown (1974), *Rush Hour* (1998), *The Green*

Hornet (2011), *Dragon Seed* (1944), *Made of Honor* (2008) and many television programs.

Exit from the East Gate, where you entered, on North Broadway.

14. To your left is **Phoenix Bakery** (969 North Broadway), the oldest business in Chinatown. Its strawberry whipped cream cakes are a local treat.

15. On North Broadway, turn right, and walk to the corner of West College Street. Turn left, onto West College Street. You'll see the Chinatown Metro stop one block away, at the intersection of Spring Street. The **Chinatown Station** is on the Gold Line within the LA Metro system. It's a short ride to Union Station, the next stop.

Phoenix Bakery

Chinatown Station

BUNKER HILL WALKING TOUR

In 1867 Prudent Beaudry purchased and developed Bunker Hill, with lavish two-story Victorian houses for the upper-class residents. In the late twentieth century, through the Bunker Hill Redevelopment Project, the hill was lowered in elevation, and the entire area was redeveloped with modern high rises.

There's world-famous architecture, too, in downtown Los Angeles—most

❶ Pershing Square

❷ Biltmore Hotel

❸ One Bunker Hill

❹ Bonaventure Hotel

❺ Los Angeles Public Library

❻ Night Sail (Statue)

❼ Sequi (Statue)

❽ Pre-Natal Memories (Statue)

❾ Museum of Contemporary Art

❿ Walt Disney Concert Hall

⓫ Music Center

⓬ Dorothy Chandler Pavilion

⓭ Mark Taper Forum

⓮ Ahmanson Theater

⓯ Cathedral of Our Lady of the Angels

⓰ Grand Park

⓱ City Center/Grand Park Station

START:
Metro: Pershing Square
Station

END:
Metro: City Center/Grand
Park Station

Tour Time:
About 3 hours

Chapters:
9, 15, 19, 22

impressive when measured on a human scale. *For this tour, leave the car behind.*

We'll start and end at underground Metro stations, walking in a loop through Bunker Hill. Wear sunscreen and walking shoes, but don't dress too casually. We'll visit a cathedral and Walt Disney Concert Hall, and some tempting restaurants.

Take the Red Line (the underground Metro Rail) to the Pershing Square Station.

1. Take the escalator up to **Pershing Square**, at the corner of Hill and Fifth streets.

Pershing Square

2. To your west, across the park, you'll see the **Biltmore Hotel**. Walk west on Fifth Street to the corner of Olive Street. Cross Olive Street and turn left, toward the Biltmore Hotel's entrance for pedestrians.

When it opened in 1923, the Biltmore was the largest hotel west of Chicago. Its architects combined the Beaux Arts style with Spanish Baroque to stunning effect. The dazzling interior craftsmanship has earned it a place as an LA Historic-Cultural Landmark.

Biltmore Hotel

Don't be surprised if the interior appears familiar. It's one of Hollywood filmmakers' favorite locations for simulating East Coast cities. The Biltmore served as every upscale Washington D.C. venue in the TV series *The West Wing*. Other TV shows in which the

Interior of the Biltmore Hotel

Biltmore depicts East Coast locations: *ER, NYPD Blue, CSI: NY, Ally McBeal* and *Mad Men*. Among the many movies filmed here: *Ghostbusters, Spider-Man, Beverly Hills Cop, True Lies, Splash*, and *Chinatown*.

Interior of the Biltmore

In 1960 the Democratic Convention was held in LA, and the Biltmore was the headquarters for nominees John F. Kennedy and Lyndon B. Johnson. Archival photos show the Biltmore during that era.

Johnson at the Biltmore, 1960

Pass the ballroom and conference rooms on the western side of the building. The Biltmore was the site of the Academy Awards presentations for eight years in the 1930s and 40s.

Exiting on the western side puts you on Grand Avenue. Walk a short distance to the right, to the corner of Fifth Street, then turn to the left, continuing west. Walk westward on Fifth Street.

One Bunker Hill

3. At the corner of Fifth Street and Grand Avenue, you'll see the Art Deco treasure called **One Bunker Hill**, the original home of the Southern California Edison Company. When it was completed in 1931, this was the first building in the west to be heated and air-conditioned solely by electricity.

Bonaventure Hotel

4. In the distance (to the west), the cylindrical building is the famous **Bonaventure Hotel**, an ingenious architectural feat that even includes a jogging track around its perimeter. Its glass elevators ascend on the building's exterior, a radical concept at the time of its construction. The Bonaventure is another favorite filming location. Films include: *Rain Man, In The*

Rain Man, 1988

Los Angeles Public Library

View of the rotunda, c. 1929

Atrium of the Library

History of California murals

Steps lead up Bunker Hill

Line Of Fire, Wonderland, True Lies and *Alien Nation.*

5. At the end of the block, you'll come to the intersection of Fifth Street and Flower Street. (Do not cross the street.) Turn left on Flower Street where you'll see the front entrance to **The Los Angeles Public Library**.

One of the most-visited buildings in America, the Central Library is a National Landmark, with the third-largest collection of books in the U.S. This building was constructed in 1926.

Take the escalators, just past the gift shop, up one level to the second floor, then walk straight ahead toward the glass balcony. Although the building appears to be four stories tall from the exterior façade, inside it's an eight-story atrium, with California sunlight from giant skylights illuminating all the way to the lowest level, four stories underground.

Turn 180 degrees and head in the opposite direction, away from the glass balcony toward the oldest section of the building. In 1933, muralist Dean Cornwell painted this four-panel history of California. How many of the characters described in this book's early chapters can you identify?

Return to the first floor, then use the side exit that returns you to Fifth Street. Ahead are steps (and escalator) that lead up Bunker Hill. Ascend to the top of Bunker Hill. Look behind you for a terrific view of the Library's mosaic roof, crowned with a torch atop the pyramid that represents the "Light of Learning."

You're standing at the intersection of Hope Street and 4th Street. Walk straight ahead to the red granite building. Modern construction on Bunker Hill includes courtyards where employees from office towers meet for lunch. Turn right (east) and climb the stairs into the courtyard. Walk through the courtyard. Ahead, you'll see Grand Avenue.

Stairs leading to the courtyard

6. Beside you, see Louise Nevelson's sculpture, entitled **Night Sail**. With her art installed at New York's Museum of Modern Art and major museums around the world, Nevelson is famous for assembling found objects and transforming them with black paint. *Night Sail* is one of her rare pieces that is not constructed of found objects.

Grand Avenue

Turn left to see another commission for this Wells Fargo site.

Night Sail, by Louise Nevelson

7. Nancy Graves created this colorful sculpture, entitled **Sequi**. A graduate of Vassar and Yale, Graves was awarded the Yale Arts Award for Distinguished Artistic Achievement just weeks before the installation of this artwork.

Turn left; walk north to the corner of 3rd Street, then cross Grand Avenue, heading east.

Sequi, by Nancy Graves

8. On the east side of Grand Avenue, here's another public plaza with an intriguing sculpture, the perfect response to Louise Nevelson's *Night Sail*. Inspired by Nevelson's technique, artist Mark di Suvero assembled found objects to create **Pre-Natal Memories**. The steel beams are found objects, painted black, like Nevelson's works. Unlike *Night*

Pre-Natal Memories, di Suvero

MoCA

MoCA night

Walt Disney Concert Hall

Lillian and Walt Disney

View of the stage

Sail (Nevelson's, created in a foundry), di Suvero takes the concept to a higher level, actually using heavy steel "found objects" to assemble something completely new. *Pre-Natal Memories* is part of the permanent collection of the Museum of Contemporary Art (MoCA) to the north.

Walk back to the Grand Avenue sidewalk and head north, toward the red sandstone building's front entrance.

9. Completed in 1986, the first U.S. commission for Japanese architect Arata Isozaki, the **Museum of Contemporary Art** opened to great acclaim. The MoCA's exhibition spaces are under the courtyard level, lit from above by pyramidal skylights. Arata's idea inspired the natural light concept of the Getty Center.

10. Continue walking north on Grand Avenue. You can't miss one of the most celebrated architectural achievements on earth: the **Walt Disney Concert Hall**.

When Walt Disney died, his widow Lillian donated $50 million from her personal fortune to build the adjacent concert hall, dedicated for the LA Philharmonic's use. Mrs. Disney's donation was the largest single gift in U.S. history for a cultural building. Local architect Frank Gehry won the competition.

Enter from Grand Avenue, beside the Concert Hall Café. You'll face the desk that welcomes visitors with audio players for the self-guided tour. See www.laphil.com for tour details.

Take a tour. Like the exterior, there are no flat walls or 90-degree corners inside Disney Hall. You'll be dazzled by the combination of textured building materials illuminated by sunlight streaming from unexpected angles.

Curved walls of the concert hall

An avid gardener, Mrs. Disney insisted the hall include a garden. In the roof garden, concertgoers can wind through paths and stroll between the hall's shimmering sails.

Concert Hall's roof garden

Next, return to the ground level and Grand Avenue. Continue to the Music Center across the street.

There are several places of note on the ground floor:

LA Phil Store

On the south side of the building, Chef Joachim Splichal's Patina is one of the most exquisite restaurants in LA. There's also a terrific self-service café on this ground level.

The LA Phil Store is a delightful gift shop for music lovers, with recordings and videos of the LA Philharmonic and other performers, plus books and memorabilia about LA.

Disney Hall and Music Center

The Box Office for Disney Hall is outdoors on Grand Avenue. From September until June, the acclaimed Los Angeles Philharmonic is in residence at Disney Hall.

11. Remain on the west side of Grand Avenue. Cross 1st Street to enter the **Music Center** from its side staircase. Ascend the stairs and walk straight ahead to the Music Center Plaza.

Music Center

Dorothy Chandler Pavilion

Music Center Plaza

Mark Taper Forum

Ahmanson Theater

View of City Hall

12. You're walking beside the famous **Dorothy Chandler Pavilion**. This theater is the former home of the LA Philharmonic, now the dedicated home for the LA Opera, also used by visiting dance companies. It is best known for hosting the Academy Awards ceremonies for decades.

Inspired by New York's Lincoln Center, Dorothy Buffum Chandler (wife of *Los Angeles Times* publisher Norman Chandler) led an effort to build a central home for the performing arts in downtown LA. Her nine-year campaign raised 19 million dollars from LA's wealthiest citizens and corporations; their names appear in gold throughout the Music Center complex.

13. The Mark Taper Forum (named for a real estate developer who donated to Mrs. Chandler's cause) at the Music Center is the site for plays. Many important plays began at the Taper before heading to Broadway and regional success. The most intimate theater in the complex, with less than 1000 seats, the Taper is hailed for its great sight lines and acoustics.

14. The **Ahmanson Theater** is the Music Center's big stage for musicals, and has hosted many pre-Broadway tryouts, along with touring productions of large-scale shows.

From the center of the Music Center Plaza, face east, with your back to the central fountain. Ahead, down the graceful slope, is a view of City Hall.

Constructed in 1928, City Hall is retrofitted to withstand a magnitude 8.2 earthquake. Symbolically, the concrete that forms its base is made of sand from all fifty-eight counties in California, with water taken from all twenty-one original missions.

City Hall opening, 1928

You've seen LA City Hall in the movies. Films include: *War of the Worlds* (1953), *The Bad News Bears* (1976), *L.A. Confidential* (1997) and *Gangster Squad* (2013); TV shows include: *Perry Mason, Dragnet, Adam-12* and *The Adventures of Superman*—where it serves as the offices for *The Daily Planet*.

Music Center

15. Next, turn to the left and head north, past the Mark Taper Forum and the Ahmanson Theater, down the stairs. Come to the corner of Grand Avenue and Temple Street, the site of our last major stop. Diagonally across the street, you'll see the **Cathedral of Our Lady of the Angels**.

Stairs to Temple Street

With more than five million Catholics in 287 parishes, LA is home to the largest Roman Catholic archdiocese on the continent. This modern cathedral is its mother church.

Cathedral, Our Lady of the Angels

Observe the traffic lights, then cross Grand Avenue and Temple Street. Walk down Temple Street (east) beside the Cathedral to this entrance, called the "sheepgate," a reference to Jesus Christ, a shepherd leading his flock, welcoming all.

"Sheepgate" entrance

Step into the Cathedral courtyard. To the left, a staircase leads to the Upper Plaza and a full view of the Cathedral.

Cathedral, Our Lady of the Angels

Interior of Cathedral

Cathedral interior

The statue of the Virgin Mary over the entrance to the Cathedral refers to the first name bestowed on this territory by the first Spanish explorers: Nuestra Señora la Reina de los Ángeles.

Enter the Cathedral. Designed by Pritzker Prize-winning Spanish architect Rafael Moneo, the building was completed in September 2002, with controversy over the cost ($190 million, not including the land), and Moneo's deconstructivist design.

The nave and transepts seat approximately 3,000 worshippers. The presbytery to the left of the altar can seat up to 300 priests. A fun fact: the Cathedral is one foot longer than St. Patrick's Cathedral in New York City!

The lower level is a mausoleum containing 1,270 crypts and 4,746 columbarium niches for burials. Among the notable names buried at the Cathedral: Saint Vibiana, patron saint of the Archdiocese of LA, and Oscar-winning actor Gregory Peck.

After exploring the Cathedral, go back to the sheepgate on the lower plaza, and exit onto Temple Street. Turn left (east) and continue down the hill. At the end of the block, turn right (south) onto Hill Street.

16. Walk south on Hill Street. We're heading toward the slope between the Music Center and City Hall, known as the Grand Park.

The park offers views of City Hall and a great view of the headquarters for the *Los Angeles*

Courtyard of the Cathedral

St. Vibiana's, former parish of the Catholic Archdiocese of LA, 1885

Times at 1st and Spring streets. Since the building opened in 1935, it's been the site of protests and takeover schemes, yet it is famous for magnificent murals (inside) its iconic Art Moderne architecture, and an impressive collection of Pulitzer Prizes. (Free tours are available, with reservations in advance. Phone 213-237-5757 for tour information.) The Grand Park is also notable for its collection of exotic trees from all continents. Each is labeled with an explanation of its origins.

17. On Hill Street, just south of the Grand Park, you'll find the entrance to **Civic Center/Grand Park Station**, where our tour ends.

LA Times building from Grand Park

Civic Center/Grand Park Station

HOLLYWOOD DRIVING TOUR

Explore this route by car to visit the Hollywood sign and the earliest houses built in the Hollywood Hills, the enclave originally known as Hollywoodland. These are not palatial estates, but the quaint, historic homes of entertainment industry professionals for nearly a century. The tour continues to Paramount Studios and the Hollywood Forever Cemetery, Windsor Square and Larchmont Village.

❶ Hollywood Boulevard & Vine Street
❷ Avalon
❸ Capitol Records Building
❹ Hollywood Tower Apartments
❺ Entrance to Hollywoodland
❻ Hollywoodland Realty office
❼ Sunset Ranch
❽ Rodgerton Drive

❾ Sunset-Gower Studios
❿ Hollywood Forever Cemetery
⓫ Raleigh Studios
⓬ Paramount Studios
⓭ Windsor Square
⓮ Former home of Norman Chandler
⓯ Former home of George Getty II
⓰ Larchmont Village

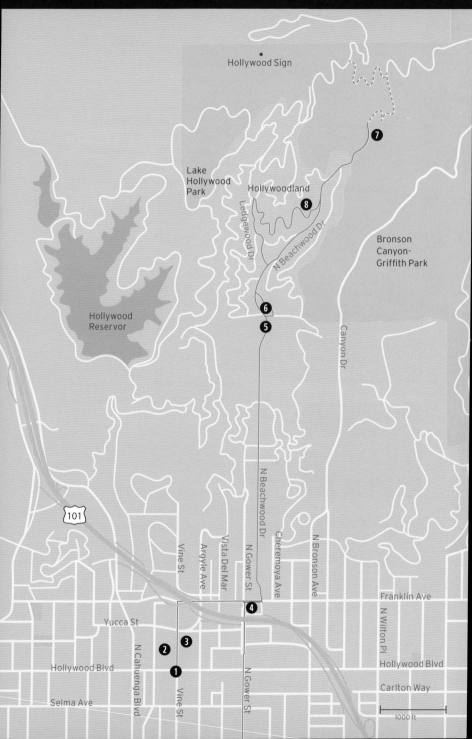

START:
Hollywood Boulevard and Vine Street

END:
Larchmont Village

Tour Time:
About 5 hours

Chapters:
9, 10, 12, 18, 24

Ever wonder how Hollywood got its name? One story credits Canadian developer Hobart Johnstone Whitley (1847-1931), who became a U.S. citizen in 1870, then visited Los Angeles on his honeymoon with his second wife, Gigi, in 1886. They devised the name Hollywood when, years later, Whitely bought 400 acres to construct Whitley Heights, the first residences for silent movie stars. Whitley Heights became a National Historic District in 1982.

Walk of Stars

Avalon

Capitol Records building

1. Start at the **corner of Hollywood Boulevard and Vine Street**. This is where the Walk of Fame begins, extending for many blocks to the east and west across Hollywood Blvd. and north-south on Vine Street. This corner is dedicated to real out-of-this-world stars— the first American astronauts to land on the moon, who also accomplished one of the most significant feats in the history of television.

Stay in the right lane; head north on Vine Street.

2. Across Vine Street, on the left (west), notice **Avalon** (1735 Vine Street), a dance club today, but known for decades as the Palace Theater. Built in 1927 for live radio broadcasts, it was converted to a television studio for the *Jerry Lewis Show*, then *Live from the Hollywood Palace*, the *Sammy Davis Jr. Show*, and many more. It was here that Richard Nixon aired his infamous "Checkers" speech.

3. On the right, you'll pass the **Capitol Records**

Building, resembling a stack of vinyl records on a spindle. The biggest stars in the music industry continue to record in its underground studios. Artists who recorded here include Frank Sinatra, the Foo Fighters, The Beatles, The Beach Boys, Nat King Cole, Duran Duran, Aretha Franklin and many, many more.

Hollywood Tower Apartments

Continue north to the intersection. Turn right onto Franklin Avenue and navigate into the center lane.

4. Head east on Franklin Avenue, passing the **Hollywood Tower Apartments** on the right. Built by actor George Raft in 1929, it's now a National Landmark, and home to decades of entertainment luminaries. Brazilian actress Carmen Miranda, famous for introducing the samba and her "tutti-frutti hat" to the world, was married here in 1947.

Beechwood Drive

5. Continuing east, navigate into the left-turning lane; prepare to turn left at Beechwood Drive. With a left turn onto Beechwood Drive, the famous Hollywood sign comes into view. Continue north toward the sign. Drive north on Beechwood Drive for approximately one mile to the stone gates that mark the **entrance to Hollywoodland**.

Entrance to Hollywoodland

6. Turn right, just past the eastern tower, to view the original **Hollywoodland Realty** office on the left (north; officially 2700 Beechwood Drive), where the original tracts were sold.

Hollywoodland Realty office

7. Pass the realty office, and turn left onto Woodhaven Drive for a view of some original Hollywoodland houses. Though not protected

Sunset Ranch

Entrance to the park

The iconic Hollywood sign

View of the city

Hollywoodland, c. 1920s

View from Rodgerton Drive

as landmarks, it's easy to spot the original houses that first comprised this enclave. At the intersection of Beechwood Drive, turn right and continue up the hill for approximately 3/4 mile. Continue on Beechwood Drive (past the billboard for the **Sunset Ranch**), then park on the dirt shoulder. The tour continues on foot, with a visit to the famous Hollywood sign. Note that the park closes at sunset.

The road to the Hollywood sign is a broad and well-maintained dirt path (fire road). Proceed up the hill—a visit up the hill for a photo of the Hollywood sign and then back down takes about a half hour.

For hikers, there are multiple paths that wind through the canyon and provide some extraordinary views of Hollywood, Griffith Park, the Observatory and Downtown LA.

After capturing your photos, return to the car. The tour continues on wheels through historic Hollywoodland. Drive back down the hill on Beechwood Drive for 1/4 mile to Rodgerton Drive. Bear right onto Rodgerton Drive for a view of Hollywoodland and one of its historic stone walls.

8. Travel about 1/5 mile on **Rodgerton Drive**, then park on the right shoulder *briefly* for a glimpse of the historic houses built into the canyon cliffs.

Travel about 1/10 mile farther on Rodgerton Drive to a long, curving stone wall created by European stonemasons in the 1920s. It has supported houses on the street above for 100

years. Continue on Rodgerton's circuitous
route heading downhill. Another 1/5 mile is
the intersection of Rodgerton, Ledgewood
and Deronda drives. Make a sharp left onto
Ledgewood Drive and down the steep hill.

Work of European stonemasons

Enjoy the scenery on Ledgewood Drive as
you continue downhill for approximately 1/4
mile to the intersection of Beechwood Drive.
Turn right onto Beechwood Drive to exit from
Hollywoodland, heading south.

Sunset-Gower Studios

Stay in the right lane.

At the intersection of Franklin Boulevard and
Beechwood Drive, turn right onto Franklin
Blvd., then immediately navigate into the left-
turning lane at the Gower Street traffic light.
Make a left turn onto Gower Street, continuing
south.

Mr. Smith Goes To Washington, 1939

9. Continue down the hill to Sunset Boulevard.
At the corner of Gower Street and Sunset
Boulevard, turn left onto Sunset Boulevard. On
the right, you'll pass **Sunset-Gower Studios**,
famous for most of the twentieth century as
Columbia Pictures.

The Golden Girls, 1985-1992

As Columbia Pictures, this comparatively
small studio generated some of Hollywood's
most enduring hits, including *Mr. Smith Goes
To Washington, Golden Boy, Suddenly Last
Summer, Dr. Strangelove, Bye Bye Birdie, Lost
Horizon, Funny Girl, Tootsie* and many more.
As Sunset-Gower Studios, it's been home to
television hits including *The Fresh Prince of
Bel-Air, Saved By The Bell, The Golden Girls,
That's So Raven, Six Feet Under, Dexter* and

Gordon Street sign

Entrance to Hollywood Forever

Douglas Fairbanks Jr.'s grave

Rudolph Valentino funeral, 1926

Tombstone of Mel Blanc

Tombstone of Johnny Ramone

many more. *General Hospital* was filmed here for 24 years. Sunset-Gower Studios is not open to the public.

10. Continue east to the corner of Gordon Street. Turn right onto Gordon Street, then continue south to Santa Monica Boulevard. At the intersection of Gordon Street and Santa Monica Boulevard, continue straight ahead into the driveway for the **Hollywood Forever Cemetery**.

The final resting place for some of the biggest names in the entertainment industry, Hollywood Forever Cemetery first opened in 1899. The site of many special events, the cemetery is open for free to visitors on most days from 8 a.m. to 5 p.m.

A map of notable graves is available from the office to the right of the entrance. Or follow the video tour online at hollywoodforever.com.

Early film stars, like actor Douglas Fairbanks Sr., built spectacular monuments for themselves. Fairbanks is buried here facing a reflecting pond. His family crypt also includes his son, actor Douglas Fairbanks Jr. Other famous names entombed here include Mel Blanc, Rudolph Valentino, Cecil B. DeMille, Peter Lorre, Jayne Mansfield, Tyrone Power, Nelson Riddle, Carl "Alfalfa" Switzer, Faye Wray, Vampira and many more. Railroad scion William Clark Jr. is buried in a replica of a Greek temple, surrounded by a pond, seen at left, with the grave of rock star Johnny Ramone in the foreground.

Raleigh Studios

Mary Pickford

Bronson Gate, (at Paramount) 1933

New gate at Paramount Studios

Filming at Paramount Studios

Exit through the same entrance gates.

At the exit, turn right onto Santa Monica Boulevard. Travel east for two traffic lights to Van Ness Avenue. Turn right onto Van Ness Avenue and drive south, passing the eastern wall of the Hollywood Forever Cemetery.

Continue south on Van Ness Avenue and navigate into the right lane, preparing to turn right at Melrose Avenue.

11. Before turning onto Melrose Avenue, notice **Raleigh Studios**, across the street, on both sides of Van Ness Avenue. Founded in 1915, Raleigh is not the largest Hollywood studio, but it is the oldest continually running studio in the world. Silent films were made here for more than decade; the first starred Mary Pickford. Classic films made here include *In The Heat Of The Night*, *The Best Years Of Our Lives*, *What Ever Happened To Baby Jane?* and *A Star Is Born*. It was here that Ronald Reagan hosted the television series *Death Valley Days*. Other TV series include *The Adventures of Superman*, *Gunsmoke*, *Perry Mason* and *Whose Line Is It Anyway?*

12. Raleigh Studios is not open to the public. From Van Ness Avenue, turn right onto Melrose Avenue. Immediately on the right is **Paramount Studios**.

Continue west on Melrose Avenue. At Bronson Avenue, see the original Paramount gate; continue west for another block, navigating into the left lane. At the next corner, Windsor Boulevard, see the newer, larger main gate for Paramount.

More than 6,000 feature films and television episodes have been filmed on this lot. A sample includes *Forrest Gump, Rear Window, Sunset Boulevard, Transformers, Ghost, Airplane!, The Ten Commandments, Vertigo, Top Hat* and *Ordinary People*. Television series filmed here include *Glee, Star Trek, Frasier, Cheers, Happy Days, Shogun, The Odd Couple, Mork & Mindy, Bonanza, Entourage, MacGyver* and *The Brady Bunch*. Paramount Studios is not open to the public.

Sunset Boulevard, 1950

Star Trek, 1966-1969

13. From the left lane on Melrose Avenue, turn left onto Windsor Boulevard, heading south. The final destination is **Windsor Square**, an enclave of mansions built for the movie stars and robber barons of old Hollywood. Continue south on Windsor Boulevard.

Windsor Boulevard sign

Cross the intersection at Beverly Boulevard. It's the avenue that divides north and south street numbers throughout LA. Windsor Boulevard also marks the beginning of the historic Windsor Square neighborhood.

These are private residences. Some former residents of this neighborhood include actors John Barrymore, Ethel Barrymore, Cliff Robertson, Anne Heche and Ellen DeGeneres, silent screen star Dolores Costello, opera star Lawrence Tibbett, oil tycoon J. Paul Getty's son, and newspaper baron Norman Chandler.

Windsor Square, c. 1920s

14. At the corner of Windsor Boulevard and Second Street, turn left onto Second Street. Travel east for one block to Lorraine Boulevard. Turn right onto Lorraine Boulevard. Continue south, past the historic mansions on Lorraine

House number indicated on curb

Former home of Norman Chandler

Former home of George Getty II

Windsor Square vintage postcard

Larchmont sign

Larchmont Village

Boulevard. House numbers are painted on the curbs near each driveway. 455 South Lorraine Boulevard, the **former home of Norman Chandler**, was dubbed "the Western White House," for the Chandlers made it available to visiting presidents Eisenhower, Kennedy, Johnson and Nixon.

15. Turn left onto Fifth Street, heading east for one block. From Fifth Street, turn right onto Irving Boulevard, and continue to drive south across the 6th Street intersection. Just past the corner stands 605 South Irving Boulevard, the **former home of George Getty II**, son of oil baron J. Paul Getty. To provide a residence for LA's mayor, Getty donated his house to the city. However, mayors rarely sleep here. The house is ceremonial, used to receive heads of state, or for meetings with government officials.

Travel south to the end of the block at Wilshire Boulevard. Turn right, heading west. Continue west for three short blocks to Plymouth Boulevard, then turn right, past a final row of grand residences in Windsor Square.

The Windsor Square neighborhood has few palm trees, making it an ideal location for feature films, since it can substitute as almost any location. From silent movies featuring the *Keystone Kops* to *War Games*, *The Artist*, and countless television commercials, you've seen these streets in many other guises.

16. Continue north on Plymouth Boulevard to First Street. Turn left on First Street and follow its tree-lined curves to the corner of Larchmont Boulevard, known to locals as **Larchmont**

Village. Turn right, onto Larchmont Boulevard.

Here you'll find boutiques, restaurants and shopping destinations—the ideal place to end this tour.

No alcohol is served in this residentially-zoned district, but everyone is welcome to buy a bottle of wine at Larchmont Village Wine, Spirits & Cheese. Most Larchmont restaurants will provide glasses and uncork your wine for a small fee.

Larchmont Village is a favorite hangout for working actors (it's off the radar for most tourists), as well as local residents.

Larchmont Wine, Spirits & Cheese

Larchmont Boulevard, c. 1920

HOLLYWOOD HEIGHTS WALKING TOUR

Unlike the drive through historic, residential Hollywoodland, you don't need a car to visit the congested, honky-tonk section of Hollywood that's fun for visitors and locals alike.

There's more to do on Hollywood Boulevard than can be accomplished in one

❶ Hollywood and Highland Center
❷ The Hollywood Museum
❸ Hollywood Boulevard
❹ Egyptian Theatre
❺ Musso & Frank
❻ Frederick's of Hollywood
❼ Hollywood United Methodist Church
❽ El Capitan Theater
❾ Chinese Theatre

❿ Roosevelt Hotel
⓫ Magic Castle
⓬ The Freeman House
⓭ View point
⓮ High Tower
⓯ Hollywood Bowl
⓰ Hollywood Heritage Museum
⓱ 2000 North Highland Avenue

Intolerance (1916) set at the Fine Art Studio at 4500 Sunset Boulevard

START:
Hollywood and Highland
Center

END:
Hollywood and Highland
Center

TOUR TIME:
About 4 hours

CHAPTERS:
9, 22

day. This tour focuses on the historic stops, then strays into Hollywood Heights to visit landmarks that are off many tourist's itineraries. The route covers a few miles with an uphill stroll. Wear walking shoes, sunscreen, and casual clothing. While all is free, we'll visit two stops that require a (well-justified) entrance fee.

Take the Red Line (the underground LA Metro) to the Hollywood Blvd./Highland Avenue Station. Take the escalator up to Hollywood Boulevard, then step into the Hollywood and Highland complex.

Hollywood and Highland Center

1. The **Hollywood and Highland Center** is the site of the Dolby Theatre, which is the home of the annual Academy Award telecasts. From Hollywood Boulevard, step inside and ascend the glamorous staircase. Illuminated along the sides, you'll see the names of every film to win an Academy Award for Best Picture, arranged in chronological order.

Dolby Theatre

The design is based on scenery in D.W. Griffith's film *Intolerance*, one of the most elaborate spectacles in the history of silent movies.

Stairs to the theatre

On Oscar night, **Loews Hollywood Hotel** on the adjacent property is filled with hair stylists, make-up artists and dressers to assist Oscar nominees and guests before making their entrances in front of the cameras and entering the Dolby Theatre.

Take the elevators to the third or fourth floors, then use the crosswalk that faces to the north. Hollywood and Highland provides one of the best views of the Hollywood sign, and is a fun place to take a photo.

Shopping complex

Next, navigate to street level, and head to the left (east) toward the corner of Highland Avenue. Our first stop is on the diagonal corner of Highland Avenue and Hollywood Boulevard. You'll see many attractions aimed at tourists. Our destination is the most authentic attraction on the block:

View of Hollywood sign

2. The historic Max Factor studio, now called **The Hollywood Museum**.

Cross the street to the east and again to the south. Head to 1660 North Highland Avenue. This is the first stop that requires an admission fee. Take the elevator to the top floor, then work your way down. The Studio opened in 1928. See where make-up magician Max Factor hosted all of Hollywood's performers, where he invented new technology for the burgeoning film industry, and for retail sales, too.

The Hollywood Museum

The museum is filled with costumes and props from your favorite movies, old and recent. You will gain insight into the art of filmmaking, and how it evolved. See: thehollywoodmuseum.com

Front of Max Factor studio, 1939

3. Hollywood Boulevard.
From the front door of the museum, turn right (north). At the corner, turn right again, onto Hollywood Boulevard. (Turn the corner, but don't cross the street just yet.)

Hollywood Boulevard

Red sign with historic facts

Walk of Fame indicators: Film

Stage

Television

Special Accomplishments

Amidst the attractions (and the crowds), notice the 1920s architecture from the days when Hollywood Boulevard was an important shopping street for the show biz elite.

While exploring Hollywood Boulevard: look up, and look down.

Look up to see signs about the significance of where you're standing. Follow the signs, if you'd like, to take a tour of this historic street. The red signs disclose interesting facts, famous names, and vintage photos. The tour continues on both sides of Hollywood Boulevard.

Look down to see the Hollywood Walk of Fame beneath your feet. Names are honored in five categories, indicated by the brass medallion in the center of the star. See if you can spot them all. They are:

Film (designated with an old-fashioned movie camera)

Stage (designated by the masks of comedy and tragedy, the hardest ones to find!)

Music (honored with a vinyl record and stylus)

Radio (honored with a classic ribbon microphone)

Television (indicated by an old TV with rabbit-ear antennae)

There are several commemorative stars interspersed on the sidewalk too, to celebrate special accomplishments that affected the entertainment industry.

Want to snap your photo beside your favorite celebrity's star? For a list and the address for each one, see: www.walkoffame.com/starfinder

Two new stars are added each month. Unveilings start at 11:30 a.m., always attended by celebrity guest speakers. Check online to see who will receive the star treatment next, and where the ceremony will take place. Star ceremonies are free (no tickets required).

Adding a new star

There are two notable landmarks to visit as you head east on Hollywood Boulevard:

4. At 6712 Hollywood Blvd., notice the **Egyptian Theatre**, built in 1922, years before the invention of sound movies. That year, King Tutankhamen's tomb was discovered in Egypt, and an Egyptian craze swept the nation, inspiring this remarkable structure. Now a National Landmark both inside and out, the Egyptian was developed by Charles E. Toberman, who would gain even greater fame five years later with his Chinese Theatre. The Egyptian originally cost $800,000 to build; the renovation, completed in 1998, cost $12.9 million. The Egyptian is famous for the openings of silent film classics, including *Robin Hood* and *The Ten Commandments*. Owned today by the non-profit American Cinematheque, the theater is open for screenings of movie classics (from many countries), now featuring state-of-the-art sound. For a schedule, see www.americancinemathequecalendar.com

Grauman's Egyptian Theatre

Theatre building

Theatre interior, 1922

5. Cross to the north side of Hollywood Boulevard, where you'll find the oldest restaurant in Hollywood. Built in 1919, **Musso & Frank**, at 6667 Hollywood Boulevard, was the place to be seen in the days when Hollywood was first being built. It's where some of the

View from the Theatre, 1928

Musso & Frank

Musso & Frank in 1919

Sinatra and Bacall in 1955

Frederick's of Hollywood

Frederick's catalog, 1959

first movie deals were made—because Musso & Frank installed the town's first pay phone. Regular customers were Hollywood's A-List: including Charlie Chaplin, Mary Pickford and Douglas Fairbanks. Years later, it's where Joe DiMaggio wooed Marilyn Monroe, where Humphrey Bogart dated Lauren Bacall, where Greta Garbo had breakfast with Gary Cooper.

With the Writers Guild offices across the street, Musso & Frank was also the hangout for America's literary greats. John Steinbeck, Raymond Chandler, F. Scott Fitzgerald, Dorothy Parker and many others could be found at the mahogany bar. Today, the restaurant is a reminder of Hollywood's history. Even the menu remains much as it was 90 years ago.

Continue west on Hollywood Boulevard, back toward the Dolby Theatre.

6. At 6751 Hollywood Boulevard, you'll pass another famous landmark: **Frederick's of Hollywood**.

In 1946, Frederick Mellinger introduced black lingerie to the American market, revolutionizing women's intimate apparel. A few years later, he followed that success with "The Rising Star," the world's first push-up brassiere. With his designs seen on Hollywood's most glamorous actresses, his garments were an enormous success; he influenced the women's apparel industry for decades. Frederick's is open daily.

Head west, cross the intersection at Highland Avenue.

7. As you cross, look north to see the **Hollywood United Methodist Church**. We'll be there soon, taking a scenic route to approach it. Stay on the north side of Hollywood Boulevard; continue to walk west, past the Dolby Theatre.

United Methodist Church

8. You'll have a great view of the historic **El Capitan Theatre** on the south side of Hollywood Boulevard. Owned by The Walt Disney Company, it's been the site of Disney premieres for decades. Open to the public daily, the El Capitan is one of the last movie theaters in America to maintain an old-fashioned theater organ. Audiences are entertained with a live organ recital before every show, included in the ticket price.

El Capitan Theatre

On the north side of the street, you're approaching one of Hollywood's most enduring landmarks:

El Capitan Theatre, 1920s

9. The **Chinese Theatre**. Following the success of his Egyptian Theatre down the street, developer Charles E. Toberman built this giant Chinese pagoda for entrepreneur Sid Grauman five years later. The theater opened in May 1927, five months before the first talking picture premiered in New York; it soon became the largest theater in America to be wired for sound. With one of the largest movie screens on earth, the Chinese has always been a site for red carpet premieres, including: *A Star is Born, Star Wars*, the *Harry Potter* films, and countless other hits. During the 1940s, it was also home to the Academy Awards ceremonies.

Chinese Theatre

The forecourt at the Chinese Theatre features the handprints and signatures of nearly 200

Opening night, 1927

Handprint and signature

Roosevelt Hotel

Hotel interior

Academy Awards ceremony, 1927

Monroe at Roosevelt Hotel

movie stars, spanning every decade since the 1920s, from silent movie comics like Harold Lloyd to recent stars like Eddie Murphy. As movie promotions, some movie cowboys embedded the horseshoe prints from their horses, Al Jolson embedded his famous knees, and Daniel Radcliffe embedded *Harry Potter's* magic wand. Step inside and look for your favorite performers.

10. Farther west, at the intersection of Orange Drive, cross to the south side of Hollywood Boulevard for a visit to the **Roosevelt Hotel**.

Built in 1927, the Roosevelt is one of the oldest structures in Hollywood, yet still one of the trendiest. Invitations to latenight cocktail parties by the pool are highly prized. Marilyn Monroe lived here for two years; Clark Gable and Carole Lombard occupied the penthouse, which is now named for them.

In 1929, the Roosevelt's ballroom was the site of the first Academy Awards ceremony. (They presented awards in 12 categories in 15 minutes, then everyone had dinner!) More recently, artist David Hockney painted an underwater mural in its swimming pool.

A frequent location for film and television, the Roosevelt can be seen in: *The Fabulous Baker Boys* (1989), *Quiz Show* (1994), *Catch Me If You Can* (2002), and on television including: *Melrose Place, Murder She Wrote, The Bachelor, Knots Landing,* and *Moonlighting,* and others.

Exit through the front doors of the Roosevelt Hotel to return to Hollywood Boulevard. Walk left, to the corner of Orange Drive. Cross Hollywood Boulevard and stay on Orange Drive, heading north. We'll stroll through Hollywood Heights, a residential neighborhood of vintage architecture surrounded by landmarks.

Hollywood skyline

Notice some of the quaint residences that were erected to capitalize on Hollywood's flashy history. The Nirvana apartments, for example, opened after the success of the Chinese Theatre around the corner.

Nirvana apartments

11. At the north corner, Orange Drive intersects with Franklin Avenue. Ahead is the **Magic Castle**, a private club for Prestidigitators (magicians!). Guests are welcome, but only with a pass from a member. The Castle is filled with surprises and humor, also including an elegant dining room, theaters, a séance room, and hotel accommodations. See: www.magiccastle.com

Magic Castle

Turn right, onto Franklin Avenue, heading toward the Hollywood United Methodist Church. Turn left at the corner of Franklin Avenue and Hillcrest Road, beside the Hollywood United Methodist Church. Take a stroll up the steep incline at Hillcrest Road, into the residential Hollywood Heights.
The first intersection on the right is Glencoe Way. Turn right, onto Glencoe Way, and continue walking east. Follow the short street as it curves into the hills. Straight ahead: 1962 Glencoe Way, also known as:

Hillcrest Road

12. The Freeman House. The exterior conceals its size; the building is actually three stories tall, carved into the steep hillside below. It's

The Freeman House

Entrance to the Freeman House

Wright's textile block style

Architectural sketch

Along Glencoe Way's curves

View from the Heights

a spacious three-bedroom house of nearly 3,000 square feet, with views over Hollywood. Constructed in 1923 by Frank Lloyd Wright, the house for Samuel Freeman is the second construction by Frank Lloyd Wright in LA.

Not open to the public, the building is significant, for it is here that Wright perfected his concrete block construction, creating decorative blocks that are sturdy enough to support the roof. With his son Lloyd Wright as the construction manager, Wright created these hollow, concrete blocks, then aligned them atop of one another and reinforced them with steel rods through the center, similar to creating textiles. Wright's Los Angeles structures are known today as the concrete textile block houses.

Wright stated that buildings in Los Angeles should "grow right out of the soil," as he proved here on Glencoe Way, one that still continues today. In 1986, the Freemans bequeathed the house to the School of Architecture at the University of Southern California (USC).

Next, we'll walk through Hollywood Heights to appreciate some magnificent views, and appreciate more houses that are carved into these Hollywood hills. Follow Glencoe Way as it curves to the north and east.

13. You'll soon see some remarkable views over Hollywood Boulevard to the south and the Hollywood sign to the east. This view is the summit of our hillside trek, an ideal place for photos.

As you continue to walk northward, it appears that Glencoe Way reaches a dead end, but it does not. As houses were built in these hills, long public staircases were built throughout the neighborhood. We're about to visit one of the shortest of those staircases. Walk straight ahead on the stairs to the left.

Staircase, resembling Positano

Follow the stairs to the north. Walk straight. The street winds past some grand houses that were built for Hollywood's early movie stars (plus some newer arrivals, too). The original developers modeled Hollywood Heights to resemble Positano, Italy.

Grand house on the Heights

Over the rooftops, you'll soon see a slender tower that resembles an Italian campanile directly ahead. That's our next destination. Keep the tower within your view as the street curves through the hills.

A slender tower

A short distance ahead, the street intersects with Camrose Drive. Turn right (east) on Camrose Drive to head down the hill. One block down the hill, you'll reach the intersection of High Tower Drive. Turn left onto High Tower Drive.

High Tower Drive

14. The **High Tower** is an elevator. When the original houses were built into the hillside to resemble Positano, sidewalks and steep staircases were installed for access, but residents soon tired of the climb. This elevator, controlled by a key, is for residents' use only.

High Tower

Feel free to climb the stairs and sidewalks if you'd like to explore this quaint Hollywood cul-de-sac. (Sidewalk entrance to the stairs is

The Long Goodbye, 1973

Hollywood Bowl

Art Deco fountain

Hollywood Bowl Museum

Box Office

on the left.) Most buildings are actually divided into apartments with addresses on Broadview Terrace and Los Altos Place, the streets above.

It was here that Robert Altman filmed *The Long Goodbye* in 1973, starring Elliott Gould as detective Philip Marlowe.

Stroll back to Camrose Drive and continue down the hill, where the street intersects with Highland Avenue. Do not cross Highland Avenue. Turn left and continue north.

15. We're heading to the historic **Hollywood Bowl**. Ahead, you'll see the Art Deco fountain that marks the entrance.

The Hollywood Bowl is the largest concert venue in Los Angeles (not including stadiums and arenas like the Staples Center). It's the summer home for the LA Philharmonic when they're not performing in Disney Hall.

Turn left to enter the Hollywood Bowl driveway and walkways. The facility is open to the public for free when performances are not in session. Visit the Hollywood Bowl Museum on the left, a free exhibit open to the public year-round. It explains the history of the famous band shell and the many artists who have performed here.

Next, stroll up the hill toward the Bowl. You'll pass the Box Office, where tickets for upcoming concerts are available. Notice the covered pathway behind the Box Office windows as you continue to walk up the hill.

You'll pass the escalator that leads concertgoers

to the upper levels of the amphitheater.

Continue up the hill, bearing left. You'll see one of many entrances to the enormous Hollywood Bowl. With more than 17,000 seats, ticket holders enter on many levels. Walk inside to view the concert space.

Escalator at the Bowl

Since 1921, practically every great artist on earth has performed here, in every musical style. Rock, jazz, country, ballet, folk tunes, show tunes, pop tunes all sound great under the stars. From Bill Cosby to The Beatles, from Black Sabbath to Barbra Streisand, events continue every summer, many with fireworks!

Hollywood Bowl, 1929

Feel like climbing? Exit the amphitheater from one of the upper levels.

Then, make your way down through the walkways that lead past picnic areas with views of the Hollywood Hills. Many ticket holders pack a meal (or buy one from the café near the Box Office). You'll also discover the *Hollywood Bowl Walk*, ten panels that describe the history and significance of these eighty-eight acres.

Hollywood Bowl, 1940

Back near the Box Office, continue down the walkway, past the museum, toward Highland Avenue. At the Hollywood Bowl exit, turn right onto the Highland Avenue sidewalk. Stroll two blocks downhill to the crosswalk. Cross Highland Avenue here, at the intersection of Milner Avenue. Ahead is probably the oldest building still standing in Hollywood.

Intersection of Milner Avenue

16. Known today as the **Hollywood Heritage Museum**, this barn is director DeMille's first

Hollywood Heritage Museum

Laskey-DeMille Barn

The Squaw Man, 1914

2000 North Highland Avenue

Rudolph Valentino

Hollywood United Methodist
Church

office in Hollywood, the building used to film and edit *The Squaw Man*, Hollywood's first feature film. This is the second (and final) stop with an admission fee.

With docents on hand to explain how DeMille and company created Hollywood's first feature, this barn (moved here from its original Vine Street location) offers insight into the fledgling stages of the film industry.

After visiting the Hollywood Heritage Museum, return to the intersection of Milner and Highland avenues. Turn left. Cross Milner, but do not cross Highland Avenue. Walk downhill on Highland Avenue. You'll soon pass a tower hidden behind a massive ficus tree.

17. The address is officially: **2000 North Highland Avenue**.

It's the former home of silent movie star Rudolph Valentino, the original "Latin lover." The dashing actor starred in high-profile romantic fantasies like *The Sheik* (1921); *Blood and Sand,* (1922), in which he played a bullfighter, and the silent classic *Four Horsemen of the Apocalypse*, the biggest grossing film in history to that date. Today, Valentino's Hollywood mansion is divided into rental apartments. (Actor John Leguizamo lived here briefly in the 1990s.)

Continue the downhill walk on Highland Avenue. Cross Highland at the intersection of Franklin Avenue, heading toward the familiar Hollywood United Methodist Church.

Look into the foliage in the hillside behind the church. Nestled in the trees, you'll see the three-story Freeman House, Frank Lloyd Wright's construction, discreetly carved into the hillside as if it's part of the natural landscape.

Freeman House

To your left, the Hollywood and Highland Center is our final destination, the completion of our loop through Hollywood Heights. Head downhill for one more block.

You'll find a staircase that leads back into the main level.

Hollywood and Highland Center

SUNSET STRIP AND BEVERLY HILLS DRIVING TOUR

You'll need a car for this adventure. We're trekking from the edge of West Hollywood, across the Sunset Strip, to Beverly Hills. The number of famous places within such close proximity will surprise you.

1. Guitar Center
2. Directors Guild of America
3. Laugh Factory
4. Chateau Marmont
5. The Standard
6. Carney's
7. Sunset Tower Hotel
8. The Comedy Club
9. The House of Blues
10. The Mondrian
11. Mel's Drive-In
12. Sunset Plaza
13. Eveleigh
14. The Viper Room
15. Whisky a Go Go
16. Hustler

17. The Roxy
18. One Oak
19. Former office of Geffen Records
20. Sierra Tower
21. Greystone Mansion
22. Beverly Hills Hotel
23. Will Rogers Memorial Park
24. Former home of Gloria Swanson
25. Former home of Milton Berle
26. Former home of Gene Kelly
27. Beverly Hills City Hall
28. Via Rodeo
29. Beverly Wilshire
30. Paley Center for Media
31. Church of the Good Shepherd

START:
Sunset Boulevard and
Vista Street

END:
Church of the Good
Shepherd

TOUR TIME:
About 4 hours

CHAPTERS:
12, 13, 18

There's plenty of walking involved too, so wear sunscreen and walking shoes, but don't dress too casually. We'll visit the famous Polo Lounge in the exclusive Beverly Hills Hotel, and leave you among some of Beverly Hills' most tempting restaurants and shops. Although the tour ends in upscale style, it begins with Sunset Strip's honky-tonk fun.

Drive west on Sunset Boulevard, leaving the Hollywood city limits at the intersection of Vista Street. (You'll see "Hollywood" on the pillar that supports the traffic sign. Here's where the city of West Hollywood begins.) Just west of Vista Street, pull over on the right.

Guitar Center

B.B. King's "Lucille"

1. 7425 Sunset Boulevard is known as the **Guitar Center**. Some of the biggest names in rock-and-roll buy their instruments here, and the area is home to many performers. It's a treasure trove for music lovers, with some of rock's most famous guitars on display, including B.B. King's beloved "Lucille." A decade before the Rock-and-Roll Hall of Fame opened in Cleveland, rock musicians preserved their hands on the sidewalk here. Hollywood may have its movie stars, but rock stars rule the Sunset Strip at the Guitar Center.

Directors Guild of America

2. Drive west. As you cross Fairfax Boulevard, stay in the right lane. On the opposite side of the street you'll see this modern building: the **Directors Guild of America**.

In addition to the Academy of Motion Picture Arts and Sciences that bestows the Oscars, each craft in the entertainment industry has its own guild, or union. SAG-AFTRA, the actors union, is largest, but the Writer's Guild is also nearby, and this place for the Director's Guild.

As you cross the intersection at Hayworth Avenue, look to the right.

3. On the corner ahead, you'll see the **Laugh Factory**, the club that launched many comedy careers. Every famous stand-up comic, from Robin Williams to Roseanne Barr, has performed here. Famous comics like Jerry Seinfeld arrive unannounced to try out new material on a delighted audience.

4. Three blocks ahead, you'll come to Marmont Lane on the right. Drive up the ramp for a quick lap around this history-laden hotel. The **Chateau Marmont** is the Strip's most storied address, where writers, musicians and performers check in for months at a time to be pampered yet left alone.

Robert DeNiro lived in the penthouse for months. John Belushi died in Bungalow #3 after a wild night of narcotics. Tony Randall lived here for years while filming *The Odd Couple* for television; it's where Paul Newman met his future wife Joanne Woodward, where actress Greta Garbo famously hid from the paparazzi to "be alone," and where Sting tried out his new songs on the lobby piano. *Butch Cassidy and the Sundance Kid* was written here, plus *The Music Man, Day of the Locust* and other screenplays. Artists David Hockney, Jasper Johns, Robert Motherwell and Frank Stella have all lived and worked here.

Laugh Factory

Chateau Marmont

Greta Garbo

Entrance of Chateau Marmont

Butch Cassidy and the Sundance Kid, 1969

Googie's

The Standard

Pool at The Standard

Old-time Sunset Strip

Carney's

Coming down Selma, see the open intersection to the left. During the 1960s this was the place for Flower Power, where young Angelenos congregated. The shopping complex beyond was the site of **Googie's**, the coffee shop for which an architectural style is named.

Turn right, back onto Sunset, heading west.

5. Continue west on Sunset Boulevard. Crossing Sweetzer Avenue, you'll discover **The Standard**. The opposite of the Chateau Marmont, The Standard is a place to be *seen*. The lobby gained notoriety for the "installation art" over the front desk, built with a one-way mirror, where spectators watch an attractive guest prepare for bedtime in full view of the lobby. The 24/7 Coffee Shop is open day and night. The pool is a popular venue for glamorous parties.

Continue west on Sunset Boulevard. You're now in the thickest of the old-time Sunset Strip, with billboards, fast-food, and congestion at all times.

6. Carney's is a fast-food joint built inside a repurposed train car. Enormously popular and affordably priced, it's open until 3 a.m. on weekends, and midnight during the week.

7. Continuing west, the Art Deco landmark on the left has had many names: The St. James Club, The Argyle; Marilyn Monroe's former address is now the **Sunset Tower Hotel**, open to the public. The Tower Bar restaurant is an elegant nightspot frequented by Hollywood's A-list.

In its tawdry past: Howard Hughes lived in the penthouse and kept apartments for his mistresses below. John Wayne kept a cow on its terrace. In 1944, Bugsy Siegel got kicked out for running a bookmaking operation from here. Past residents include: Quincy Jones, Zsa Zsa Gabor, Michael Caine, Truman Capote, Paulette Goddard, Clark Gable, and Errol Flynn.

Sunset Tower Hotel

IN THE MOVIES: *Get Shorty* (1995), *The Italian Job* (2003), *The Player* (1992).

Bugsy Siegel

8. Heading west, there are two legendary nightspots at the intersection of Olive Drive. On the right: **The Comedy Club**, where Jim Carrey, David Letterman, Howie Mandel and many others found fame. It was formerly Ciro's, the Strip's first glamorous nightclub, built when Hollywood's early stars had money but not many places to frolic. Gossip columnists eavesdropped on revelers like Ronald Reagan, Judy Garland, Frank Sinatra, Ava Gardner, Marilyn Monroe, Lucille Ball and Desi Arnaz. Onstage, stars like Sammy Davis Jr. entertained their friends.

The Comedy Club

9. On the left is **The House of Blues**, the club owned by John Belushi and Dan Aykroyd, with guest artists each night. The Gospel Brunch packs them in every Sunday. Reservations are a must. www.houseofblues.com/losangeles

The House of Blues

10. Across Olive Drive, those gigantic doors open on **The Mondrian**, the hotel developed by Ian Schrager, cofounder of New York's Studio 54. The Mondrian's Sky Bar is packed with hip, young professionals, and is a favorite among fashion models.

The Mondrian

Mel's Drive-In

11. Cross the busy intersections at LaCienaga Boulevard and Alta Loma. Next on the right: **Mel's Drive-In**, open 24 hours, is recognizable from films and TV shows. Formerly Ben Frank's, this is one of the last authentic Googie structures in LA.

Sunset Plaza

12. Leaving the honky-tonk section of the Strip, these next several blocks comprise **Sunset Plaza**, a collection of upscale boutiques and some of LA's most splendid restaurants.

Eveleigh

13. Eveleigh is one of Sunset Plaza's most alluring restaurants, at 8752 Sunset Boulevard. For decades, actors have been partial owners in many West Hollywood restaurants, including Ryan Seacrest, Rob Lowe, Tori Spelling, Elton John, Ashton Kutcher, Sylvester Stallone and more.

Mickey Cohen's "front" Michael's

Continuing west, exit Sunset Plaza and return to the Strip's colorful past. The road makes a slight curve at Holloway Drive. The modern building on the left corner was the site of gangster Mickey Cohen's storefronts for his bookmaking operation.

The Viper Room

14. On the next block, also on the left, you'll see **The Viper Room**, formerly owned by Johnny Depp. Actor River Phoenix died of a drug overdose here on October 31, 1993. Depp closed the club every year on that date until he finally sold his shares in 2004. In the 1940s, this was the Melody Room, an intimate jazz bar that was allegedly the site of illegal gambling, run by Mickey Cohen and Bugsy Siegel.

15. Coming up on the right, on the corner of Clark Street: that's the **Whisky a Go Go**, 8901 Sunset Boulevard, the epicenter of the 1960s rock-and-roll scene on the Strip. Young women in miniskirts danced in cages: the original go-go dancers. The Doors, featuring Jim Morrison, was the house band. Everybody from Janis Joplin to Frank Zappa played here, loudly.

Whisky a Go Go

16. Approaching Hilldale Avenue, the shop across the street that occupies most of the block is publisher Larry Flynt's contribution to the Strip: the **Hustler** retail store and coffee bar. Not to be upstaged by Hollywood stars, Flynt's sidewalk is a tribute to porn stars; their handprints are preserved in plaques, including his own.

Hustler

Tribute to porn stars

17. Crossing the intersection at Hammond Street, you'll pass **The Roxy**, 9009 Sunset Boulevard, on the right. Bruce Springsteen gave his breakthrough performance here in 1975. Other major players here have included David Bowie, Neil Young, and Prince.

The Roxy

18. Continuing west, **One Oak** is a two-story dance club at 9039 Sunset Boulevard, where Kanye West, Katy Perry and friends are known to celebrate. It's a popular place following events like the Golden Globe Awards, when celebrities descend en masse for private parties.

One Oak

19. Across the street at 9130 Sunset Boulevard is the former office of **Geffen Records**. Owner David Geffen sold the building when he teamed with Steven Spielberg and Jeffrey Katzenberg to form Dreamworks SKG.

Former office of Geffen Records

Doheny Road

Sierra Tower

Greystone Mansion

Gardens of Greystone Mansion

That's the end of the Sunset Strip.

You just crossed Doheny *Drive*. You're headed toward Doheny *Road*. Make sure you're in the right lane. Sunset Boulevard curves to the left, but you don't. We're about to enter Beverly Hills. Drive straight ahead, past the triangular traffic island that leads to Doheny Road.

20. You'll pass the high-rise **Sierra Tower**. Past and current residents include: Cher, Elton John, Sidney Poitier, Diahann Carroll, Evander Holyfield, Courtney Cox, Matthew Perry, Ozzie and Sharon Osbourne, and many more.

21. You've left West Hollywood. In Beverly Hills, for the rest of this adventure, all street signs are white. We're heading to the **Greystone Mansion**. Drive to the intersection of Loma Vista Drive, then turn right. A short distance ahead, signs direct you to free parking at the Greystone Mansion. Turn left. (The gates close at 5 p.m.)

Park and follow the sidewalk that leads to this palatial courtyard. This is the home of Ned Doheny, scion of Edward L. Doheny, the wealthiest oilman in the world. Ned was shot to death here in 1929.

Today, the Doheny estate is owned by the City of Beverly Hills. It's comprised of 18.3 acres, including unpaved bridle paths that are easy hikes. Explore the paths and the mansion. The place will seem familiar from films and television shows.

Then return to the car. Retrace your route to the park entrance, then turn right, back to Doheny

Road. Turn right on Doheny Road and observe residential Beverly Hills. At the intersection of Schuyler Road, turn left (south). The tour heads downhill, back to Sunset Boulevard. Continue down Schuyler Road to Mountain Drive. Bear right. Mountain Drive curves, delivering you to the intersection of Sunset Boulevard. Turn right, onto Sunset Boulevard, continuing west.

Beverly Hills mansion

You'll pass mansions on this busy street. It's the architecture that Billy Wilder had in mind when he made the film *Sunset Boulevard*. But today's celebrities cannot live within view of the street, for the paparazzi watch their every move.

Beverly Hills Hotel

22. After passing Rexford Drive, stay in the right lane. You're approaching the intersection of several streets. Bypass Beverly and Crescent drives in quick succession. Aim to turn right at the most distant option, farthest west. It's the driveway to the famous **Beverly Hills Hotel**, one of the grandest inns on earth. Lovingly known as The Pink Palace, the hotel was built in 1912, before the city of Beverly Hills even existed.

Hotel front

Beverly Hills Hotel, 1930

There are two options for parking. The first (and easiest) option is to give your car to the valet for a small fee. Or drive past the valet, into the self-parking lot.

Follow the red carpet to the front door of the Beverly Hills Hotel, then step inside. Explore this five-star hotel. Our primary destination is the fabled **Polo Lounge**.

Polo Lounge

From the front entrance, bear to the left, past the concierge desk. Walk to the mahogany

The Lounge's outdoor patio

Bungalows

Hepburn and Tracy

Will Rogers Memorial Park

Beverly Hills Hotel on the Eagles'
Hotel California jacket, 1977

wall. Step inside the Polo Lounge. When movie moguls ran the studios, this restaurant was the center of power. Long before cellphones, Hollywood dealmakers could have hardwired phones brought to their tables. The indoor bar was a favorite meeting place for Frank Sinatra, Dean Martin and other cronies. It's one of the most cherished hideaways in all of LA.

"Hideaway" is a literal term at the Beverly Hills Hotel. There are 21 unique bungalows for privacy. Stroll outside (back into the lobby, then turn right) to explore. To avoid scandals in the twentieth century, movie studios rented bungalows for movie star trysts that had to stay out of the press. In these bungalows, Katharine Hepburn and Spencer Tracy had a secret affair, and Carole Lombard dallied with Clark Gable. Elizabeth Taylor honeymooned here—more than once.

23. From the front entrance, walk back to the crosswalk at Sunset Boulevard. Wait for the light, then cross Sunset Boulevard to the park across the street. In 1926, popular vaudeville and movie star Will Rogers was named the "Honorary Mayor" of Beverly Hills. A generous philanthropist, years after his death, the park was renamed in his honor as the **Will Rogers Memorial Park**.

After your park visit, return to the car and exit the Beverly Hills Hotel.

You'll be on the hotel's western border. Turn left, head east for a short distance, and pass the entrance. Turn left on Crescent Drive, heading north (slightly uphill). On your left will be private entrances to the hotel's bungalows.

24. Look to the right as you drive up the street. Here are the former residences of two major celebrities. 904 North Crescent Drive is the former home of actress **Gloria Swanson**.

Former home of Gloria Swanson

25. Two doors away at 908 North Crescent Drive is the former home of **Milton Berle**, one of the pioneers of early television.

Gloria Swanson

Continue up Crescent Drive. At the intersection of Lexington Road, continue straight. Crescent Drive curves, and you'll see multi-million-dollar residences here. This is a sample of the sumptuous housing in Beverly Hills.

The alternative: these are public streets with sidewalks and free parking. Leave the car, then take a stroll on the tree-lined sidewalks, past Beverly Hills mansions.

Former home of Milton Berle

This tour now heads south, to Rodeo Drive and the famous shopping district in downtown Beverly Hills. As Crescent Drive completes its arc, the street name changes to Oxford Way. Continue down the hill, heading south. The street name changes again shortly. Oxford Way merges with Hartford Way for one short block. Proceed straight ahead at the Sunset Boulevard intersection. This is the starting point for **Rodeo Drive**.

Milton Berie

The area of Beverly Hills south of Sunset Boulevard is known as Beverly Flats (no joke!) to distinguish it as the shopping district. A few blocks ahead, the zoning changes, and there are no more residences.

Rodeo Drive

Former home of Gene Kelly

Gene Kelly in *Singin' in the Rain*

Beverly Hills City Hall

Shopping district

Special turquoise sign

Continue south on Rodeo Drive, crossing the intersection of Lomitas Avenue. In the days when the outer limits of Beverly Hills had no paved roads or water service, these centrally located residences were popular with early Hollywood stars.

26. 725 Rodeo Drive is the former home of **Gene Kelly**, who received an honorary Oscar in 1952 for his "versatility as an actor, singer, director and dancer, and specifically for brilliant achievements in the art of choreography on film."

Continue south on Rodeo Drive. **Santa Monica Boulevard** is the shopping district's northern boundary. The district is comprised of about 18 blocks, with Rodeo Drive in the center.

27. Looking east, this beautiful structure with the mosaic dome is **Beverly Hills City Hall** (at Santa Monica Boulevard and Rexford Drive.) It's also the site of the Police Department, Fire Department and Public Library.

As you cross Santa Monica Boulevard, look for the turquoise signs. They indicate free parking provided by the City of Beverly Hills. You'll find entrances mid-block. There's one on almost every block within the shopping district.

From here, you're on your own. Enjoy the restaurants, fashions, gifts, hotels, and window-shopping.

28. There's a popular place for photos as you stroll down Rodeo Drive. Look for **Via Rodeo**, between Dayton Way and Wilshire Boulevard.

Via Rodeo is a charming cobblestone cul-de-sac that leads to the Versace showroom and Tiffany & Co., among other shops.

29. Just south of Via Rodeo, the grand hotel on the corner of Rodeo Drive and Wilshire Boulevard is the **Beverly Wilshire**. Look familiar? It's where Julia Roberts fell in love with Richard Gere in *Pretty Woman* (1990). Elvis Presley lived here for years when filming at Paramount. A decade later, John Lennon stayed here, too. Why? Because he heard that Elvis lived here!

30. In addition to restaurants and boutiques, consider a visit to the **Paley Center for Media**, formerly the Museum of Television and Radio, at 465 North Beverly Drive. With about 150,000 television shows and commercials, it's the place for television research or reminiscence. Founded by William S. Paley, who built CBS Television, the Center is dedicated to the preservation of television programs as art, history, and a record of our culture.

31. The **Church of the Good Shepherd**, 501 North Bedford Drive, is the only Catholic Church in Beverly Hills, the place where Frank Sinatra and many other famous Catholics have been laid to rest.

Via Rodeo

Beverly Wilshire

Pretty Woman, 1990

Paley Center for Media

Church of the Good Shepherd

SANTA MONICA AND VENICE BEACH DRIVING TOUR

Three unforgettable places are explored on this day by the ocean, all free (except for food and parking). We're traveling from Pacific Palisades to Santa Monica to Venice. You'll need a car to drive along the Pacific Coast, then walking shoes and sunscreen for garden paths, sandy beaches and a busy boardwalk.

SANTA MONICA
1. Santa Monica Pier
2. Santa Monica State Beach
3. Muscle Beach

VENICE BEACH
4. The Venice Canals
5. Mural of Abbot Kinney
6. Venice Boardwalk
7. Mural of Jim Morrison
8. Mural, *Homage to A Starry Night*

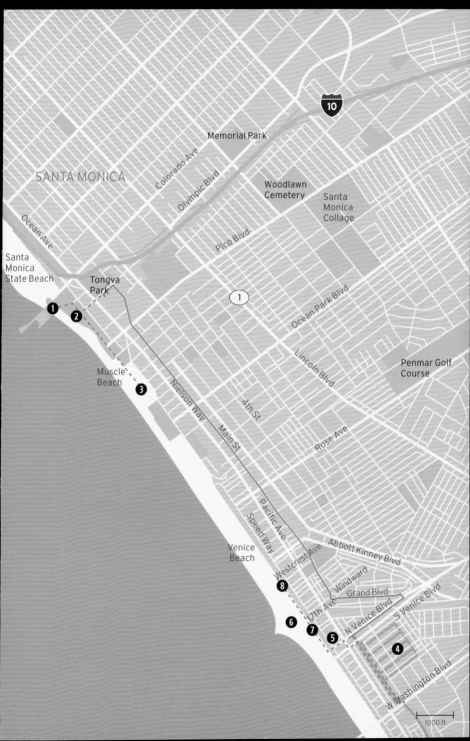

START:
Santa Monica Pier

END:
Wave Crest Avenue

TOUR TIME:
About 3 hours

CHAPTERS:
7, 9, 11, 14, 20

Route 66 was the first U.S. Highway to connect Chicago to the Pacific Ocean. For much of the twentieth century, locals called it the Main Street of America, the road that migrant workers followed as they populated the West. It all ended here, at Santa Monica Pier.

∽∾

1. Santa Monica Pier

Whether you're parked to the north or south, you can't miss the sidewalks leading to the **Santa Monica Pier**. Your destination is the wooden pier, built in 1909.

Today you'll find restaurants and rides. The Santa Monica Looff Hippodrome houses one of America's oldest carousels, built in 1922, now a National Landmark.

Exit the Pier on the south side (toward parking lots 3 and 4) for a stroll on the sand and the paths.

Entrance to Santa Monica

Santa Monica Pier

State Beach

2. Santa Monica State Beach

Paths for bicycles and pedestrians weave along the coastline. Take a stroll where palm trees meet the Pacific sands. You'll pass volleyball courts, beach cafés, checkerboards, and ...

3. Muscle Beach

Created in the 1930s as a WPA project, then rededicated by the City of Santa Monica in 1989, this was the workout area for famed body builders Jack LaLanne and Joe Gold, among others.

Provided by the City of Santa Monica, the equipment is free to use. Try out the gymnastics equipment, the soft lawn for acrobats, calisthenics bars, and the tight-rope.

The rings at Muscle Beach

Return to the car to leave the City of Santa Monica by traveling south, crossing back into LA in the neighborhood called Venice. We'll get there via Main Street in Santa Monica.

If you're parked in Lots 3 or 4 (south of the Pier), drive two blocks east, away from the ocean. When you reach Main Street, turn right, heading south.

View of the Pier from the beach

If you're parked in Lots 1 or 2 (north of the Pier), follow the Exit signs; you'll land on Pacific Coast Highway heading south. Bear right. Avoid the traffic heading into the tunnel and the freeway beyond. Drive up the surface road ramp to the right. It's called Moomat Ahiko Way. (You'll see the sign overhead.) Turn right onto Ocean Avenue. Continue on for almost a half-mile. At the intersection of Pico Boulevard, turn left, east, away from the ocean. Travel for one block, get in the right lane, and turn right. Now you're on Main Street.

Santa Monica Beach, 1880

Main Street

The streets are lined with one-of-a-kind shops and restaurants. Zuma Jay, the proprietor of The Boarding House, where Hollywood's coolest kids get their surfboards and wetsuits, was elected to the City Council in Malibu in 2008. After one term, he gave it up to return to the boards and the business he loves.

Zuma Jay

Continue south on Main Street for almost two miles. The street changes from Main Street in

Windward Avenue

Venice Beach, 1912

Ship Cafe at the Pier, 1906

The Venice Canals

House on the Canal

Santa Monica to Main Street in Venice.

Straight ahead, you approach a traffic circle. Drive around 3/4 of the traffic circle to Grand Boulevard. Stay in the right lane. (Don't be confused by signs pointing to South Venice Boulevard. We're heading to North Venice Boulevard.)

Drive for three blocks (past Andalusia Avenue; that's your marker). When you come to this intersection, turn right, and follow the curve onto North Venice Boulevard. That turn reverses your direction; you're now heading directly west toward the Pacific Ocean.

There's a parking lot on your left as you approach Pacific Avenue. Park here, or continue straight, across Pacific Avenue. There's indoor parking on the left, closer to the beach. If you're lucky, you may find parallel parking on either side of this one-way street.

Welcome to Venice, originally developed by Abbot Kinney, who was so inspired by the canals in Venice, Italy, that he built a community connected by a network of canals. To visit the canals, walk south on Pacific Avenue, then turn left onto South Venice Boulevard. Walk east for a few paces and you'll find an unforgettable oasis.

4. The Venice Canals
Created in 1905, the Venice Canal district was honored as a National Landmark in 1982. There are sidewalks along the canals. Step forward to experience the surreal beauty. Every house has a dock with a boat mooring.

Continue walking south along the canal. Traffic crosses at West Washington Boulevard. Cross the bridge, then follow the sign to stroll back on the opposite side of the canal (toward your car).

Less than a quarter of Abbot Kinney's canals exist today. Nearby canals once included a dance hall, an auditorium, a ship restaurant and a block-long shopping arcade. When Venice became part of the City of Los Angeles in 1911, Huntington's Red Cars stopped here, but when the trolleys were dismantled, LA paved many canals into streets. Remember Grand Boulevard? It was originally the Grand Canal.

Your stroll ends at South Venice Boulevard, where you started. From the Boulevard, walk to Pacific Avenue. Turn Left on North Venice Boulevard, heading toward the ocean.

5. You'll pass the giant mural of Venice's founder, **Abbot Kinney**. The 50-foot by 20-foot mural was created by Rip Cronk, one of America's most prominent muralists. This tour visits two more murals by Rip Cronk.

At the corner where North Venice Boulevard meets the intersection, turn right to visit the famous . . .

6. Venice Boardwalk
Different from the Santa Monica waterfront, the Boardwalk in Venice is a more honky-tonk affair, with vendors selling everything from fast food to T-shirts and henna tattoos.

The Venice community includes a number of

North Venice Boulevard

Venice Beach, 1905

Abbot Kinney mural

Venice Boardwalk

Bathhouse, c. 1925

Venice Beach, 1920s

The Boardwalk

Pumping Iron, 1977

Xtreme Sports

Marijuana, by prescription

rich eccentrics, and an assortment of famous artists, writers, actors and musicians. Each summer, more than 200,000 people from all over the world visit the boardwalk daily.

It was here at Ocean Park Beach in Venice that Sister Aimee Semple McPherson went for a dip and didn't come up in 1926. It is also the site where thousands of followers fell to their knees to pray for McPherson's entrance into heaven.

And, the other half of Muscle Beach is installed here. The concrete structure on the left features weight lifting equipment and a posing amphitheater now maintained as a club. Young Arnold Schwarzenegger made this place famous. You can see young Schwarzenegger work out at this site in the 1977 documentary film *Pumping Iron*.

More than 200 movies and television episodes have been filmed on the Venice Beach and Boardwalk. Other titles include *White Men Can't Jump* (1992), *Get Shorty* (1995), *American Gigolo* (1980), *The Doors* (1991), *Thirteen* (2003), *Lords of Dogtown* (2005) and, of course, television's *Baywatch, NCIS: Los Angeles, Three's Company* and *Beverly Hills 90210*.

Near the sand, across from the bookstore, you'll discover Xtreme Sports, where skateboarders perform tricks that seem to defy gravity.

In California, marijuana is legally dispensed to adults with a prescription. One of the attractions on today's boardwalk: a proliferation of medical professionals selling marijuana prescriptions.

Final destinations: Continue north on the boardwalk to visit two of Rip Cronk's murals.

7. At 17th Avenue, turn right, away from the ocean. The parallel street is called the Speedway. Turn right on the Speedway to see Rip Cronk's **mural of The Doors frontman *Jim Morrison***, painted in 1980, nine years after Morrison's death. Morrison grew up in LA, a friend to the Venice arts community for years.

8. Back on the Boardwalk, head north to see another of Cronk's murals. Walk north on the Boardwalk, to Wave Crest Avenue. Turn right to see ***Homage to A Starry Night***. Measuring 17-feet tall and 37-feet wide, the work was completed in 1990.

The day comes to an end. You can retrace your steps along the Boardwalk and the sand to reach your car.

Jim Morrison mural

Homage to A Starry Night

Sennett girls on the beach

INDEX

24/7 Coffee Shop *274*
500 Days of Summer *224*

A
Abbott and Costello Meet
   the Keystone Kops *48*
Academy Awards *94, 99,*
   191, 233, 238, 261, 262
Aykroyd, Dan *121, 275*
Adam-12 *239*
Aguilar, Antonio *222, 225*
Ahmanson Theater *230,*
   238, 239
Ain't Misbehavin' *218*
Airplane! *251*
Albuquerque Morning
   Journal *117*
Alice's Wonderland *95, 96*
Alien Nation *234*
All of Me *121*
Ally McBeal *233*
Alston, Walter *170, 172*
Alta California *10, 12, 16, 23*
Ambassador Hotel *160,*
   161, 186, 188, 190, 191
American Gigolo *185, 290*

América Tropical *130, 132,*
   133, 134, 222, 226
Angelus-Rosedale Cemetery *218*
Angelus Temple *106,*
   108, 109, 110, 111
Animated Cartoons: How
   They Are Made, Their Origin
   and Development *95*
Aniston, Jennifer *121*
Annie Hall *129*
A Place in the Sun *161*
Apollo 13 *191*
Argo *105*
Arizona *14*
Armstrong, Louis *160*
Arnaz, Desi *275*
A Star is Born *250, 261*
A Starry Night *284, 291*
Atchison, Topeka and Santa
   Fe Railroad *47, 54*
Autry, Gene *48, 104*
Avalon *242, 244*
Avery, Charlie *79*
Avila Adobe *222, 225, 226*
Avila, Francisco José *225*

B
Bacall, Lauren *164, 260*
Bahia de los Fumos *10*

Baker, City Marshal Frank *37*
Bale, Christian *121*
Ball, Lucille *217, 275*
Barr, Roseanne *273*
Barrymore, Ethel *100, 251*
Barrymore, John *191, 192, 251*
Barrymore, Lionel *192*
Basie, Count *160*
Batman *121, 176*
Baum, L. Frank *217*
Baxter, Leone *140, 141*
Bay of Smokes *10, 13, 16, 45*
Baywatch *290*
Beach Boys *5, 178,*
   183, 184, 245
Beatles *212, 245, 267*
Beatty, Ned *105*
Beaudry, Prudent *230*
Beechwood Canyon *100, 105*
Beechwood Drive *103,*
   245, 246, 247
Beginners *198*
Bell, Horace *32*
Belushi, John *214,*
   215, 273, 275
Ben Hur *89*
Benny, Jack *218*
Bergman, Ingrid *164*
Berle, Milton *218, 270, 281*

Betzhold, Estelle *112*
Beverly Hills *20, 25, 91, 112,*
115, 116, 120, 121, 122, 124,
129, 162, 214, 215, 217
Beverly Hills 90210 *25, 290*
Beverly Hills Cop *91, 129, 233*
Beverly Hills Hotel *270,*
272, 279, 280
Beverly Wilshire *270, 283*
Big Four *42, 44, 45*
Bilderrain, Jesús *36, 37*
Biltmore Hotel *55, 230, 232*
Birth of a Nation *92, 98, 217*
Black Sabbath *267*
Blade Runner *224*
Blake, Tom *181, 182*
Blanc, Mel *248*
Blood and Sand *268*
Bogart, Humphrey *105,*
126, 162, 164, 260
Bonanza *251*
Bonaventure Hotel *230, 233*
Borgnine, Ernest *121*
Bounds, Lillian *95*
Bowie, David *277*
Bowron, Fletcher *150, 152*
Brice, Fannie *218*
Bridges, Jeff *121*
Bronson, Charles *121*
Brother *152*
Buena Vista Café *270*
Buena Vista Drive *21*
Bugsy *105, 124, 125, 212, 214,*
215, 217, 224, 275, 276
Bundle of Joy *166*
Bunker Hill *6, 220, 230,*
232, 233, 234, 235
Burbank *21, 47*
Burns, County Sheriff James *37*
Burton, Richard *167*
Butch Cassidy and the
Sundance Kid *273*
Butterfield 8 *167*
Bye Bye Birdie *247*

C
Cabrillo *10, 12*
Cadillac Café *156*
Caine, Michael *275*
Cain, James *105*
Cajon Pass *45*
California Constitution *31*
California Institute of
the Arts *132*
Calle de los Negros *29, 37*
Calle del Toro *21*

Cab Calloway *160*
Cambridge, Godfrey *218*
Campaigns Inc. *140,*
141, 142, 143
Canfield *50, 52, 53, 54*
Cantor, Eddie *218*
Capitol Records *242, 244*
Capote, Truman *218, 275*
Carney's *270, 274*
Carradine, David *217*
Carrey, Jim *275*
Carroll, Diahann *278*
Carter, Nell *218*
Casablanca *164*
Catch Me If You Can *224, 262*
Cathedral of Our Lady of the
Angels *33, 230, 231, 239*
Cession Treaty *31*
Chalifour, Martin *202*
Chandler, Harry *59,*
71, 100, 102, 140
Chandler, Norman *238,*
242, 251, 252
Chandler, Otis *144*
Chandler, Raymond *260*
Chan, Jackie *121*
Charlie Chaplin *17, 78, 79,*
81, 87, 92, 97, 98, 138,
146, 150, 217, 260
Chateau Marmont *214,*
270, 273, 274
Chavez, Julian *172*
Chavez Ravine *5, 172,*
173, 174, 175, 301
Chee Long Tong *38*
Cheers *251*
Cher *278*
Chinatown *6, 21, 38, 40, 41,*
75, 129, 220, 222, 224, 227,
228, 229, 233, 300, 301
Chinese American
Museum *222, 226, 227*
Chinese Exclusion Act *40*
Chinese Theatre *76, 219,*
254, 255, 259, 261, 263
Chinigchinich *12, 15*
Chiye Nagano *149*
Chouinard School *132*
Church of the Good
Shepherd *270, 283*
Citizen Kane *138, 185*
City Cemetery *39*
City Hall *10, 39, 231, 238,*
239, 240, 270, 282
Civil War *30, 32, 98, 217*
Clark, Eli P. *100*

Clark Jr., William *248*
Cleopatra *167, 168*
Clooney, George *121*
Club Alabam *154, 159, 160, 161*
Cobb, Lee J. *218*
Cocoanut Grove *160,*
162, 188, 191, 192
Cohan, George M. *164*
Cohen, Meyer H. *126*
Cohen, Mickey *5, 122, 124,*
125, 126, 218, 276, 300
Cole, Nat King *217, 245*
Colors *137*
Colt, Samuel *29*
Comedy Club *270, 275*
Commercial Street *38*
Cooke, John *214*
Cook, James *178*
Coolidge, Calvin *117*
Cooper, Alice *104*
Cooper, Chris *121*
Cooper, Gary *260*
Cornwell, Dean *234*
Coronel Building *36, 37, 38*
Cosby, Bill *267*
Costello, Dolores *251*
Costner, Kevin *121*
Courtley's Exclusive Jewelry *125*
Cox, Courtney *278*
Crabtree, Lotta *4*
Crocker *18, 44, 46*
Cronk, Rip *135, 289, 291, 301*
Cryer, George *159*
CSI: NY *233*

D
Damaged Goods *144*
Dana, Jr., Richard Henry *23*
Darren, James *182, 185*
Davis, Bette *121, 217*
Davis, Clive *216*
Davis Jr., Sammy *217, 244, 275*
Day, Doris *105*
Day-Lewis, Daniel *121*
Day of the Locust *105, 273*
Dead Ringer *121*
Death Becomes Her *121*
Death Valley Days *250*
Death Wish II *25*
de Batuc, Alfredo *135*
Dee, Sandra *182, 185*
DeGeneres, Ellen *251*
DeMille, Cecil B. *82,*
85, 87, 217, 248
DeNiro, Robert *273*
De Palma, Brian *121*

Depp, Johnny 215, 276
Devil in a Blue Dress 161
Dexter 247
Diaz, Porfirio 53
DiMaggio, Joe 218, 260
Directors Guild of
America 270, 272
Disneyland 201, 207, 210
Disney, Lillian 96, 201
Disney, Roy O. 95
Disney, Walt 21, 50, 95,
97, 104, 174, 201, 202,
203, 217, 300, 304
di Suvero, Mark 235
Dodger Stadium 52,
153, 175, 176, 177
Doheny, Edward L. 50, 52,
53, 54, 55, 112, 114, 115,
116, 117, 118, 119, 120, 300
Dolby Theatre 260, 256, 261
Dolemite 161
Dolores del Rio 135
Dora, Miki 182, 183
Dorothy Chandler
Pavilion 230, 238
Double Indemnity 17
Downey, John G. 45
Dragnet 239
Dragon Seed 41, 229
Dr. Strangelove 247
DuBois, W.E.B. 157, 158, 159
Dunbar Hotel 159, 161
Dunbar, Paul Lawrence 159
Duncan, U.S. Corporal Lee 99
DuPont 140
Duran Duran 245

E
E.T. Earl 71
Easy Rider 185
Eaton, Fred 68, 70, 73
Ed Sullivan Show 183
Egyptian Theatre 254, 259, 261
Einstein 144
Eisenberg, Jesse 121
Eisenhower 143, 252
El Camino Real 12
El Capitan Theatre 254, 261
Eli P. Clark, 100
Ellington, Duke 160
Elliot, "Mama" Cass 218
El Pueblo 6, 13, 18, 220,
222, 224, 225, 226
El Pueblo de Nuestra Señora
la Reina de Los Angeles
de Porciúnculá 13, 18

El Rio de Nuestra Señora
la Reina de Los Angeles
de Porciúnculá 13
Embarcadero 6
Entourage 251
Entwistle, Peg 103, 104
ER 233
Eraserhead 121
Essanay 80
Eveleigh 270, 276

F
Fairbanks, Douglas 100,
116, 248, 260
Fall, Albert B. 50, 52,
114, 115, 116, 117
Fandango 18, 21
Farnum, Dustin 82, 83
Fast and Furious 4 41
Fatty Arbuckle 79, 87
Ferenz, F. K. 132
Fields, Totie 218
Firehouse 222, 226
Firestone Tires 56, 62
Fisher, Carrie 166, 168
Fisher, Eddie 166, 167
Fisher, Todd 166
Fitzgerald, F. Scott 260
Flynn, Errol 275
Flynt, Larry 105, 277
Foo Fighters 245
Foreign Miners Tax Law 28
Forest Lawn Cemetery 111, 166
Forest Lawn Glendale 216, 217
Forest Lawn Hollywood
Hills 215, 217
Forrest Gump 191, 251
Fort Hill 33
Four Horsemen of the
Apocalypse 268
Francis, Anne 105
Franciscan Friars 12, 16
Franklin, Aretha 245
Franklin, Bonnie 218
Frasier 251
Frederick's of
Hollywood 254, 260
Freeman House 254,
263, 264, 269
Freeth, George 178,
180, 181, 184
Freleng, Friz 95
Frémont 24, 25
Fresh Prince of Bel Air 247
Funicello, Annette 218
Funny Girl 247

G
Gable, Clark 162, 165,
217, 262, 275, 280
Gabor, Zsa Zsa 275
Gandhi, Mahatma 111
Gangster Squad 41,
63, 105, 239
Greta Garbo 260, 273
Gardner, Ava 125, 126, 191, 275
Garfield II 121
Garland, Judy 89, 125, 126, 275
Gaye, Marvin 215
Gay Pride Parade 128
Geffen, David 277
Geffen Records 270, 277, 278
Gehry, Frank 201, 236, 300
General Hospital 248
General Motors 56, 62
Gere, Richard 283
Get Shorty 275, 290
Getty Center 204, 209,
210, 236, 301
George Getty II 242, 252
Getty, J. Paul 6, 204, 206,
207, 251, 252, 300, 301
Getty Oil Company 207
Getty Villa 206, 207, 209
Ghost 251
Ghostbusters 121, 233
Ghostbusters II 121
Gibb, Andy 218
Gibson, Mel 121
Gibson's Gambling House 23
Gidget 5, 178, 182,
183, 184, 185
Glee 251
Glenn, John 188
Goddard, Paulette 275
God Is The Bigger Elvis 169
Goldberg, Whoopi 121
Golden Boy 247
Goldfish, Samuel 82
Gold, Joe 286
Gold Mountain 30
Goldwyn, Samuel 85
Gone With the Wind 166, 192
Goodman, John 121
Googie's 199, 201, 274
Grand Boulevard 288, 289
Grand Park 230, 231,
232, 240, 241
Grauman, Sid 261
Graves, Nancy 235
Grease 185
Great Depression 75, 103, 111,
120, 138, 140, 149, 159, 165

Great Plains Indians 12
Greystone Mansion 112, 116,
  117, 118, 120, 121, 270, 278
Grier, Rosey 188
Griffith, D. W. 79, 98
Guber, Peter 176
Guitar Center 270, 272
Gulf Oil 114
Gunsmoke 250

H
Hampton, Lionel 154
Hanks, Tom 104
Happy Days 251
Harding 50, 114, 116, 117
Hardwick, Lois 95
Harlow, Jean 86, 192
Harman, Hugh 95
Harman, Walker 95
Harriman, E. H. 71
Harrison, George 212, 214
Harry Potter 261, 262
Hart, Dolores 169
Hartman, Brynn 215
Hartman, Phil 215
Hawn, Goldie 121
Hay, Harry 127
Hearst, William Randolph 109,
  138, 141, 142
Heche, Anne 251
Hefner, Hugh 104, 126, 217
Hepburn, Katharine 191
High Tower 254, 255, 265
Hillside Memorial
  Cemetery 91, 126
Hillside Memorial Park 218
Hit Man 137, 161
Hockney, David 262, 273
Holliday, Billie 160
Hollyhock House 194, 196, 197
Hollywood and Highland
  Center 254, 256
Hollywood Bowl 85,
  254, 255, 266, 267
Hollywood Chamber of
  Commerce 104, 105, 300
Hollywood Forever 212, 214,
  216, 217, 218, 242, 248, 250
Hollywood Heights 6, 220,
  256, 263, 264, 265, 269
Hollywood Heritage
  Museum 254, 267, 268
Hollywoodland 4, 63, 100,
  102, 103, 104, 105, 242,
  245, 246, 247, 254, 301
Hollywood Museum 90,

254, 255, 257, 301
Hollywood Nite Life 125
Hollywood Sign Trust 105
Hollywood Tower
  Apartments 242, 245
Hollywood United Methodist
  Church 254, 261, 263, 268
Holyfield, Evander 278
Honeysuckle Rose 218
Hong Chow 36
Hopkins, Mark 44
Hedda Hopper 162
Horne, Lena 160
Horton, Edward Everett 105
House of Blues 270, 275
Houston, Whitney 121, 216
Howard, Moe 126
Hubbard, Sir Charles 126
Hudson, Jennifer 217
Hughes, Howard 191, 275
Humphrey, Hubert 190
Hunt, Helen 121
Huntington, Collis 56, 63
Huntington, Arabella 58, 63, 64
Huntington, Henry 47, 58,
  62, 63, 68, 71, 146, 180
Huntington Library,
  Art Collections and
  Botanical Gardens 63
Hustler 224, 270, 277
Hyde Street Pier 270

I
Immigration Act of 1924 149
Inception 185
Indecent Proposal 121
Independence Day 105
Indian Removal Act 15
International Church of the
  Foursquare Gospel 106
In The Heat Of The Night 250
In The Line Of Fire 233
Intolerance 98, 254, 256
Ising, Rudolph 95
Isozaki, Arata 236
It Happened One Night 165
Iwerks-Disney Commercial
  Artists 95
Iwerks, Ub 95
J
Jackman, Hugh 121
Jackson, Michael 212, 216, 217
Jan and Dean 183
Jay, Zuma 184, 287
Jennings, Dale 127
Jessel, George 92, 218

Jimmie Higgins 144
John, Elton 276, 278
Johns, Jasper 273
Johnson, Lyndon 233
Johnson, Magic 176
Johnson Rafer 188, 189
Jolson, Al 92, 94, 218, 262
Jones, Quincy 275
Janis Joplin 214, 215,
  277, 301, 303
J. Paul Getty Museum 206, 207
Judge Olvera 22
Jumpin' Jack Flash 121

K
Kahanamoku, Duke 178,
  180, 181, 182, 183
Katzenberg, Jeffrey 277
Keaton, Buster 87
Kelly, Gene 270, 282
Kennedy, Beth 108
Kennedy, John F. 186,
  189, 190, 200, 233
Kennedy, Robert F. 186, 190, 191
Kewen, Edward J. C. 29
Keystone Kops 48, 79, 252
Keystone Studios 81, 78, 79
KFSG radio 111
Kid Auto Races At Venice 79
King, B.B. 272
King Creole 169
King of Spain 12
Kinney, Abbot 65, 66,
  284, 288, 289
Klugman, Jack 218
Knots Landing 262
Kohner, Frederick 182
Kohner, Kathy 182, 183
Kostelanetz, André 105
Kutcher, Ashton 276

L
L.A. Confidential 63,
  129, 198, 239
LA Dodgers 146
LaLanne, Jack 286
Lamas, Fernando 218
Lancaster, Burt 218
Lane, Abbe 122
Lansky, Meyer 124
LA Phil Store 237
La Placita 227
Larchmont Village 242,
  244, 252, 253
Lasky, Blanche 82
Lasky, Jesse L. 82, 85

LA Times *141, 203, 207, 241*
Laugh Factory *270, 273*
Laugh-O-Gram *95*
Laurel, Stan *218*
Lautner, John *199*
Law of Capture *54*
Lee, Pinky *218*
Leguizamo, John *268*
Leigh, Vivien *192*
Lemmon, Jack *218*
Lennon, John *283*
Lethal Weapon *3 17, 4, 41*
Letterman, David *275*
Lewis, Jerry *121, 244*
Liberace *217*
Lippincott, Joseph B. *70*
Little Tokyo *146, 148, 149, 152*
Little Tramp *79, 80, 81*
Live from the Hollywood
    Palace *244*
Lloyd, Harold *262*
Lombard, Carole *67,*
    162, 165, 262
London, Jack *178, 180*
Lord Jim *180*
Lorre, Peter *248*
Los Angeles Examiner *109,*
    119, 140, 142, 144
Los Angeles News *30, 33, 34*
Los Angeles Public
    Library *230, 234*
Los Angeles Rangers *32, 33*
Los Angeles Times *29,*
    59, 71, 100, 102, 118, 119,
    140, 144, 150, 186, 214,
    238, 241, 300, 301
Lost Horizon *247*
Lovell House *198*
Lovell Residence *197*
Loving You *169*
Lowe, Rob *276*
Lugosi, Bela *105*
Lumiére Brothers *76*
Lund, Robina *206*
Lutz, Edwin G. *95*
Lynch, David *121*

M
Mabel at the Wheel *80*
Mabel's Strange Predicament *79*
MacGyver *251*
Mad Men *233*
Magic Castle *254, 263*
Maguire, Tobey *121*
Main Street *37, 59, 161,*
    286, 287, 288

Making A Living *78, 80*
Malden, Karl *121*
Malibu *182, 184, 204,*
    207, 209, 287
Manchester, Melissa *105*
Mandel, Howie *275*
Manifest Destiny *26, 28, 30*
Mansfield, Jayne *217, 248*
Manzanar War Relocation
    Center *146, 150, 151*
Marked Woman *164*
Mark Taper Forum *230,*
    238, 239
Martin, Dean *280*
Martin, Steve *121*
Mattachine Society *127*
Matthau, Walter *218*
Max Factor *86, 87, 88,*
    89, 90, 91, 218, 300
Mayer, Louis B. *84, 141*
McAllister, Wayne *199*
McCarthy, Joe *173*
McDaniel, Hattie *218*
McPherson, Aimee Semple *106,*
    110, 111, 142, 217, 290, 300
McPherson, Harold *108*
Meier, Richard *209*
Mellinger, Frederick *260*
Melrose Place *262*
Mel's Drive-In *270, 276*
Mercer, Johnny *88*
Merchants Exchange
    Building *242*
Merriam, Frank *141*
Methot, Mayo *164*
Metro-Goldwyn-Mayer *84*
Mexican-American
    War *25, 26, 29*
Mexican Petroleum Company *53*
MGM *84, 89, 141, 165,*
    166, 167, 169, 304
Michael's Exclusive
    Haberdashery *124*
Mickey Mouse *96, 97*
Mildred Pierce *185*
Mill's Building *242*
Mills, Hayley *121*
Miranda, Carmen *245*
Mister Roberts *180*
Mitchum, Robert *126*
Mondrian *270, 275*
Moneo, Rafael *240*
Monroe, Marilyn *217, 218,*
    219, 260, 262, 274, 275
Monterey *14, 22*
Moomat Ahiko Way *287*

Moonlighting *262*
Moore, Demi *121*
Mork & Mindy *251*
Morrison, Jim *277, 284, 291*
Morse, Robert *121*
Mortimer Mouse *96*
Morton, Jelly Roll *156*
Moses, Robert *170, 172, 175*
Motherwell, Robert *273*
Mount Saint Mary's College *120*
Mount Sinai Memorial Park *218*
Mr. Smith Goes To
    Washington *247*
Mulholland, William *68,*
    70, 75, 300
Murder She Wrote *262*
Murphy, Eddie *121, 262*
Murray, Bill *121*
Muscle Beach *185, 284,*
    286, 287, 290
Museum of Contemporary
    Art *230, 231, 236*
Music Center *54, 201, 230,*
    231, 237, 238, 239, 240
Musso & Frank *254, 259, 260*
My Man Godfrey *165*

N
National Historic Landmark
47, 85, 137, 152 , 154, 196, 197,
    234, 245, 259, 286, 288
National Register of Historic
    Places *16, 67, 111, 161*
NCIS: Los Angeles *290*
Nelson, Harriet *218*
Nelson, Ozzie *218, 278*
Nelson, Ricky *218*
Neutra, Richard *173, 197*
Neve, Felipe de *13, 14, 15*
Nevelson, Louise *235*
Newman, Paul *168, 273*
New Spain *10*
New Yorker *136, 301*
New York Stock Exchange *44*
New York Times *39, 97, 301*
New York Volunteers *29*
Nigger Alley *29, 30, 31, 36, 40*
Night Sail *230, 235*
Nin Yung *36*
Nirvana apartments *263*
Nisei Week *146, 150, 151, 152*
Nixon, Richard M. *143,*
    144, 190, 244, 252
No Man of Her Own *162, 165*
North By Northwest *48*
NYPD Blue *233*

O

Ocean Avenue 287
Ocean Park Beach 109, 290
Oil! 4, 50, 138
Oil Queen of California 55
Olson, Culbert 143
Olvera Street 16, 22, 25, 130,
    133, 134, 222, 225, 226
O'Malley, Walter 170, 172
One Oak 270, 277
Ordinary People 251
Orozco, José Clemente 130, 132
Oswald the Lucky Rabbit 96
Otis, Harrison Gray 71
Our Lady, Queen of the
    Angels 13, 222, 225, 227
Owens River Gorge Dam 75
Owens Valley 68, 70,
    71, 73, 75, 149

P

Pacific Avenue 288, 289
Pacific Electric Railway 58,
    60, 61, 71, 146, 180
Pacific Light and Power
    Company 54
Pacific Power and Light
    Company 58, 59
Paley Center for
    Media 270, 283
Paley, William S. 283
Pallette, Eugene 99
Paramount Pictures 84
Paramount Studios 242,
    249, 250, 251
Parker, Dorothy 260
Parsons, Louella 162
Pearl Harbor 150, 224
Peck, Gregory 240
Perez, Jesus 188
Pérouse, Galaup de la 14
Perry, Katy 277
Perry Mason 239, 250
Perry, Matthew 278
Pershing Square 55,
    230, 231, 232
Pfeiffer, Michelle 121
Phantom of the Paradise 121
Phoenix Bakery 222, 229
Phoenix, River 215, 276
Pickford, Mary 81, 92,
    116, 250, 260
Pio Pico 23, 24, 225
Playboy Club 126
Plaza Art Center 132
Plunkett, Hugh 115, 116, 117, 120

Point Break 185
Poitier, Sidney 278
Polo Lounge 272, 279, 280
Portolá 12, 13, 20
Post 303
Power, Tyrone 248
Pre-Natal Memories 230,
    235, 236
President Franklin D.
    Roosevelt 140
Presley, Elvis 169, 283
Pretty Woman 105, 191, 283
Price, Vincent 105
Prince 247, 277
Prohibition 116, 124
Promontory Summit 42, 47
Pryor, Richard 216
Pueblo de Los Angeles
    Historic Monument 134
Pumping Iron 290

Q

Queen Hotel 55
Quintero 20
Quiz Show 262

R

Radcliffe, Daniel 262
Raft, George 245
Rain Man 176, 233
Raleigh Studios 242, 249, 250
Ramone, Johnny 216, 217, 248
Rancho San Pedro 21
Rancho San Rafael 21
Randall, Tony 273
Razaf, Andy 218
Reagan, Ronald 217, 250, 275
Rear Window 251
Red Car 64, 109, 301
Redford, Robert 121
Reminiscences of a Ranger 32
Reynolds, Debbie 166, 168
Rice, George 23
Richard Meier & Partners 209
Ricochet 137
Riddle, Nelson 248
Rin Tin Tin 92, 94, 99
Riperton, Minnie 218
Ritter, John 218
Rivera, Diego 130, 132
Roberts, Julia 283
Robertson, Cliff 182, 185, 251
Robin Hood 259
Rockefeller, John D. 53
Rock Star 121
Rodeo de las Aguas 20

Rodeo Drive 281, 282, 283
Rodgerton Drive 242, 246, 247
Rodia, Simon 136, 137
Rogers, Will 270, 280
Roman Catholics 12
Rooney, Mickey 191
Roosevelt Hotel 254, 262
Roosevelt, Theodore 73
Rosa, Esther 86
Route 66 127, 228, 286
Roxy 270, 277
Royal Sport: Surfing
    in Waikiki 180
Runaway Jury 25
Rush Hour 41, 121, 228
Russell, Jane 219
Russell, Rosalind 121

S

Saint Vibiana 240
Salonen, Esa-Pekka 202
Salt Lake Railroad 47
San Bernardino 45, 47
Sanchez, Esteban 36
San Fernando Mountain 45, 46
San Fernando tunnel 42, 46
San Francisco 12, 14, 36, 37,
    39, 42, 45, 47, 60, 112, 138,
    146, 165, 172, 300, 301
San Francisco Examiner 39, 138
San Gabriel 10, 13,
    16, 22, 24, 31
San Pedro 21, 36, 45,
    46, 47, 148
San Pedro Bay 21
Santa Monica Mountains 100
Santa Monica Pier 157,
    284, 286
Santa Monica State
    Beach 284, 286
Sarandon, Susan 121
Savalas, Telly 218
Saved By The Bell 247
Scarface 129
Schindler House 197, 198
Schindler, Rudolph 197
Schrager, Ian 275
Schulberg, Budd 188
Schwarzenegger,
    Arnold 121, 290
Seacrest, Ryan 276
Segel, Jason 121
Seinfeld, Jerry 273
Sellecca, Connie 105
Semple, Robert 108
Sennett, Mack 67, 78, 79, 81

Sepulveda House *222, 226*
Sequi *230, 235*
Sherman, M. H. *100*
Sherman, Moses H. *71*
Shogun *251*
Shore, Dinah *218*
Shoults, Tracy E. *102*
Showdown in Little Tokyo *152*
Siegel, Bugsy *105, 125,*
212, 214, 275, 276
Siege of Los Angeles *24*
Sierra Tower *270, 278*
Silvers, Phil *218*
Simon Rodia Watts Towers
Jazz Festival *137*
Sinatra, Frank *125, 126,*
245, 275, 280, 283
Sinclair Oil *114*
Sinclair, Upton *110, 138,*
140, 142, 144, 300
Singing in the Rain *166, 282*
Siqueiros, David Alfaro *130,*
132, 134, 226
Sirhan Bishara Sirhan *189*
Sister Aimee *106, 108,*
109, 110, 111, 290, 300
Six Feet Under *137, 247, 304*
Slovak, Hillel *218*
Smith, Cathy *214*
Smith, Lucy *115, 119*
Somerville *154, 156, 157,*
158, 159, 160, 161, 301
Southern California Edison *54*
Southern California Fruit
Growers Exchange *49*
Southern California
Gas Company *59*
Southern Pacific *42, 45,*
46, 48, 49, 56, 58, 59,
61, 62, 72, 156, 300, 301
Spelling, Aaron *218*
Spelling, Tori *276*
Spider-Man *121, 233*
Spielberg, Steven *277*
Splash *233*
Splichal, Joachim *237*
Springsteen, Bruce *277*
Stallone, Sylvester *276*
Standard Oil *53, 56,*
62, 114, 140
Star Trek *176, 210, 251*
Star Wars *261*
Steamboat Willie *97*
Stein, Gertrude *56*
Steinbeck, John *260*
Stella, Frank *273*

Stewart, Patrick *121*
Sting *273*
Stockton, Commodore
Robert *24, 25, 300*
Streep, Meryl *121*
Street of the Blacks *29*
Streisand, Barbra *267*
Stripes *121*
Suddenly Last Summer *247*
Summers, Emma *54, 55*
Sunkist *49*
Sunset Boulevard *122, 124,*
126, 129, 209, 212, 228,
247, 251, 272, 274, 277,
278, 279, 280, 281, 301
Sunset-Gower Studios *242,*
247, 248
Sunset Plaza *270, 276*
Sunset Ranch *242, 245, 246*
Sunset Strip *6, 122, 126,*
127, 165, 199, 215, 218,
220, 270, 272, 274, 278
Sunset Tower Hotel *270,*
274, 275
Superman Returns *176*
Surfin' Safari *184*
Suriya Thomas *135*
Swanson, Gloria *67,*
104, 270, 281
Switzer, Carl "Alfalfa" *248*

T
Tarzan *180, 181*
Taylor, Elizabeth *121,*
167, 168, 217, 280
Teapot Dome, Wyoming *114*
Temple, John *23*
Terrigno, Valerie *128*
Texas Rangers *32*
That's So Raven *247*
The Adventurer *144*
The Adventures of
Superman *239, 250*
The Artist *252*
The Bachelor *262*
The Bad News Bears *239*
The Beach Boys *183*
The Best Years Of
Our Lives *250*
The Big Lebowski *121, 129*
The Blue Dahlia *129*
The Bodyguard *121, 152*
The Brady Bunch *251*
The Color Purple *176*
The Crimson Kimono *152*
The Daily Planet *239*

The Defiant Ones *48*
The Department of Building
and Safety *136*
The Dirty Dozen *121*
The Disorderly Orderly *121*
The Doors *126, 129,*
277, 290, 291
The Dragon Seed *41*
The Fabulous Baker Boys *262*
The Fast and the Furious *176*
The Getty Conservation
Institute *133, 210*
The Gnome-Mobile *144*
The Golden Child *121*
The Golden Girls *247*
The Green Hornet *41, 228*
The Hangover *129*
The Hollywood
Reporter *142, 162, 301*
The Human Tornado *161*
The Hustler *224*
The Italian Job *275*
The Jazz Singer *92, 93, 94, 96*
The Jungle *138, 144*
The Karate Kid *185*
The Kid *17*
The Long Goodbye *266*
The Long, Hot Summer *168*
The Loved One *121*
The Magnificent Ambersons *161*
The Money Changers *144*
The Muppets *121*
The Music Man *273*
The Naked Gun *176*
The Odd Couple *251, 273*
The People vs. Larry Flynt *105*
The Plaza *222, 225*
The Pleasure of His
Company *169*
The Prestige *121*
There Will Be Blood *121, 138, 144*
The Roy Rogers and Dale
Evans Show *17*
These Old Broads *168*
The Sheik *192, 268*
The Simpsons *137, 215*
The Social Network *121*
The Squaw Man *82, 83,*
84, 85, 87, 88, 268
The Standard *270, 274*
The Ten Commandments *251,*
259
The Three Stooges *126*
The Trouble With Angels *121*
The Viper Room *215, 270, 276*
The Way We Were *224*

The Wedding Singer *191*
The West Wing *232*
The Wet Parade *144*
The Witches of Eastwick *121*
Thirteen *120, 290*
Thomas, Richard *105*
Thor *210*
Three's Company *290*
Tibbett, Lawrence *251*
Tiffany & Co. *104, 283*
Timberlake, Justin *121*
Time *138, 256, 286*
Toberman, Charles E. *259, 261*
Todd, Mike *167*
Tomlin, Lily *121*
Tootsie *92, 247*
Top Hat *251*
Torero, Mario *135*
Tork, Peter *105*
Toyota, Yasuhisa *202*
Tracy, Spencer *280*
Transcontinental Railroad *30, 40, 42, 46, 78*
Transformers *176, 251*
Triangle Film Corporation *79*
Trillin, Calvin *136*
Trousdale Estates *120*
True Lies *233, 234*
Truman, President *172*
Tucker, Chris *121*
Twilight *198*
Twin Dragon Gateway *222, 228*
Two Years Before the Mast *23, 300*

U
Union Pacific *42, 46, 48*
Union Square *6, 242*
Union Station *37, 40, 110, 176, 222, 223, 224, 229*
Universal Studios *96, 200*

V
Valentino, Rudolph *192, 217, 248, 268*
Valley of the Dolls *185*
Vampira *217, 248*
Van Gogh *210*
Variety *97*
Venice Beach *284*
Venice Boardwalk *284, 289*
Venice Blvd *285, 288, 289*
Venice Canals *284, 288*
Venice Reconstituted *135*
Verdugo, Jose Maria *21*
Vertigo *251*

Via Rodeo *270, 282, 283*
Viceroy *12*
Viceroyalty *10*
Villaraigosa, Mayor Antonio *134*
Vitaphone *93*

W
Wahlberg, Mark *121*
Walk of Stars *244*
Walt Disney Concert Hall *50, 201, 202, 203, 230, 232, 236*
Walt Disney Studios *21*
War Games *252*
Warner Brothers *92, 94, 99, 164*
Warner, Harry *92, 94*
Warner, Jack *92, 94*
Warner, Sam *93, 94*
War of the Worlds *239*
Waterworld *75*
Watts *136, 137, 156*
Watts Towers *136*
Watts Towers of Simon Rodia State Historic Park *137*
Wayne, John *275*
We Are Not A Minority *135*
Weissmuller, Johnny *180, 185*
West Coast Land and Water Company *59*
Western Addition *6*
West Hollywood *3, 5, 122, 127, 128, 129, 197, 270, 272, 276, 278, 301*
West, Kanye *277*
West, Mae *82*
West Washington Boulevard *218, 289*
Westwood Memorial Park *218*
What Ever Happened To Baby Jane? *250*
What Women Want *121*
Where The Boys Are *169*
Whisky a Go Go *126, 270, 277*
Whitaker, Clem *140, 141*
Whiteman, Paul *105*
White Men Can't Jump *290*
Whitley Heights *244*
Whitley, Hobart Johnstone *244*
Who Framed Roger Rabbit? *56, 63*
Whose Line Is It Anyway? *250*
Widney, Robert M. *39*
Wiggins *48, 49, 301*
Wilder, Billy *218, 279*
Williams, Andy *104, 188*
Williams, Harold M. *208*

Williams, Robin *273*
Will Rogers Memorial Park *270, 280*
Wilson, Carl *218*
Wilson, President *98*
Windsor Square *100, 102, 103, 242, 251, 252*
Winkler, Margaret *95, 96*
Winkler, Otto *166*
Winter Kills *121*
Winters, Jonathan *121*
Wonderful Wizard of Oz *217*
Wonderland *95, 96, 234*
Wong, Anna May *218*
Wood, Natalie *218*
Woodruff, S. H. *102*
Woodward, Joanne *168, 273*
World War I *53, 74, 99, 114*
Wray, Faye *217, 248*
Wright, Frank Lloyd *194, 196, 201, 264, 269, 300*
Writers Guild *260*
Wyman, Jane *217*
Wyman, Roz *175*

X
X-Men *121*
Xtreme Sports *290*

Y
Yang-na *10, 12, 13, 15, 16*
You are the Star *135*
Young, Neil *277*
Yut Ho *34, 36, 40*

Z
Zappa, Frank *277*

BIBLIOGRAPHY

Books:

Basten, Fred E., *Max Factor's Hollywood*, General Publishing Group, Los Angeles, 1995.

Beebe, Lucius, *The Central Pacific and Southern Pacific Railroads*, Howell-North Books, Berkeley, California, 1963.

Bennett, Shelley M., *The Art of Wealth*, The Huntington Library, San Marino, California, 2013.

Berges, Marshall, *The Life and Times of Los Angeles: A Newspaper, A Family and A City*, Atheneum, New York, 1984.

Bonino, Mary Ann, *The Doheny Mansion*, Edizioni Casa Animata, Los Angeles, 2008.

Bottles, Scott L., *Los Angeles and the Automobile*, University of California Press, Los Angeles, 1987.

Buntin, John, L.A. *Noir*, Harmony Books, New York, 2009.

Burke, Margaret Tante, *Are The Stars Out Tonight*, Round Table West, Los Angeles, 1980.

Carr, Harry, *Los Angeles City of Dreams*, Grosset & Dunlap Publishers, New York 1935.

Chang, Iris, *The Chinese in America*, Viking, New York, 2003.

Chaplin, Charles, *My Autobiography*, Simon and Schuster, New York, 1964.

Cho, Jenny and the Chinese Historical Society of Southern California, *Chinatown in Los Angeles*, Arcadia Publishing, San Francisco, 2009.

Comer, Virginia Linden, *Los Angeles, A View from Crown Hill*, Talbot Press, Los Angeles, 1986.

Dana, Richard Henry, *Two Years Before the Mast*, The World Publishing Company, Cleveland, Ohio, 1946.

Davis, Margaret Leslie, *Dark Side of Fortune*, University of California Press, Los Angeles, 1998.

Davis, Margaret Leslie, *Rivers in the Desert*, Olmstead Press, Chicago, 2001.

DeMarco, Gordon, *A Short History of Los Angeles*, Lexikos, San Francisco, CA, 1988.

Epstein, Daniel Mark , *Sister Aimee: The Life of Aimee Semple McPherson*, Harcourt Brace & Company, New York, 1993.

Felch, Jason and Frammolino, Ralph, *Chasing Aphrodite*, Houghton Mifflin Harcourt, New York, 2011.

Flamming, Douglas, *Bound for Freedom: Black Los Angeles in Jim Crow America*,

University of California Press, Ltd., Los Angeles, 2006.

Gebhard, David, *Romanza: The California Architecture of Frank Lloyd Wright*, Chronicle Books, San Francisco, 1988.

Friedricks, William B., *Henry E. Huntington and the Creation of Southern California*, Ohio State University Press, Columbus, Ohio, 1992.

Greenberg, Mark, editor-in-chief, *Inside the Getty*, J. Paul Getty Trust, Los Angeles, 2008.

Greenberger, Howard, *Bogey's Baby*, St. Martin's Press, New York 1978.

Guralnik, David, Editor-in-Chief, *Webster's New World Dictionary of the American Language*, William Collins & World Publishing Co., Inc., Cleveland, Ohio, 1976.

Harris, Warren G., *Gable & Lombard*, Simon & Schuster, New York, 1974.

Herr, Jeffrey, *Landmark L.A.*, Angel City Press, Los Angeles, 2002.

Hess, Alan, *Googie*, Chronicle Books, San Francisco, 1985.

Houseman, Victoria, *Made in Heaven*, Bonus Books, Inc., Chicago, 1991.

Kaplan, Sam Hall, *LA Lost and Found*, Crown Publishers Inc., New York, 1987.

Koshalek, Richard; Hutt, Dana; Reese, Carol McMichael; and Webb, Michael, *Symphony: Frank Gehry's Walt Disney Concert Hall*, Harry N. Abrams Inc., New York, 2003.

Kronzek, Lynn C. et al, *Los Angeles, Place of Possibilities*, Heritage Media Corporation, Carlsbad, California, 1998.

Kurashige, Lon, *Japanese American Celebration and Conflict*, University of California Press, Los Angeles, 2002.

LaBotz, Dan, *Edward L. Doheny: Petroleum, Power, and Politics in the United States and Mexico*, Praeger Publishers, New York, 1991.

Lately, Thomas, *The Vanishing Evangelist*, Viking Press, New York, 1959.

Longstreet, Stephen, *All Star Cast*, Thomas Y. Crowell Company, New York, 1977.

Mahoney, Erin, Walking L.A., Wilderness Press, Berkeley, CA, 2006.

Marcus, Ben, *Surfing USA!*, Voyageur Press Inc., Stillwater, Minnesota, 2005.

Mason, William M. and McKinstry, John A., *The Japanese of Los Angeles*, Los Angeles County Museum of Natural History, Los Angeles, 1969.

Matson, Robert William, William Mulholland, *A Forgotten Forefather*, University of the Pacific, Stockton, CA, 1976.

Mattson, Kevin, *Upton Sinclair and the Other American Century*, John Wiley & Sons, Inc., Hoboken, NJ, 2006.

Mulholland, Catherine, *William Mulholland and the Rise of Los Angeles*, University of California Press, Los Angeles, 2000.

O'Flaherty, Joseph S., *An End and a Beginning*, Exposition Press, New York, 1972.

Orsi, Richard J., *Sunset Limited*, University of California Press, Los Angeles, 2005.

Pitt, Leonard and Dale, *Los Angeles A to Z*, University of California Press, Los Angeles, 1997.

Poole, Jean Bruce and Ball, Tevvy, *El Pueblo*, Getty Conservation Institute, J. Paul Getty Trust, Los Angeles, 2002.

Rasmussen, Cecelia, *LA Unconventional*, Los Angeles Times, Los Angeles, 1998.

Rayner, Richard, *The Associates*, W.W. Norton & Co. Inc., New York, 2008.

Reavill, Gil, *Los Angeles*, Compass American Guides, Oakland, CA, 1992.

Robinson, Greg, *After Camp*, University of California Press, Los Angeles, 2012.

Robinson, W. W., *History of the Miracle Mile*, Columbia Savings and Loan Association, Los Angeles, 1965.

Robinson, W. W., *Los Angeles from the Days of the Pueblo*, California Historical Society, Chronicle Books, San Francisco, 2002.

Sanderson, Arlene, *Wright Sites*, The Preservation Press, 1991.

Schiller, Gerald A., *It Happened In Hollywood*, Morris Book Publishing LLC, Guilford, Connecticut, 2010.

Sinclair, Upton, I, *Candidate for Governor: And How I Got Licked*, published by the author in 1935, republished by University of California Press, Los Angeles, 1994.

Smith, R.J., *The Great Black Way*, Public Affairs, New York, 2006.

Stanton, Jeffrey, *Venice California, Coney Island of the Pacific*, Donahue Publishing, Los Angeles, 1987.

Stein, Philip, *Siqueiros*, International Publishers, New York, 1994.

Storer, William Allin, *The Architecture of Frank Lloyd Wright*, third edition, University of Chicago Press, Chicago, 2007.

Tereba, Tere, *Mickey Cohen: the Life and Crimes of LA's Notorious Mobster*, ECW Press, Toronto, Ontario, Canada, 2012.

Torrence, Bruce, *Hollywood: the First 100 Years*, Hollywood Chamber of Commerce, Hollywood, CA, 1979.

Walker, Jim, *Pacific Electric Red Cars*, Arcadia Publishing, San Francisco, CA, 2006.

Weaver, John D., *El Pueblo Grande*, Ward Ritchie Press, Los Angeles, 1973.

Weber, Msgr. Francis J., *Southern California's First Family: the Dohenys of Los Angeles*, Lorson's Books and Prints, Fullerton, California, 1993.

White, Richard, *Railroaded*, W. W. Norton & Company, Inc., New York, 2011.

Wilcock, John, *Los Angeles*, APA Publications, Hong Kong, 1991.

Williams, Greg, *The Story of Hollywoodland*, Papavasilopoulos Press, 1992.

Wilson, Neill C. and Taylor, Frank J., *Southern Pacific*, McGraw-Hill Book Company, Inc., New York, 1952.

Young, Nat, *The History of Surfing*, The Body Press, Tucson, Arizona. 1987.

Zesch, Scott, *The Chinatown War*, Oxford University Press, New York, 2012.

Video:

Djokic, Kristina and Nash, Bruce, *Los Angeles*, The History Channel, 2001.

Lin, Selena, Sunset Boulevard: *Paradise Lost*, A&E Television Network, 2002.

Maysles, Albert, *Concert of Wills: Making the Getty Center*, J. Paul Getty Trust, 2003.

Tajonar, Hector, *Siqueiros: Artist and Warrior*, Getty Conservation Institute, 1998.

Periodicals:

Becerra, Hector, "Decades Later, Bitter Memories of Chavez Ravine," *Los Angeles Times*, April 5, 2012.

Blake, Gene, "Belushi's Last Days," *Los Angeles Times*, March 16, 1982.

Branson-Potts, Hailey, "Diversity in a Gay Haven," *Los Angeles Times*, March 7, 2014.

Endicott, William, "Janis Joplin Death Laid to Drug Overdose," *Los Angeles Times*, October 6, 1970.

Hernandez, Daniel, "The Big Stink," *LA Weekly*, August 9, 2006.

Hodenfield, Chris, "Tales of the Chateau," *Los Angeles Times*, September 14, 1986.

Im, Jimmy, Rest In "A-List Peace," *The Hollywood Reporter*, November 1, 2013.

Johnson, John Jr., "How Los Angeles Covered Up the Massacre of 17 Chinese," *LA Weekly*, March 10, 2011.

Kahrl, William, "Mulholland's Long Shadow," *Los Angeles Times*, November 3, 2012.

Keck, William, "Scandal's History for 'These Old Broads,'" *Los Angeles Times*, February 12, 2011.

King, Susan, "Evolution of a Tramp," *Los Angeles Times*, January 26, 2014.

King, Susan, "Lifelong Role Suits Her," *Los Angeles Times*, July 12, 2013.

King, Susan, "Sunset Gower Studio Marks 100 Years," *Los Angeles Times*, October 16, 2012.

Knight, Christopher, "At Last, For All To See," *Los Angeles Times*, October 9, 2012.

Lepore, Jill, "The Lie Factory," *The New Yorker*, September 24, 2012.

Lifton, Sarah, "Man of Color: The Incredible Life of John Alexander Somerville," USC Trojan Family, University of Southern California Department of Special Collections, Los Angeles, 1994.

Los Angeles Times, Editorial, March 23, 1896.

Los Angeles Times, "O'Malley Lost Some Chavez Ravine Battles, but Won War," April 10, 1962.

Muchnic, Suzanne, "More Space for Sailing the Nevelson Legend," *Los Angeles Times*, June 21, 1985.

Muchnic, Suzanne, "A Nancy Graves Sculpture Grows," *Los Angeles Times*, February 21, 1986.

New York Times, "Justice, Hollywood Style," November 10, 2002.

Norman, Geraldine and Hoving, Thomas, "The Getty Scandals," *Connoisseur*, May 1987.

Ouroussoff, Nicolai, "A Reflection of the City Around It," *Los Angeles Times*, October 19, 2003.

Pool, Bob, "Bright Idea for a Boulevard," *Los Angeles Times*, September 2, 2013.

Pool, Bob, "Rebirth of a Jazz Sanctuary," *Los Angeles Times*, June 12, 2013.

Rugeroni, Joyce, transcriber, "Frank Wiggins," Press Reference Library, International News Service, Los Angeles, 1913.

Saillant, Catherine, "L.A. Lifts Its Ban on Public Murals," *Los Angeles Times*, August 30, 2013.

Soteriou, Helen, I"nterview with Venice Beach Muralist Rip Cronk," *Juxtapoz* Magazine, June 18, 2010.

Snow, Shauna, Arts and Entertainment Report, *Los Angeles Times*, May 3, 1997.

Vankin, Deborah, "Arranging Walls," *Los Angeles Times*, July 7, 2013.

Whitman, Alden, Obituary: "J. Paul Getty Dead at 83," *New York Times*, June 6, 1976.

Williams, Carlton, "Supreme Court Approves Chavez Dodger Park," *Los Angeles Times*, October 20, 1959.

Zimmerman, Tom, "The California Cure The Land of Sunshine," *Los Angeles Times Magazine*, October 2009.

Interviews:

Hon. John Jude Duran, Mayor of West Hollywood, August 13, 2013.

Brian Mylius, muralist, September 5, 2013.

Donelle Dadigan, president, The Hollywood Museum, November 23, 2013.

Broadcast:

Take Two, The Great Red Car Conspiracy: Is It Real?, KPCC Southern California Public Radio, March 29, 2013.

SoCal Focus, Chavez Ravine: Community to Controversial Real Estate, KCET, September 13, 2012.

ACKNOWLEDGEMENTS

James Roman and Museyon Guides would like to thank the following organizations and individuals for their guidance and assistance in creating *Chronicles of Old Los Angeles*.

Hon. John Duran
Los Angeles Public Library
Beverly Hills Public Library
Donelle Dadigan
Steve Nyclemoe
Dave Schlesinger
Carol Merrill-Mirsky
Jim Geiger
Rob Gordon
Doug Hutchinson
Brian Mylius
Paul Neumann
Rusty Hamrick
David Ahlander
Phebe Arlen
Cyril Nishimoto
Bill Watanabe
Jessica Kaye
Library of Congress
UCLA Library
University of Southern California Libraries
Pacific Electric Railway Historical Society
Water and Power Associates, Inc.

CREDITS

Page 10:
San Gabriel Mission near Pasadena, Cal., 1900-1920, Library of Congress, LC-DIG-stereo-1s01714

Page 40:
The anti-Chinese wall—The American wall goes up as the Chinese original goes down / F. Grätz, 1882, Library of Congress, LC-USZC4-4138

Page 43:
South Pacific Train to San Francisco entering Newhall Tunnel about 1898. C.C. Pierce, photographer. Probably the south entrance to the tunnel.

Page 46:
Detail of an 1876 Southern Pacific map, showing the railroad's lines through Southern California, Bancroft Library, UC Berkeley.
BANC PIC 1963.002:1822—A

Page 52:
Albert B. Fall, Ed Doheny, 11/24/26, Library of Congress, LC-DIG-npcc-16240

Page 53:
Signal Hill in Los Angeles County, c. 1923,

Library of Congress, PAN US GEOG

Page 60:
Huntington Beach Municipal Pier, c. 1914; Pacific Electric Railway Car (upper left), concession stands (lower left), bandshell (right), and pier in background, Library of Congress, HAER CAL,30-HUBE,1-103

Page 67:
A Pacific Electric car rolls along the shoreline of the blue Pacific, Charles D. Savage Photo, Donald Duke Collection, Pacific Electric Railway Historical Society Collection

Page 75:
Two men examining kit of dynamite and wire found during sabotage incidents of Owens Valley Aqueduct, Calif., circa 1924, UCLA Library Special Collections, Charles E. Young Research Library, UCLA.

Page 116:
A 1924 cartoon depicting Washington officials racing down an oil-slicked road to the White House, trying to outpace the Teapot Dome Scandal of President Warren G. Harding's administration; The Granger Collection

Page 127:
Members of the Mattachine Society in a rare group photograph. Photo by James Gruber.

Page 129:
West Hollywood, photo by James Roman

Page 145:
Toward Los Angeles, California, Dorothea Lange, 1937, Library of Congress, LC-DIG-fsa-8b31801

Page 146:
Farm and farm workers, Mt. Williamson in background, Manzanar War Relocation Center, California; photograph by Ansel Adams, 1943, Library of Congress, LC-DIG-pprs-00370

Page 148:
Grand Parade at First Street and San Pedro Street, Toyo Miyatake Studios, 1951

Page 149:
Los Angeles, CA. The evacuation of Japanese Americans from West Coast areas under United States Army war emergency orders. Sign on store owned by Japanese in Little Tokyo, Lee Russell, 1942, Library of Congress, LC-USF34-T01-072263-D

Page 149:
Los Angeles, CA. The evacuation of the Japanese-Americans from West Coast areas under U.S. Army war emergency order. Japanese Americans going to camp at Owens Valley gather around

baggage car at the old Santa Fe Station, Lee Russell, April 1942, Library of Congress, LC-DIG-fsa-8a31149

Page 150:
Mess line, noon, Manzanar War Relocation Center, CA, photograph by Ansel Adams, 1943, Library of Congress, LC-DIG-pprs-00368

Page 151:
Nisei Parade, 1951, Japanese girls dancing in the street for Nisei Week celebration, 25 August 1951, University of Southern California Libraries

Page 152:
Nisei Festival Week Queen contestants, Los Angeles, 1966, Copyright Regents of the University of California, UCLA Library.

Page 155:
Lionel Hampton, at far left, rides in a Cadillac convertible in front of Club Alabam on Central Avenue, c. 1953 / Los Angeles Public Library

Page 171:
Manager Walt Alston being mobbed by players and wellwishers in the tunnel en route to the clubhouse, 1959, Herald-Examiner Collection / Los Angeles Public Library

Page 189:
Kennedy family members depart the Capitol, 1963. Photograph by Abbie Rowe, National Park Service. in the John F. Kennedy Presidential Library and Museum, Boston.

Page 195:
The "Hollyhock House," in the East Hollywood neighborhood of Los Angeles, California, Carol M. Highsmith, 2013, Library of Congress, LC-DIG-highsm-24261

Page 196:
Living room (View Southwest) - Hollyhock House, 1965, Library of Congress, HABS CAL,19-LOSAN,28-10

Page 213:
Michael Jackson in concert at Wembley Stadium History World Tour '97, Starstock/Photoshot Photo UIW 013482/C-18 12.07.1997 Photoshot/Everett Collection

Page 216:
Johnny Ramone's tomb at Hollywood Forever Cemetery, photo by Maria Bukhonina

Page 224-291:
Touring photographs in the section by James Roman